THE GREATEST

"Haile Gebrselassie has won many great victories
as an African athlete. He is a great ambassador
for his people, and through his numerous humanitarian
and charitable works a vitally important citizen
for the future growth and development of Africa."

—Nelson Mandela

THE GREATEST

The Haile Gebrselassie Story

Jim Denison

BREAKAWAY BOOKS
HALCOTTSVILLE, NEW YORK
2004

ISBN: 1-891369-48-2
Library of Congress Control Number: 2004106531

Published by Breakaway Books
P.O. Box 24
Halcottsville, NY 12438
(800) 548-4348
(212) 898-0408
www.breakawaybooks.com

FIRST EDITION

To the future of Ethiopia—
Eden, Melat, Bete, and all her other children.

Contents

Foreword   9
Prologue   11

Part One: From the Start

1. Monday Mornings   17
2. Moscow, July 27, 1980   23
3. A Time to Run   41
4. Haile's Office   49
5. On Track   61
6. Six Seconds High   77
7. Jos Hermens   95
8. The Greatest   111

Part Two: Into the Lead

9. Birmingham, February 21, 2003   155
10. Atlanta, July 29, 1996   175
11. Haile at Home   187
12. Sydney, September 25, 2000   211
13. Coming Back   227
14. The Road to Athens   245
15. Athens, August 20, 2004   271
Epilogue   277
Acknowledgments   279
Appendices   281

Foreword

While Jim was writing this book I used to say to him: "Make sure you do a good job so that when I'm asked questions at press conferences I can just refer to page numbers in the book for the answers." I'm happy to say that from now on my press conferences will be a lot easier. For more than twenty years running has been my life and has given me so many unforgettable experiences. This book documents these moments and describes the people close to me who have helped me achieve my goals. It has been a pleasure collaborating with Jim on this book. I hope that everyone reading it will find something to inspire them in their own running.

Haile Gebrselassie
Addis Ababa, 2004

Prologue

The final lap. Sweat lines Haile Gebrselassie's face; his forehead shines under the strain. At the top of the backstretch the Kenyan Paul Tergat leads. His elegant stride extends into the night; the ground rushes beneath him in a torrent. With 200 meters to go it's still Tergat, so often a runner-up to the man now inches in arrears. Tergat and Gebrselassie have broken clear; they hit the homestretch determined: They're side by side, shoulder to shoulder. The air around them is still as if they are running in a vacuum. And this after 24 laps of suspicious surges, sideways glances, and questionable team tactics. Tergat's in with a fighting chance this time. Not like Atlanta. This is going to come down to the last step. It will definitely be decided at the line. Tergat knows it. At this point—100 meters to go—everyone does. It's his best chance in years. Oh, but for that unstoppable force behind him: a bundle of power, expression, and light. So a packed Olympic stadium rises, a television audience in the billions shift to the edge of their seats. Could this be Tergat's day? That must be what he's repeating. *I can win this. I can win this . . .*

Magic seemingly intervened that September Monday night in Sydney, 2000—a collective gasp of disbelief, a flutter of pleasure, the world mesmerized as the men's 10,000-meter final drew to a close. Only two could have possibly won gold: Paul Tergat, a majestic, proud champion, or Ethiopia's favorite son, Haile Gebrselassie.

Over each passing kilometer, from the 1st through to the 10th, time had moved fast and time had moved slow. The pace fluctuated like a nervous day on Wall Street—62 seconds for one lap, 72 for another, 56 for another still. Such is the effect of earnest confrontation—and at an Olympic Games in particular, where unknown possibilities are so often reconfigured into a new order. The result being, as journalists would later describe this race, "A sublime and fantastically super-charged climax."

When the gun signaled the start of this Olympic 10,000 meter final, Gebrselassie had everything to lose. He was the defending Olympic champion from Atlanta four years earlier, the world record holder, and four times the world champion. Tergat was a cross-country specialist, winning that world title consecutively between 1995 and 1999. Gebrselassie didn't run cross-country. And Tergat had never beaten Gebrselassie on the track, finishing second to him in Atlanta and at two of those world championships—1997 and 1999.

But for Sydney Tergat had never prepared more strenuously: "I would be on the track, running hard, collapsing, getting up, and running hard again. And when I was done I couldn't stand. I was so tired. I couldn't eat. I felt sick. I had no energy to do anything other than take a drink of water and lie down. Then I'd think of Haile, and know that he was training even harder."

So in a move meant to level their Olympic score, Tergat had surged to the lead from a pack of six with 250 meters remaining. And only Gebrselassie could respond.

Now with just 50 meters of racing ahead of them virtually nothing separates these two, not the thickness of their vests, a sliver of paper, or an invisible line. Twenty runners had responded to the starter's gun some 27 minutes earlier, but it's come down to this: a lean, a half stride, the weight of one man's breath.

Gebrselassie had carefully maintained second place the entire race, closely monitoring all six lead changes. But Tergat surprised him, slingshotting to the front on the final backstretch. And as hard as he's pumping his fists and as high as he's lifting his knees, Gebrselassie isn't gaining. Tergat's holding on, and the finish line is fast approaching.

These two rivals offer a study in contrasts: Tergat 5-feet-11 with a tailor-tapered torso, Gebrselassie 5-feet-4 and barrel-chested, but with an albatross-sized stride. Tergat's height and width fill his lane. Gebrselassie's narrow shoulders center him in his. But their hard-edged grimaces demonstrate an equal capacity to tolerate pain.

Their struggle continues down the homestretch as their cheek-bones rise and their faces bunch. Deep lines cut across their brows, giving them a wind-whipped, tortured appearance as if they had just thrust their hands into a sack of broken glass. Their anguish fills the camera, a synchronized trajectory of speed and determination, and it stuns the world. This is raw, this is reality, this is unfiltered drama.

However, despite their parity in talent, effort, and resolve, and the subfractional distance that separates them, one of these champions will have to lose. But who will it be? How will this scene close? Only 15 meters of track remain and these two are in each other's skin.

There's clear desperation in their last yelps for air. Their every pore discharges thick steam, deep heat, solid tension. They're pulling at their roots to sprint their hardest, digging deep, doing whatever might help them reach that painted white line across the track first.

On top of all this, Gebrselassie's hearing things. One simple word over and over: *Yichala, Yichala,* It is possible, It is possible. Five meters out . . . now three, and this single word is still circulating in Gebrselassie's head. He can only feel Tergat by his side now; his vision is clouding, his ears are ringing. Then somehow he remembers, *Lean, Lean.* It's a beautiful dip, too: graceful and balanced with his arms out to his sides like wings. He's taken off; he's across the line first for an incredible nine one-hundredths of a second victory. It's a race that will never be forgotten. The day the world proclaimed this humble Ethiopian the greatest distance runner of all time.

Part One

FROM THE START

Everything you can imagine is real.
—Pablo Picasso

1

Monday Mornings

Come Monday morning most people in Addis Ababa, Ethiopia's capital city, don't go to work. They aren't woken up by a smart-sounding alarm. They don't step into a warm shower, or run a hot bath. They're more likely to be woken up by the year-round 6 A.M. equatorial sunrise, or a pack of barking dogs, or religious hymns coming over the loudspeakers from Saint Ourael's church in the city center. And it's squatting beside a slow-moving stream that's mostly rock and soil that most people wash themselves first thing in the morning.

Neither is breakfast in Addis Ababa likely to include a steaming cup of fresh-ground coffee, cereal, toast, or two eggs easy-over. Forget about wide pages of an early-edition newspaper to turn, or the plastic faces of morning television hosts to stare into. Neither will there be lunch bags to fill, school runs to make, or a scheduled commuter train to catch.

Come Monday morning in Addis Ababa crowds of people hit the streets—kids hawk small bags of sweets or tiny packs of tissue, adults, with glassy, liquid eyes, think, *It's Monday, a new week. Maybe a new opportunity . . . Maybe life will get easier.*

Ethiopia isn't a country of clock towers and chimes; fixed shifts and hard schedules are rare. Work can be elusive; the opportunity to earn a day's wage unpredictable—a hole to dig, goods to deliver, a floor to sweep, a pile to stack . . .

Scarce traffic lights and unpainted crosswalks can hardly organize the parade of humanity along the streets and sidewalks of Addis come Monday morning. Commerce and communication operate in the open like an expansive 24-hour street bazaar. Deals aren't forged in offices high above the ground. Myriad voices, sounds, and gestures complement every interaction: a kiss on both cheeks, the press of handshakes and hugs, chatter, traffic, mobile phones. Events in Addis largely carry on outdoors, like nature. Everyone here touches and reaches his neighbor. Private space is not something that's taken for granted.

Only a few good roads within central Addis handle all the Monday morning foot traffic. The men have on pleated trousers cast in earthy tones, dark shoes, and patterned sport jackets. Their pants' creases have flattened, though, and any shine on their shoes has faded. The women wear long skirts and bright white shawls, and their soft brown faces go unmade. These men and women reach the streets from every direction, emerging out of makeshift dwellings constructed from rusted sheets of corrugated iron, splintered timber, and chipped cinder blocks.

Unemployment in Addis is 30 percent for men and 41 percent for women, but come Monday morning you find very few people alone at home. What would be the point? No fat welfare check is going to pop through the door. Better to walk the streets and see what's possible. Time and opportunity must be read through a paradigm of patience and goodwill, not synchronization and control. What will come will come—*Yemetaw yemetal, yetebalew aykerim.* So Addis hums as Monday dawns, everyone eager to discover what's next, or what might change.

Downtown Addis Ababa projects a baby skyline scattered above a surprisingly large number of tall treetops. Green is a much stronger color here than you'd expect. And cranes punctuate open spaces like ships' masts in a rejuvinated port city. Flatbed trucks and car roofs laden with concrete mix, wood, bricks, and iron chug up and down the avenues. But where are they headed? Even on a Monday morning most of the construction sites around the city sit quiet, with heavy machinery idle and not a single worker in sight. As is often the case here, momentum is easily lost as funds disappear, the rain comes, and initiative is washed away. So frustration infects anyone with an eye toward renewal or change. But somehow despair remains in check . . .

Whether it's a taxi driver in his blue-and-white cab hailing passengers out his rolled-down window, or a goat and cattle herder directing his brood across a busy intersection, or a homeless man quietly rubbing a few small coins together, all Ethiopians have been inspired by enduring national traditions of hope and optimism. "We are full of self-determination . . . we never succumbed to a European colonizer," says local businessman Girma Neda. "We bask in our country's beauty—deep cliffs, rivers, expansive pastureland—and like our long line of distance running champions, we ooze courage and reek of willpower. That's why it is that every Ethiopian feels a call from inside his soul to dream and declare himself free."

But without a proper plan, or the necessary support, one's dreams will never materialize. And therein lies the problem: Progress is slow in Ethiopia. The majority of the population continues to live without electricity. Men urinate down drainpipes. And water in many towns and villages has to be collected by hand, sometimes from as far away as 10 miles. Days can advance slowly, as if time wasn't marked by seconds, minutes, and hours but instead by the shadows moving across the land, or the changes in weather a new season brings.

To land in Ethiopia is to arrive in a vastly different age. The calendar is divided into 13 months, 12 with 30 days each, and an intercalary month at the end of the year with five or six days. While the year is 2004 in the West, it's 1996 in Ethiopia. The West has used the Julian calendar, which in 1582 was supplanted by the Gregorian calendar. The Egyptians have used the ancient Coptic calendar. The Ethiopic calendar is related to all of these, but different from all of them, too.

Daily time remains constant throughout the year, where day and night are always the same length: counting starts at dawn and sunset, which is the Western 6:00 A.M. and 6:00 P.M. So Western 7:00 A.M. is Ethiopia's one o'clock; Western noon is six; Western 6:00 P.M. is twelve o'clock, and so on.

Farmers use oxen to plow their fields, and donkeys, sheep, and cattle run loose in the street. The facts of life can also be grim: Food is often scarce due to drought, poor distribution channels, and crop and livestock disease. Ethiopia has the third highest number of people living with HIV/AIDS in the world. Malaria is a constant worry, with close to six million cases occurring annually. Garbage that has spilled onto the street from overstuffed dumpsters is tempting enough to provide many with their daily meal. United Nations and Red Cross all-terrain vehicles are regularly on patrol. The average Ethiopian man will only live to 53. The average woman, 55. Child mortality rates are 175 per 1000. The yearly per capita income throughout Ethiopia is $100, the fifth lowest in the world, says the World Bank. Subsequently, most Ethiopians are resigned to the fact that their life will be short—but not, they hope, inconsequential. *Egziabher yalew neger aykerim*. This must be what God has planned for us.

Life in Addis not only on Mondays but every day of the week offers constant reminders of suffering and discomfort: men sleeping on the streets, families of 10 crowded into single-room dwellings. It can be difficult to see anything but despair, although, thankfully, some can. And these special few imagine the possibilities and concentrate on satisfying them one step at a time. They are the brave Ethiopian men and women who resist foreign dependency—a trap, they argue, that imprisons one's spirit and restricts one's imagination. The Ethiopian optimist, the dreamer, searches for some way to make his life meaningful, and in that process he hopes that he can affect others similarly. Through such a course of action he becomes his own man: a man with a vision, a man who continues to smile as he works tirelessly for a new future. No expectation or responsibility is too great for such a man; his ambitions materialize as he fills in the outlines of his imagination with the toil of labor.

A legendary distance runner must be such an imaginative laborer. That status doesn't come from sheer hard work and victories alone. To log over 100 miles in training each week, to accept the pressure of Olympic and world championship competition, and to battle back from injuries and other low points is simply expected of a champion. Similarly, the ordinary champion must be prepared to stand on a starting line and accept the pain that will follow. The well-traveled long-distance runner understands his body well: He can forecast the exact moment in a race when his muscles will begin to scream. Despite that, however, he carries on.

But the distance runner who seeks what others are unable to know or conceive, and in his mind's eye pictures what no one else can—prosperity where there is despair, opportunity where there is hopelessness, change where there is fear—and works that much harder to make his dreams come true, is no ordinary champion. That's the sign of a genius, a legend: a man who lives a story all his own. A life story so full of wonder and amazement that it's almost impossible to believe. A man whose people consider him to be close to God and pray every time before he runs. Haile Gebrselassie, a great Ethiopian runner who happens to be an even greater man, has imagined such a story, and in all possible ways he continues to live it today. And this is that story: the story of Haile Gebrselassie's politics of hope and his dream of Olympic gold.

2

Moscow, July 27, 1980

Steps forward. Not steps, strides. Long, powerful, resolute strides. Click, click; pop, pop; tap, tap. The sound of moving feet—firm, flexible, soft . . . mesmerizing. A metronome in full swing drawing a constant up-down beat. Long distance running is four levers—two arms, two legs—set to a precise tempo.

The long-distance runner generates countless strides forward. Forward on the road, over grass, around a track. And each step is in sync with the one before it, the one after it . . . pop, pop, pop. Here legs resemble wings as they mark their path across the sky: one stroke, one beat, one cycle, and then another . . . and another.

Moving forward for miles—in this case 6.2 miles divided into oval 400-meter laps, 25 to be exact—is the 10,000-meter runner. And his event is the longest race contested entirely around a track. It's the surest test of courage and skill for an Olympic long-distance runner. Much more so than the marathon. The 10,000 demands stricter degrees of stamina, speed, and smarts. The stamina to endure stinging midrace surges and the exacting toll of running just above 4-minute-mile pace for nearly 30 minutes. The speed to dodge contact and collisions—all those elbows, knees, and feet fighting for space. Speed, too, to accelerate and sprint the last half lap or more and secure a place among the medals. And to execute these dimensions requires a calm, composed, tactical mind-set: the insight to evaluate others' strengths and weaknesses, the intuition to gauge an opportunity, the confidence to work through a rough patch. As a result, the 10,000-meter Olympic champion stands tall before an audience of billions as he is hailed by many as the leading distance runner in the world.

Launching an Olympic campaign over 10,000 meters can never be an impulsive decision. That would be foolish as well as a fiction. Success at 10,000 meters takes time most of all. Time to prepare that's measured in years, not hour blocks or convenient monthly chunks. Maybe 10 years, maybe 20, all for one race.

A 10,000-meter runner's Olympic ambitions, therefore, are never spontaneous. Like an astronaut on the launch pad, or a major-leaguer in the on-deck circle, a 10,000-meter runner's arrival into the Olympic stadium is almost always fashioned out of childhood dreams—*One day that'll be me*. And dreaming is the antithesis of impulsiveness. Moreover, a child's Olympic fantasy is normally grounded in the material properties of gold: an Olympic gold medal dangling from the neck of a similar other. One's countryman, perhaps. That's the alchemy of sport, taking base desires—recognition, success, achievement—and spinning them into dreams of gold.

It would have been impossible for Miruts Yifter to have known as he was sprinting away from the other 14 Olympic 10,000-meter finalists in Moscow on July 27, 1980, that among the millions back home in Ethiopia celebrating his triumph on the world's largest sporting stage there was a small seven-year-old boy alone in a dry, hot field with a radio the same size as his head held close to his ear and his features frozen in suspense at what he was hearing. "Yes, it's Miruts Yifter. Yes, Miruts Yifter wins for Ethiopia! Miruts Yifter wins the Olympic 10,000-meter gold medal." And how impossible it would have been for Yifter to realize the impact he was having on this boy's conception of who he wanted to be, and what he wanted to achieve in life most of all—*I want to win the Olympic 10,000 meters like Miruts Yifter; I want to do something special, something big; I want to be the greatest distance runner of all time.* And so life began for the boy, all thanks to Yifter.

The Olympic 10,000-meter final in 1980 was predicted by most track and field experts to go Yifter's way. Unlike any distance runner before him, Yifter could so dramatically change gears over the last lap of a long-distance race and transform himself into a sprinter—arms pumping, knees lifting—that he had earned the nickname "Yifter the Shifter," and a reputation for being unbeatable.

It resembled magic, a dozen roses appearing out of thin air, a missing person discovered behind a black cape, so immediate and surprising was Yifter's metamorphosis from distance runner to sprinter. Audiences around the world gasped at his rapid acceleration. The mind boggled: all those long, ordinary laps and then suddenly this: a man taking to the air. His lead seemed created out of thin air. The juxtaposition of fast and slow dumbfounded people. It was in such an instant, too, at the snap of a finger, the blink of an eye, that Yifter could display his trick of speed. And what frustrated his competitors, but tantalized his fans, was predicting the moment Yifter would choose to fly away. This was always a mystery.

In his Olympic 10,000-meter semifinal in Moscow on July 24, Yifter sprinted clear of the pack and into a certain qualifying position for the final with exactly one lap to go—400 meters out. Up until that point he had been content to allow a chasing pack of two to follow in his wake.

It was intolerably hot that July afternoon in the Lenin Stadium. A sequence of gentle rainstorms the previous three days had passed, leaving the track bathed in a bright blaze of sun. The infield grass had gone brown; in between events a band of Soviet workers dressed in communist olive green heaved a hose around the track to cool its scorching surface. The 13 men in the second 10,000-meter semifinal, including Miruts Yifter, were in no hurry to begin racing when the gun sounded at 5:05 P.M., sending them on their 25-lap trial.

The early leader in Yifter's semi-final was a barefoot Zambian named Damiano Ngwila. Beads of water shot from the back of his heels as he made his way in front for the first eight laps. The 85,000 spectators were delighted by Ngwila's shoeless display, just as they would have been by a bear riding a bicycle, or a juggler on stilts. Muscovites love the circus and the absurd, and a man running without shoes struck them as that strange. They applauded and stomped the ground in time with Ngwila's steps. For a moment these Olympics organized by the "Evil Empire," as Americans were wont to say, were pure carnival. By the race's midway point, however, the Zambian had fallen back through the pack and a new sense of seriousness took over. It was at this point that Yifter moved to the lead. And with him came Britain's Brendan Foster, and the East German Peter Jorg.

The qualification procedure for the 10,000 meters guaranteed a spot in the final to the first four finishers from each semi-final. And Yifter seemed determined to arrange those places sooner rather than later. He began to surge, easily breaking the lesser runners hanging off the tail of the pack. Without notice he would extend his stride a fraction, lift his knees ever so slightly higher, and instantly he would be on his own enjoying a 15-meter advantage. The effect of his random spurts was immediate and significant. Down would go the heads of the other runners, up would go their shoulders as they dug into the ground and pushed on. It was either that or find themselves half a lap behind and their Olympic dream unraveled.

Yifter, it was clear to everyone, was a distance running revolutionary. His speedy tactics reconfigured the sport. The Ethiopian people loved his bold dominance, his reinvention of tradition. So it was that radios all across Ethiopia were tuned in to events as they transpired half a world away in Moscow. Farmers sought a spot of shade to sit down and listen, schools adjourned early, and trade and traffic in Addis Ababa slowed. Even the magic of the wireless couldn't compare to Yifter's brilliance and how proud he made his people feel.

Prior to Yifter, success as a distance runner had everything to do with endurance and pacing, and less so speed and positioning. Who could endure the mounting miles and increasing pain? Whose well-plotted pace would see him through to the bitter end? These were the tactical conundrums faced by such mid-20th-century runners as Emil Zatopek of Czechoslovakia and Ron Clarke from Australia. For them the 10,000 meters was an extreme race, so they prepared and raced cautiously. But Yifter's uncanny ability to jump a field made acceleration and surprise distance running's new virtues. With the ascent of Yifter the Shifter the world saw intelligence and innovation brought to the 10,000.

Quite interestingly, Yifter didn't become serious about running until the late age of 20, in 1965. As a child, sport was just for play, he believed. And among the games he enjoyed with his friends was chasing apes barefoot over the land. But as Yifter began to run more systematically, his sights soon fixed on the Olympics. Despite an impoverished family life, and with little food to eat at times, Yifter carried on running. He became a man beset with a dream; he became a runner with a clear vision.

By 1968 Ethiopia's national running coach, Nigusse Roba, had encouraged Yifter to move from his home in the countryside to Addis Ababa where he could train with the national squad. Yifter was admitted into the Ethiopian Air Force, and with financial support to run full-time without actually having to become involved in active military duty—a relic of the old amateur days of sport when a position in the armed services acted as a guise under which to train professionally—success on the track for Yifter quickly followed.

Immediately Yifter developed the reputation of possessing an iron will. He relished winning; he thrived on competition. He was confident and controlled, and he remained calm in the most trying competitive situations. Out of these circumstances Yifter developed his unique winning tactic, that potent blend of speed, stamina, and surprise that would forever redefine the 10,000 meters.

So talented and prepared for the 25 laps of a 10,000-meter race was Yifter that his rivals' best chance of disarming his vicious sprint finish was to find a way to unnerve or unsettle him. But in his Moscow semifinal it was difficult to imagine who in the field could disturb Yifter's steadfast demeanor. By the eighth kilometer, Yifter, Foster, and Jorg had opened up a 25-second gap on the chasing group. Certainly, these three would advance automatically to the final.

Past 9 kilometers they were still three in a row—Yifter, Foster, Jorg—with their lead over the rest of the field now half a lap. But not content to sit still and breeze into the final, Yifter rushed well ahead of the Brit and the East German at the start of the last lap. Foster and Jorg were taken aback. The crowd, however, was delighted. Once again there was a spectacle to cheer. No real advantage came from winning a 10,000 semifinal—unlike winning one's 100 meter semifinal which guaranteed a better lane for the final. With a secure place in the top four, Yifter only had to manage one more lap of the track. Surely conserving his energy instead of sprinting hard the entire last lap would have been the wiser tactic? Which was why Foster and Jorg let Yifter go, watching bemused as he quickly opened up a nine-second gap. Was this an indication of what to expect from Yifter in the final? Perhaps, then, there was some advantage to winning one's semifinal so dramatically? Because as the other finalists began to consider how that race might ultimately go, most of them were thinking about what Yifter was going to do instead of fashioning their own race plan.

Moscow was certainly going to be Miruts Yifter's final grasp at Olympic glory. He was already 35 years old, one of the most senior of all the 10,000-meter finalists. Eight years earlier in Munich, at the 1972 Olympics, he had earned a bronze medal in the 10,000 and all signs were that by the Montreal Olympics, four years later, he would be favored to move into the gold medal position. But by 1976 the world's conscience had finally awoken to the horror that was South Africa's racial policy of apartheid, and an international sports ban was placed on South Africa, prohibiting them from participating in any form of international competition. However, when New Zealand ignored the ban and traveled to South Africa for a series of rugby matches in 1975, 17 African and Arab nations, including Ethiopia, threatened to boycott the 1976 Olympics if New Zealand wasn't banned from competing.

Negotiations between the International Olympic Committee (IOC) and a strong and determined cadre of African diplomats were tense. Yifter continued to train in the hope that some form of reconciliation could be reached. He knew he was in his prime; he knew the 10,000 meter gold medal was his for the taking. If only he could make it to the starting line.

In the end, talks stalled as the IOC refused to take action over a charge concerning a non-Olympic sport—rugby. The African boycott ensued. In total, 48 nations withdrew from those Olympics. Yifter was devastated, forced to sit at home while Finland's Lasse Viren, the defending champion, had an easy run to the top of the 10,000 meter podium. Yifter would have to wait another four years for his chance at Olympic gold.

Unbelievably, four years on from Montreal talk began of another Olympic boycott: Moscow 1980. The United States was behind the protest of the Soviet Union's occupation of Afghanistan. Jimmy Carter, the American president, claimed "that continued aggressive actions by the Soviets would endanger the participation of athletes and travel to Moscow by spectators." A further 60 nations supported Carter's stand, but thankfully for Yifter, Ethiopia wasn't among them. Ethiopia's allegiance to Moscow was a foregone conclusion. Following a 1974 communist-backed revolt and the removal of the long-serving Ethiopian emperor, Haile Selassie, Ethiopia had become a Soviet satellite. As such, she would do what she was told. And in 1980 what Ethiopia's athletes were told to do was go to Moscow.

Prior to 1974 Haile Selassie was synonymous with modern Ethiopia. His overthrow and death one year later (Selassie died under mysterious circumstances, perhaps from the aftereffects of a prostate gland operation, or from suffocation at the hands of a revolutionary) marked the end of an era of Royal Ethiopian absolutism. Selassie had ruled Ethiopia like a medieval autocrat, and for almost the entire span of his 44-year leadership he was without question the most powerful and dominant politician in the country. Ethiopian scholar Peter Schwab described him as "haughty and regal . . . in control of all decision-making, and at the pinnacle of an imperial palace structure so patrimonial that all others in the system, including his family, were regarded by the great Emperor as retainers."

Through a combination of charisma, heritage, and feudalism Selassie maintained his imperial authority. He believed his power to rule was bestowed upon him by God, with the positive qualities of all previous Ethiopian emperors transmitted to him by biological descent, and by the sacred act of consecration whereby he also became the self-anointed head of the Ethiopian Orthodox Church. His officers in the palace were continuously courting his favor and fawning over him. Failure to do so could give the appearance of thinking too independently, a characteristic Selassie discouraged. In this way, and through a feudal system of land ownership, distribution, and taxation, Selassie prevented for years any form of mass opposition. Selassie's

Ethiopia, Africa's oldest nation, was little more than a footnote to the great stories of the day. But through Selassie's direct personal actions this would change.

Haile Selassie traveled widely across Europe, the first Ethiopian ruler to do so. Inspired by what he saw in Paris, London, and Rome, he designed progressive policies and attempted to modernize Ethiopia through greater technological advances and membership in the world's economic community. He took steps to improve legislation, bureaucracy, schooling, health, and social services. And on the diplomatic front, Selassie acted to promote Ethiopian power and sovereignty by securing allies overseas. He abolished the slave trade in Ethiopia, introduced the Ethiopian currency, and created the first national constitution.

Selassie achieved worldwide acclaim on the back of his rousing 1936 speech to the League of Nations following Italy's unprovoked invasion of Ethiopia by Mussolini earlier that year. His passionate call for retribution prompted sanctions against Italy and marked the first time in modern history that an African nation had worked effectively to defy the arrogance of a European one.

In 1941, with British backing, Selassie returned to Ethiopia from his place of exile in Bath, England, to defeat the Italian army and reclaim Ethiopia's long tradition of independence and freedom. His fortitude earned him the nickname "the Lion," and his actions against colonial oppression were said to inspire Nelson Mandela, Martin Luther King, and Malcolm X.

But the 1974 communist-backed revolt brought a dramatic transformation to Ethiopian life and culture. During the later Selassie years, public services had dwindled as poverty and unemployment soared. Administrative practices that had worked well in the 1950s were inefficient by the 1970s. The immediate years prior to 1974 were filled with rising inflation, corruption, and famine. Support for an uprising began among organized urban groups, unions, and students. And in June 1974, 120 military officers formed a group known as the Dergue, which represented the military and worked behind closed doors to gain power. Although they continued to claim allegiance to the emperor, officers operating under the Dergue's mandate began to arrest certain members of parliament and various aristocrats associated with Selassie's order. Dergue members effectively removed Selassie's means of governing as they held complete military control. In July they demanded a new constitution, but when it was found to be unsatisfactory to their "Ethiopia First" ideology, they continued to undermine the emperor's authority.

Emperor Selassie's estate and palace were eventually seized in August 1974, and soon thereafter he was found responsible for covering up a terrible famine that had struck Ethiopia in 1973, killing hundreds of thousands of people. Finally, on September 12, 1974, Selassie was formally deposed and arrested and power was assumed by the Dergue, officially renamed the Provincial Military Administrative Council and led by an American-educated Ethiopian, Lieutenant-Colonel Mengistu Haile Mariam.

While the revolution had general support from a large number of Ethiopians, Mengistu's campaign of "Red Terror" that followed his takeover was a travesty. Meant to flush out any and all opposition, it was founded on nothing but fear and suspicion, and lasted for over two years; it resulted in thousands of people, many of them innocent, being tortured or killed. But by 1977 the Red Terror eased, and the Ethiopian government began to assume the rhythms of its new age: to become an extreme socialist state. As a result, formal relations with the Soviet Union began. This led to the nationalization of practically every Ethiopian industry and organization—including, of course, sport.

For the Soviet Union, sport provided an effective vehicle to gain a political, military, and strategic inroad into Ethiopian culture and society. Soviet leaders understood sport's cohesive effect, and how athletic success, particularly at the international level, could galvanize the population, maintain stability, and distract people's attention from pressing social problems or uncomfortable structural or organizational circumstances. So began a period of widespread Soviet influence over the provision of sport in Ethiopia. Soviet-backed coaching schemes were launched, new stadiums and gyms were built, and exchange programs enabled top Ethiopian athletes to travel to Moscow or other Eastern Bloc nations for advanced training. Ethiopia, therefore, was directly tied into a successful 1980 Moscow Olympic Games, and would without question be sending a full contingent of athletes.

By 1980 Miruts Yifter had become Ethiopia's top sportsman. He had completed impressive victories over 5000 meters and 10,000 meters at the 1977 and 1979 World Cup of track and field. He was labeled "invincible" over a last-lap sprint, and his powers of endurance appeared limitless. Yifter was a highly visible symbol of Ethiopian national identity; he represented a level of success that was designed to inspire vast numbers of Ethiopians to support their new socialist state. The Moscow games presented the ideal opportunity for Yifter's talents to be displayed, and as well the superiority and strength of Ethiopia's socialist way of life. So when Yifter and his teammates Mohammed Kedir and Tolossa Kotu stepped up to the starting line on July 27, 1980 for the 10,000 meter Olympic final, they were carrying far more than their own personal ambitions. They were carrying the hopes of an entire nation. In particular, those of a small seven-year-old boy from the tiny farming village of Asela, 150 miles south of Addis Ababa. A seven-year-old boy named Haile Gebrselassie.

A fast early pace administered with relentless precision and determination lap after lap after lap is one way to extinguish the kick in a runner like Miruts Yifter. But no one can push the opening circuits of a 10,000-meter race alone. Or at least not for very long. There are too many laps to negotiate, and they pass too slowly. Such a tactic demands support and encouragement. It requires the mobilization of a team, and a common will to share the load.

Finland had the potential for such a team in Moscow. Two-time defending champion Lasse Viren had reached the 10,000-meter final along with his countrymen Kaarlo Maaninka and Martti Vainio. But distance running is most of all an individual sport. Preparation is solitary, at times lonely. An analyst's evaluation of a distance runner's psyche might read: introverted, goal-oriented. Yifter certainly recognized those traits in himself. Every coach and sportswriter in Moscow also knew this about distance runners. Which was why they all expected Yifter to win. Not necessarily because he couldn't be beaten, or because he was the best trained or the most talented in the field, but because the only way to upset him ran counter to the psychological makeup of his opponents. They would have to work together to wear Yifter down. And none of them had come to Moscow prepared to execute such a plan. They were largely there to protect their own interests and finish as high as they could.

With the family radio by his side as the early laps of the 10,000-meter final passed, Haile, too, realized that he understood something about psychology. He knew, for instance, how to please others, and that the reward from an unexpected good deed—praise, celebrity—was most satisfying. He'd often perform additional chores around the family farm—chopping extra firewood, feeding the cattle in some innovative way—so that he might enjoy the surprise and happiness it brought to his father and subsequently reflected back on him. "Oh, that's good. You're a very good boy. Thank you. Thank you. You are the best boy in my house." Such praise meant the world to a young boy trying to distinguish himself from his nine siblings.

Haile also understood something about the psychology of success. He knew, for example, that he had a mind and a body willing to endure. Already by age seven he had experienced untold sweat and strain: plowing rocky, dusty fields behind an unbalanced ox, fetching water miles away, and at 6:30 A.M. six days a week running 6 miles to school, and then 6 miles home. Patience, the delay of gratification . . . these were attributes already representative of Haile's character. As such, he believed that qualified him to run long distances; to run long and hard just like Yifter. *I can last . . . I can push myself . . .*

And for Haile that realization was a very great thing. Because in Yifter he saw how special it was to be a runner—especially running for an Olympic gold medal. After all, what other circumstance could bring a nation to a standstill? For a young boy with practically nothing of his own, the idea of attracting so much attention through something as simple as running—something he did every day anyway—was overwhelming. *How is it possible? How can one man be so special? To be on the radio every day he must not be a normal person. He must be very different.* So as early as seven years old Haile had his motivation and his life's work defined . . . *I want to be like Miruts Yifter.*

Without a television for miles around, and even without a newspaper to read, Haile had no idea what kind of man his new hero and role model Yifter was. Listening to the radio his imagination ran wild. *Is this man, Yifter, someone tall? Or someone fat? Or maybe he's something altogether different from what I know about people, like a god or a spirit?*

Yifter was only an image and a name to Haile. The image of a champion, a name every person in Ethiopia knew. It wasn't for another 10 years, in the spring of 1990, that Haile finally came to understand what kind of man Yifter truly was.

"I had come to Addis Ababa to run a race in the national stadium and I was with a friend of mine. He was an older boy, and he knew a few more things than me. We were in the stands sitting quietly when suddenly he grabbed my shirt and yelled. 'Haile, Haile, look, look, sitting over there, it's Miruts Yifter.' And I said, 'Oh, is that Yifter? It can't be. Are you sure?' My friend pushed me to go shake his hand, but I was too nervous. I also couldn't believe it was really him. He was not what I expected: a strong and powerful man, a real force. He was actually very normal looking. Kind of small, bald, and a little bit old. In the ten years since Moscow I had been living with my own image of Yifter. I imagined he was someone grand and important . . . almost majestic. Whether I was running to school, or on a training run, or working in the fields, or lying awake at night, I'd picture Yifter as strong and powerful and ageless. Also playing over and over in my head would be the song that was written to commemorate Yifter's great victory in Moscow . . . *Miruts Yifter, Miruts Yifter, You are our champion, You are our hero, Miruts Yifter, Miruts Yifter* . . . That song made me think I could fly over the ground. It still does. It makes me feel young again, like a boy discovering the beauty and freedom of running for the first time. But what I also understood when I first saw Yifter was that it must be possible for an ordinary man to win an Olympic gold medal. Listening to his race on the radio I thought such a thing must require a miracle. But after seeing him that day in the stadium I started to think that maybe someone normal like me could do it, too."

Someone normal like him? Haile Gebrselassie normal? It's a strange thought, that. Because even from the beginning there has never been anything normal about Haile. Take the day of Yifter's 10,000-meter final in Moscow. Haile actually risked a great deal to listen to that race. Control over the family radio was the sole province of Haile's father. And it was only to be used for the news: "My father only cared about the news, nothing else. Not music, and certainly not sport. You see, the late 1970s and the early 1980s were turbulent times in Ethiopia with the removal of Haile Selassie, the rise of Mengistu, and the counter-revolutionary groups that were always forming and breaking apart. My father wanted to know what the government was saying, what they were planning. Changes were taking place at this time, like the redistribution and collectivization of land. That was Mengistu's idea of a socialist economy. As a farmer, my father needed to know these things. So every evening after the news he would remove the batteries from the radio and hide them. Because, you see, to get money for new batteries was a very difficult thing. They had to last a long time, and not be wasted on anything unimportant like music or sport. That was my father's thinking, anyway. But on the day that Miruts Yifter ran the 10,000-meter final in Moscow, I stole the batteries and grabbed the radio and ran into the fields far, far away from our house. I knew what I was doing was wrong. My father hated thieves, and he would have been very angry with me for stealing those batteries. But inside my heart, I knew that what I wanted to know and hear from the radio was not a bad thing. It was a good thing, actually. And also very important for Ethiopia. That was what I truly felt. That was what gave me the courage to do what I did. I wasn't afraid of being punished or beaten. I only cared about one thing: I had to know what Miruts Yifter would do in Moscow."

And by the eighth lap Haile began to know. Yifter and his team-mates—Kedir and Kotu—had opened up a two-second lead. They were throwing in hard, random surges to prevent anyone else from assuming control.

Halfway, at the 5000-meter mark, the three Ethiopians had doubled the size of their lead. And still no single lap resembled another in time or design. The Ethiopians' constant surges kept the field on edge. They were drafting off each other, sharing the pacing, and changing the lead as often as five times a lap. They were trying to orchestrate a breakaway and secure a clean sweep of the medals—gold, silver, and bronze—to Ethiopia.

The others in the field appeared to be ambushed. The unpredictability of the surges, the pressure the Ethiopians were applying, was crushing their spirit, casting them farther and farther adrift. Their faces were ashen. They needed a lifeline—a slow lap to catch their breath—but the three Ethiopians were relentless. Compared to the flowing strides of the Ethiopians, Viren, Maaninka, Foster, and Jorg looked dejected and isolated.

But distance running is never such a sure thing. Pain can recede, one's wind can return; the possibilities of renewal are as limitless as the mind can invent and absorb. What else could explain what happened on the 17th lap? What Frank McKay, a British sports journalist, described this way in his reporter's notepad. "Lap seventeen . . . Viren is striking out . . . out on his own. He's jumped to the lead. He's in the lead. What a burst! He's trying to disrupt the Ethiopian style . . . he won't be taken so easily by the African challenge, he's doing all he can . . . anything to try and retain his title . . ."

But Yifter and company quickly regrouped and attached themselves to Viren's heels as if they were simply taking their place in a queue to board a bus.

With three laps remaining the lead group was down to five—three Ethiopians and two Finns. Their gap on the rest of the field was 10 seconds.

At the start of the penultimate lap, Viren was still leading, with Kedir directly off his right shoulder and Yifter content in third.

As hard as he tried, evidenced by his sharp, wincing expression, Viren couldn't shake his shadow, Kedir, or—farther back in his slipstream—Yifter. This was his attempt to burn off Yifter's kick and give himself a chance for a medal. But could he do it all by himself? Time only would tell as Viren pulled the three Ethiopians and his teammate, Maaninka into the homestretch for the next to last time.

With the sound of the bell signaling the last lap, a hush descended on the stadium. Would the running order change? Indeed, would the world's running order change? Distance running up to this point in history had largely been a European affair. But here in Moscow the Africans were asserting their might.

Into the turn the arrangement up front remained unchanged: Kedir studied Viren from behind, Viren listened for a break in Kedir's steps, and Yifter, from his vantage point in third, studied them both.

With just 350 meters to go still nothing changed—Viren, Kedir, Yifter, Koto, Maaninka. Perhaps Viren's strategy had worked? Maybe Yifter couldn't find his sprint? Surely he would have charged past Viren by now? Finnish flags quickly became evident across the stands, swaying from side to side in expectant triumph and jubilation. Hope welled in Viren, too, and with the prospect of an Olympic 10,000-meter hat trick he carried on pounding forward.

On the backstretch there were still five men in the hunt for just three medals. The stadium was electric. Here were 85,000 people waiting for a burning fuse to reach its end, bracing themselves for some kind of bang. When would it come? How loud would it be? Someone was going to have to make some type of move sometime. But who?

The Ethiopian radio announcer sitting among the world's media along the homestretch was considering exactly this as he screamed into his microphone. "Miruts Yifter is still following the Finn. Miruts Yifter is still right there, very close to the lead."

Then it happened, the trigger was pulled. With 300 meters to go Yifter inserted a hard, deep surge. "Yifter has changed gears," Haile heard straight into his ear. "He's changed gears . . . Yifter the Shifter. He's leading now. Yes, Miruts Yifter is leading now. He's still leading. Yes, he's still leading." Yifter was a wild shark running out a fisherman's line. He was a locomotive. He was in complete ascendancy as the four runners behind him crumbled. Instead of fireworks over the final half lap—two men battling for the lead step by step down the homestretch—Yifter had extinguished everyone's suspense in an instant. Part amazing and unnerving, part anticlimatic, too, Yifter's incredible kick left no one in doubt. Especially young Haile, who suddenly realized, *The Olympic 10,000 meter champion is an Ethiopian . . . an Ethiopian like me.*

3

A Time to Run

Once known as Abyssinia, Ethiopia is mentioned by both Homer and Herodotus in their great texts. Ethiopia is Africa's oldest continuously identifiable nation, and is referred to more than 30 times in the Old Testament as a site of wondrous religious significance and happenings. There are tremendous natural riches to be found in Ethiopia. In places eucalyptus trees spread wild like rambling hedgerows. Staggering vistas point to bottomless cliffs and long, meandering rivers. There are boundaryless deserts, lakes that light up the valleys, deep green pastures, thick sugarcane fields, and rows of mango trees.

Ethiopia is twice the size of Texas, and five times larger than the United Kingdom. Lions, leopards, and cheetahs are among the mammals living here. Roughly two-thirds of Ethiopia rises high above northeast Africa's lowlands to form part of the Great Rift Valley. Expansive mountain ranges and cratered cones mark Ethiopia's average elevation at 7000 feet above sea level.

The original Ethiopians arrived from Arabia in the first half of the first millennium B.C. Immediately they became a dominant power in the Red Sea region. According to tradition, the Ethiopian nation was founded by Etiopik, the great-grandson of Noah. The queen of Sheba also ruled vast stretches of present-day Ethiopia, and even ventured as far north as Jerusalem, where she consorted with King Solomon and later bore him a son, Menelik. This established Ethiopia's link to the mighty Solomonic Dynasty, a connection that held sway in determining Ethiopia's leadership up until 1974.

Ethiopians also believe that on a paternal visit to Jerusalem, Menelik stole the Ark of the Covenant and brought it back to rest in Ethiopia. So it was that Ethiopia's association with Christianity strengthened—Menelik was considered to be related to Christ through his holy father, Solomon, a man thought to be the personification of God's will on earth. And it's this ancient connection to the Holy Land that explains why the majority of Ethiopians are still Christian today.

Ethiopia's riches and traditions have also fed her runners across time. It's a story that's widely seen to begin with Abebe Bikila, who ran the 1960 Olympic marathon in bare feet over Rome's cobbled streets to collect Africa's first Olympic gold medal. Bikila's victory was doubly significant as it put to rest Italy's symbolic hold on Ethiopian sovereignty.

Throughout Addis Ababa that warm evening in early September, people could be heard rejoicing at the news that Bikila had won. The chrous, "Bikila won! Bikila won!" rang out everywhere. Amhed Almaric, a shopkeeper in the center of the city, found his wife on bended knee blessing herself and thanking God for Bikila's victory. Zeleke Araya celebrated by hugging and kissing all 13 of his children. Thousands stood silent before their radios as they heard the Ethiopian national anthem played before the world for the first time. More amazing still, Bikila did it again four years later over Tokyo's marathon course, becoming the first man to win consecutive Olympic marathon titles.

Bikila was a tall, effortless runner who took up running as a schoolboy in his hometown of Jato. In Rome he wasn't even considered among the favorites. The 28-year-old bodyguard in Haile Selassie's imperial army had a best time of only 2 hours 21 minutes and 23 seconds, more than 6 minutes slower than the world record held by the Soviet Union's Sergey Popov.

To accommodate Rome's magnificent views, the marathon took place entirely outside the stadium. The race started late in the afternoon of September 10, and finished under the Arch of Constantine close to the Coliseum at dusk. After trailing quietly behind a pack of Europeans for more than half of the race, Bikila finally moved into the lead. Only Rhadi ben Abdesselem from Morocco was able to match Bikila's great strides. But the pace soon proved too demanding for him as well, and Bikila was left to run the final miles alone, eventually crossing the finish line in a new world's best time of 2:15.16.

Bikla's 1964 Olympic marathon victory also resulted in a new world record—2:12.12. And most incredibly he had had surgery to remove his appendix only six weeks prior. Upon arriving in Tokyo, Bikila was still clutching his side and limping in pain. But he was determined to display Ethiopians' heroic nature, and after a few days spent recovering in the Olympic village he was back to full training. Bikila's victory celebration in Tokyo, a rigorous set of calisthenics performed in the stadium's infield immediately after he crossed the line, left an indelible mark in the minds of millions: *This is a great man, an Olympian whose legacy will never pass.*

Tragically Bikila died at the age of 41 when he was struck down with a brain haemorrhage in 1973. This followed a serious car crash in 1969 that left him confined to a wheelchair. Yet in his short life, Bikila achieved much, including fathering four children and fostering Ethiopia's distance running tradition.

So it was that Mamo Wolde came to be, a young runner inspired by Bikila who won the next Olympic marathon in Mexico City in 1968. Wolde, however, was a reluctant gold medalist. To collect his prize he needed to beat his hero Bikila. And for this quiet man born and raised in the small village of DreDele, such an act seemed blasphemous.

As the race progressed Wolde was content to run behind Bikila for one of the lesser medals. The previous day he had won a silver medal in the 10,000 meters, so already his Olympics was a success. But as the American sportswriter, and also the fourteenth-place finisher in that 1968 Olympic marathon, Kenny Moore, later reported, Wolde had little to say about his fate over the course of that marathon run.

Moore writes, ". . . Bikila was running hurt that day in Mexico City. After ten miles, he turned and beckoned to an ebony wraith of a teammate, Mamo Wolde, a fellow officer in Emperor Haile Selassie's palace guard. Wolde wove through the pack to Bikila's side.

" 'Lieutenant Wolde.'

" 'Captain Bikila.'

" 'I'm not finishing this race.'

" 'Sorry, sir.'

" 'But Lieutenant, you will win this race.'

" 'Sir, yes sir.'

" 'Don't let me down.'

And Wolde, thinking some runners were out of sight ahead, took off. None was, but until the tape touched his chest, he couldn't be sure. He won relieved, by a masterful three minutes."

Wolde's victory also meant that Ethiopia hadn't produced a lone prodigy in Bikila, but a succession. After he returned to Addis Ababa and had his portrait enshrined inside the Olympic rings that tower above the national stadium, Ethiopia's success in future Olympics seemed a certainty. And indeed along came Yifter in 1980, who won not only the 10,000 meters, but also the 5000 meters, collecting Ethiopia's first Olympic gold medals on the track. At the Barcelona games in 1992 it was Derartu Tulu who won gold over 10,000 meters, a feat she repeated in Sydney in 2000. And so the tradition of Ethiopian gold medalists grew—Fatuma Roba, Million Wolde, Gezahegne Abera, and of course Haile.

Year after year Ethiopia produces track champions, world junior and senior record holders, and cross-country winners. To begin to understand how a country with only one synthetic track and an underfunded club system can be so successful, it's worth making a visit to Meskel Square in central Addis Ababa any day of the week.

Formerly known as Revolutionary Square, and the site where murals of Marx and Lenin once hung, Meskel Square is a huge terraced amphitheater in the center of the city comprising hundreds of 3-foot wide hard-packed dirt steps. Here all the city's promising runners come to train just after sunrise every morning. To begin their workout they hop onto the first step and run its full length of almost 400 meters. Then they move up a step and run the same distance again in the opposite direction. And it's through this process of weaving back and forth up the amphitheater one step at a time that they accumulate their triple-figure weekly mileage. Meskel Square has even been dubbed Ethiopia's "Field of Dreams." That's because few Ethiopians can imagine a future as a lawyer, doctor, or businessman. Access to education and professional experience is limited and expensive, whereas access to long-distance running is much more open and free. To begin with all one needs is the time to run and, of course, enough motivation.

Still, many Westerners ask, Isn't it the underdeveloped transport network across Ethiopia, which forces people to walk or run everywhere, especially children, some of whom cover miles a day getting to and from school, that explains where so many great runners come from? And what about the physiological benefits of living at altitude? Or the simple diet of grains, vegetables, meat, and fruit? Or maybe, others might suggest, it's genes—people blessed with light musculature, imbued with supernatural distance running qualities? But ask Haile to explain how his country can produce so many great runners and he will never forget to mention the freedom Ethiopians have to live inside their minds and imagine a better life. After all, the freedom to dream was what shaped his career most of all.

"Of course, many factors explain why we are such a strong distance running nation. The altitude is an advantage, yes. But altitude is not magical. Otherwise, there would be great runners in Switzerland or Nepal. Poverty, or many of our children having to run to school is not the only reason, either. Countries like Somalia and Sudan are also poor, but they hardly produce any world-class runners. That's why hard work, organization, and training intelligently are crucial. And we are very good at that. Patience is also very important. For example, it took Mamo Wolde 20 years before he could get his gold medal. In Ethiopia that is normal. Once someone begins to run it is very difficult to stop. And people will continue to run their whole lives despite never winning a prize or achieving a great result. My younger sister is that way. She has been running for many years despite not getting any results. But still she hopes that one day they will come. For us, running is part of our day-to-day life, like eating. There is always time to run. Training here is not so artificial like in Europe or America. It is who we are; running provides a rhythm to our day. For example, if I don't run I can't sleep well; I won't feel good; I won't be the person I believe I am—a man who runs. But it's also important to mention when explaining our success that the world only sees the best Ethiopians. No one sees us struggle to reach our form, or how we must prove our worth at home first. That's why many people think it's easy for us, and that we arrive at the Olympics or the world championships as naturally accomplished performers. But for every Ethiopian runner who is a success on the track in Europe, or on the roads in America, thousands have failed trying. Still, you see so many young boys and now also girls running hard every day. And that's down to the fact that we have so much inspiration. We want to be like Bikila, Wolde, Yifter . . . They gave us a reason to dream and hope.

They are our models; we see in them something that sparks our imagination and encourages us to change our lives."

Sport in Ethiopia was never supposed to develop this way: from inside the hearts and minds of individuals. Instead plans were put into place, logical, rational plans. In pre-Marxist Ethiopia sport's function was to foster moral training, and teach honesty, teamwork, and responsibility. And during the Marxist years that followed, writes the Ethiopian physical educator, Gordon Adane, sport's role was to "prepare the younger generation for highly productive labor for the benefit of society, and for the defence of the socialist homeland." The principles guiding the organization and provision of sport, therefore, were, Sport for struggle, Sport for production, Sport for victory and national pride, Sport for health, and Sport for friendship. Knowledge surrounding sport also became codified and operationalized across Ethiopia. As a result, prediction, control, and measurement infected how all games were to be understood and played.

This doctrine spread far and wide, even reaching Haile's tiny rural primary school. For when he ran his first organized race as an eight-year-old, his physical education teacher knew to scream at him to run faster.

"But, Teacher," Haile began when he finished, "I was so far ahead of everyone else. Why were you yelling at me to run faster?"

"Because, Haile, you can't only run for first," the teacher pronounced, as if reading straight from a government handbook. "Time is also very important."

"Time?" Haile asked confused. "What's that?"

And so it was that Haile came to understand the nature of records and comparison, and how a simple children's pastime like running could be transformed into a serious sport. Haile listened carefully to his teacher. He wanted to understand the difference between running around the measured circle behind his school and running through the fields around his home. On those latter occasions he'd stop running to look at a bird, or to climb a tree, or to jump into a river and cool off. And when he and his friends ran to school they never ran the entire way without stopping unless they were late. They'd walk for long spells and tell each other stories about different things that had happened around the village, like a donkey running loose inside someone's house. Or they'd imitate their teacher's voice and mannerisms, or repeat the odd things they overheard their older sisters and brothers talking about. But around the grass circle behind the schoolhouse all laughing and talking was forbidden. When the teacher lined everyone up and shouted, "Go," Haile knew he had to be quiet and continue running until the teacher said, "Enough."

"When I began real sport it was very strange to me," Haile explains today. "My physical education teacher was always taking times with a watch that he wore around his neck. He would give me very specific instructions on exactly how far and how hard I should run. And he was always very clear about telling me that I must never stop. At first this made me mad. *Why do I have to run this way? I just want to have fun; I want to run free like Yifter.* I didn't understand anything about sport and how a person participated and prepared."

But Haile learned quickly, and he learned well.

"By my third or fourth race I was asking my teacher straight after winning"—and he always won—"'What was my time? What was my time?' And when I'd find out I'd ask, 'Is that good? Is that good?' To be first is one thing, I learned as a boy, but to be the fastest is something even more special. Since then I have always thought about time and breaking records. Whether it's in a race, or just in practice over some of my training loops. Either way it's the same, because I believe I must always try to do better whenever I can."

4

Haile's Office

By way of an exception, as many as 500 men and women in Addis Ababa do go to work first thing every Monday morning. They travel from various neighborhoods across the city by foot or by bus, to the Bole Road, close to the airport, where they enter a newly built eight-story office building and begin their day.

The building's occupancy rate is 100 percent, which pleases the owner immensely. But not just because it earns him a good return on his investment. Creating usable, modern office space, he believes—this is the second office building in Addis he has built—will help stimulate Ethiopia's economy and inspire people to think positively about the future.

Of the few hundred people who report to work here every Monday morning, half a dozen head to the Ethiopian Airlines office on the first floor, and another ten to the United Parcel Service branch on the second floor. They sit behind their computers, or answer phones, or handle customers' queries. These are spacious offices: air-conditioned, with carpeted floors, and framed pictures of Ethiopia's varied landscape on the walls. Bay windows overlook the busy Bole Road below—a four-lane boulevard divided by a well-planted median strip. The view includes rows of clogged streetside shops; all ages scurry up and down the broken sidewalks. The traffic is slow and thick; cars' horns are constant, the smell of exhaust potent. Shirtless men strike shovels, picks, and hammers against the curb. They're digging a ditch to bury telephone wires.

Among the stores on the Bole Road are an internet café, a beauty salon, a dry cleaner, a fine dress shop, and a supermarket specializing in imported Italian foods. Taxis drop off and pickup passengers in a continual chain of revolving doors on wheels. And all manner of body parts—elbows, heads, rear ends—protrude out overstuffed buses' windows. It's a road heaving with busy offshoots, brimming with vital city scenes.

On the eighth floor a team of architects is busy first thing Monday morning drafting plans for new homes.

Salesmen wearing white collars and dark ties arrange an office furniture store's showroom on the building's fifth floor.

At an IT center on the fourth floor, computers are boxed for shipment to Kenya, Djibouti, and Sudan.

Richard Nerurkar, a former British international distance runner, reaches his eighth-floor office most Monday mornings before nine o'clock. He's the race director for the Great Ethiopian Run, a 10K road race that in its three-year history has become the biggest mass-participation event in Africa. Richard enrolls the race's 18,000 entrants, secures sponsorship, and battles all manner of bureaucratic bylaws with a magnificent view of the foothills that surround Addis Ababa.

Two young girls dressed identically in bright white canvas sneakers, tight jeans, and loose-fitting polo shirts work at a sports shop on the office block's ground floor.

Two heavily muscled men have jobs as personal trainers at the adjacent health club, where their clients include housewives, ambassadors, and tourists.

Also on the ground floor there is a café, where nearly a dozen waiters patrol 20 tables carrying small round trays in their hands and serving Pepsi, coffee, and tea. Behind a large glass-top counter a woman operates the cash register, another dishes out generous scoops of ice cream, while two other women quickly fix the drinks on order. In the café's kitchen, three chefs in white smocks prepare the always popular cheeseburgers, french fries, and slices of pizza. Popular, especially, with the building's owner.

The café's tables accommodate young couples who linger hand in hand over their coffees, children who direct their tongues over their ice cream with rattlesnake-like quickness, and well-appointed businessmen who slug shots of espresso before their next appointment, all the while clutching their mobile phones as if they provided some form of vital life support.

Connected to the office block is a modern cinema outfitted with 300 plush seats. Four men employed as technicians turn up every Monday morning to operate the sophisticated projection system imported from America. This is another one of the building owner's dreams: to operate the first privately owned movie theater in Ethiopia.

Other technicians are also employed in and around the office block. They ensure that the elevator runs smoothly, and the phone lines and energy supply don't cut out unexpectedly. They've been teamed with a band of uniformed security guards who wield thick key rings, flashlights, and billy clubs and keep watch in white plastic chairs by the building's entrance when they're not patrolling the exterior surroundings.

Also busy by the building's wide entrance and reception area first thing every Monday morning is a team of women in ankle-length blue smocks who scrub the white marble portico. They apply themselves with vigor, using mops fashioned from shredded rags attached to smoothed-over tree branches.

As is the case with any new building, some floors still need dressing before the first tenants can move in. The sound of saws, drills, and hammers echo through the stairwell. A man on a ladder attaches a stainless-steel light fixture to the ceiling in the foyer; a large wooden desk is carried upstairs to a third floor travel agency by three skinny men in heavily soiled turquoise overalls. And painters in every corner apply the finishing brushstrokes to corners and closets.

Such honest work agrees with the building's owner. He's not some absentee landlord, either. In fact, he's on site at least twice a day. And not to occupy a spacious top-floor suite equipped with a secretary to take all his calls and answer his mail. He prefers to do that himself. It's always him they ring when something needs attention. If the elevator's out of service, or the generator's down, or the accounts need going over, they know he'll drop whatever he's doing to come by and sort it out. That's just his nature: to solve problems, to address others' needs before his own.

He typically arrives for his first daily visit late in the morning, and returns again early in the evening. As he tours various floors, or strolls through the parking lot—his cell phone ringing nonstop—he might visit a tenant to see if anything in his shop needs fixing. Or he might pause to resolve a dispute over a late payment, or simply stop by the café for a cup of tea and a chat and one of those famous cheeseburgers he adores so much.

There will always be someone in the café he can talk to and swap news and information. After all, everyone knows him here. And not just because it's his building. It has more to do with his other job. His day job, you might call it. In fact, hanging from every wall in the café are pictures of him at work at that job—his homestretch battle with Paul Tergat at the Sydney Olympics, the latest promotional poster from Adidas, a clipping out of the *Addis Ababa Tribune* following his victory at the first Great Ethiopian Run. Given the café's name this decor couldn't be more appropriate. It's spelled out in large red cursive lettering above the entrance, OLYMPIC CAFÉ.

While most Ethiopians dream of a better life in Europe or America, Haile Gebrselassie—athlete, businessman, family man—dreams of a better life at home.

"It would be easy for Haile to invest his winnings abroad," Haile's older brother Assefa says. "But what would be the point of that? Like me, he is an Ethiopian. We live in Ethiopia. And Haile wants to give something back for all the support Ethiopia has given to him. He wants to set a good example to all Ethiopians who have done well personally, so hopefully everyone will want to invest in Ethiopia's future."

Assefa holds a prominent position on the board of Haile's construction company, and like Haile he believes that the potential in Ethiopia is great. "With democracy finally beginning to take hold, and less rigid bureaucracies and bribing, we have more possibilities today to attract foreign investors, foreign currency."

It's a view shared by one of Haile's best friends and the manager of the ground-floor sports shop in Haile's building, Yasin Side. "There still need to be fewer restrictions on customs and what people can bring into the country and sell, but things have gotten much better. And Haile, through his great victories on the track and his strong business sense, has been very important in advancing that change."

In many ways it's amazing how much progress Ethiopia has made in the last decade. Early in Haile's running career, when traveling to Europe and racing for money was something new and exciting, he couldn't believe how differently people lived outside Ethiopia. *Why can't Ethiopia be rich? What's our problem? Why can't we have electricity and phones lines in every house? Why can't we have plumbing and paved roads?*

While much remains to be done, at least today the Ethiopian economy is expanding and growing. "Companies know they are welcome here," Haile says. "Still, we need more dollars, pounds, and euros, and more examples of hard work. Do you realize that we have 21 national holidays. How many does America have? How many does Britain have? Not even half that. This is part of our problem: People have to learn to work. They have to become responsible for themselves and their families. To depend on foreign aid or foreign food is to stop living for yourself. I remember when I was a boy my father used to put enough grain and maize into reserve to last for a year. We always knew that we had something to live on if there was a drought or a flood. But today farmers don't do that. Not when they know that one of the 200 relief agencies based here will provide food for them. We need to change people's attitudes and teach them how to take care of themselves. We have to become better at business and management. Like they are in Europe and America."

But Haile knows how difficult it is to adopt European attitudes and still be accepted at home. "We need Ethiopian businessmen who aren't afraid to change traditions," he says. "But they can't simply follow American or British ways. They have to remain Ethiopian; they have to live and act as Ethiopians do."

It's Haile's concerns with business and the future of Ethiopia that he often turns to Assefa and Yasin to discuss. "Do you realize, Yasin," Haile might say to his friend, "that almost 85 percent of our people are farmers? What is it in the United States, less than 10 percent?"

These conversations usually take place in the morning, over tea in the Olympic Café. And as Haile expresses the finer points of one issue or another, his hands typically begin to move faster than his mouth—"In America they can produce enough food to feed the entire world while we can't even feed ourselves." They dart through the air like small black wings. Veins rise off them like narrow mountain ranges on a topographical map. His wrists are bird-like, his fingers fine like the prongs on a shrimp fork. Moreover, his entire body is slight and wisp-like. Especially when he is dressed in half tights and a T-shirt, both black and snug fitting with his chief sponsor's three stripes running down the sides, as he is most mornings sitting in the Olympic Café. Those are his work clothes. And it's outside the city where Haile's workday begins. It's just a short commute from his house, about 20 minutes by car, and all in one direction: up. Driving up 10,000 feet is how he reaches the forests and trails atop the Great Rift Valley that surrounds Addis Ababa. It's where Haile's true office is, the legendary Ethiopian training ground, Entoto.

On the road to Entoto, Haile drives past the American embassy where out front stand thick concrete blockades and stern armed servicemen ready to ward off any potential security threats. He also passes a series of monuments honoring those Ethiopians who lost their lives to Italian forces after Mussolini got the idea in 1936 that Ethiopia belonged to him. Impressive government buildings also line his route: the Ministry of Education, the Ministry of Finance, Addis Ababa University.

This is the same road Miruts Yifter used to drive, and before him Mamo Wolde, and before him Abebe Bikila. Like Haile, they all traveled to Entoto to refine their trade. So they would have driven through Shero Meda, too, the poorest district in all of Addis Ababa, where the majority of people either live on the streets with nothing but the clothes on their back, or they work 12- to 14-hour days lifting, carrying, and digging for barely enough money to buy a loaf of bread or a single orange. And perhaps like Haile, Yifter, Wolde, and Bikila also thought to themselves how lucky they were as they sat in their cars staring out at so much hardship and suffering: *My day's work running through the forests up here is easy. I can't complain. It's nothing compared to what these people must endure.*

Certainly Haile's double workouts day after day are tough and demanding, grueling in fact. And, yes, it's true that he's often sore and tired and in pain, but he's quick to remind himself, especially when he confronts the awful conditions that so many of his countrymen must live in, *Hey, I cannot feel sorry for myself. I'm very lucky. It's just sport I'm doing, after all, and so really only fun and games.*

Research has shown that a human being can survive for three weeks without food, and three days without water. But without oxygen it's three minutes at most. That still hasn't stopped Haile from purposely depriving himself of oxygen every day for hours at a time. When he reaches Entoto, the high ground of the Great Rift Valley, and steps out of his car, he stretches his arms above his head and rises onto his toes. The odd creak in his joints follows—ankle, hip, knee. He holds this pose and breathes in deeply. It's a hard pull, like the last turn of a wrench to tighten a screw. In the process his face expands and his chest swells—inside him is a massive engine of pipes, pumps, and valves. His low percentage of fat means his rib cage makes a clear impression against his shirt. He then exhales fluidly and drops onto his heels; the rush of air he expels stirs up some dirt on the ground.

Already a dozen boys and girls are around his car singing in a high-pitched, three-beat rhythm, "Haile, Haile, Haile." They clap their hands, bounce off one another, smile, and hop in place. A boy wearing torn pants and no shirt reaches out and touches Haile's arm. He wants to know if it's actually flesh and bone his superhero's made of; he's seeing what the weave of Haile's fine Adidas top feels like. Then in an instant, like the sound of a bell, or a flash of light, Haile's off. He's high-stepping into the forest waving bye-bye to the children. "I must go run now," he shouts over his shoulder. And they all understand; no one protests. They know that this is Haile's office and that this is where he comes to work.

The physiology of respiration decrees that adaptation into an efficient oxygen carrying machine requires continual stresses to the cardiovascular system that are progressively harder and harder. The primary organs involved in this intense, highly integrated act—the heart, the blood vessels, the lungs—respond to this challenge in concert: The heart pushes a liter or more of blood through the lungs where it exits fully oxygenated and begins its journey to the muscles. In the throes of strenuous exercise this cycle repeats itself, stroke after stroke, at least three times a second. That's compared to once a second at rest. A runner's breathing rate also climbs from 12 breaths a minute at rest to 50 breaths a minute by midrace or midworkout. Total expired airflow increases 30 times; blood volume pumped grows eightfold, and heat production inside a working runner's body is 100 times higher than at rest.

At conditions of altitude, where due to decreases in barometric pressure the percentage of breathable oxygen in the air is far less than it is at sea level (12 percent compared to 21 percent), these figures escalate dramatically. The heart and lungs strain to provide enough oxygen to the working muscles, and to compensate the kidneys go into overdrive and secrete the hormone erythropoietin (EPO), which stimulates the production of additional oxygen-carrying red blood cells. Stressing the cardiopulmonary system this way isn't easy. Normal breathing at 10,000 feet above sea level can feel like sucking a milk shake through a straw. Every ounce of satisfaction comes harder, thicker, slower. Running at such a height can make breathing feel like you have a sock over your head.

The added difficulty of running at altitude, however, is ultimately rewarded back down at sea level. Those additional red blood cells mean more fuel (oxygen) can reach the muscles, thus increasing an athlete's power and endurance. When Haile drops into London or Zurich, or any other lowland location he might go to race, he feels the oxygen-rich air flood his body.

"Down at sea level it's like a valve has been opened inside my lungs. Breathing becomes much easier. And although training at altitude is very hard, it's the only way to become a world class distance runner. For me, actually, it's very important. After a race in Europe or America, I like to return to Ethiopia and get back to Entoto as soon as possible. I'm not like some African runners who have a base in Europe. I don't want to lose the gains I've made; I want to continue getting the benefits of high altitude."

And the benefits Haile feels from training at Entoto are supported by good science. "It's worth as much as 3 percent," claims the exercise physiologist Tim Noakes, who has studied the effects of high altitude on runners, cross-country skiers, and cyclists. That may not seem like a lot, but the difference between Haile's gold-medal-winning time in Sydney and the time of the 15-place finisher was just that, three percent. And when Lance Armstrong won the Tour de France in 2000, a race that covered over 2000 miles, his winning time was just 3 percent faster than the 100th-place finisher's time. Three percent, then, can mean the difference between becoming the best on earth in your sport and remaining in the middle of the pack.

It wasn't actually until 1968, when the Olympics were held at almost 8000 feet above sea level in Mexico City, that coaches, athletes, and sports scientists became interested in the effects of altitude on endurance events. Besides Mamo Wolde, who won the marathon for Ethiopia, a number of Kenyan athletes who were also raised in tiny villages atop the Great Rift Valley turned in spectacular results in Mexico City. Kipchoge Keino, the 1500 meter gold medalist, blasted past a gasping Jim Ryun from America. Naftali Temu easily prevailed in the 10,000 meters. And Amos Biwott and Benjamin Kogo ran one-two in the steeplechase ahead of a field of exhausted Europeans.

In an effort to match the East Africans' altitude advantage and recalibrate their blood chemistry, many American and European distance runners today spend large chunks of their season training in places like Boulder, Colorado; Albuquerque, New Mexico; or any number of Alpine villages in France or Switzerland. The less patient among them simply inject EPO into their bloodstream, despite this practice being prohibited by the International Olympic Committee.

But catching such cheats is extremely difficult when the effects being tested for—a high red blood cell count—can also be attained naturally by training someplace high in the sky like Entoto.

In one of the latest scientific developments athletes can now simulate at sea level the conditions found at 8000 feet by living in so called "altitude houses." Into these houses excessive levels of nitrogen are pumped to reduce the availability of breathable oxygen. Athletes then live normally, carrying out everyday activities such as cooking, watching television, and sleeping. Except all the time they're quietly stimulating their kidneys to produce more EPO, and hence more red blood cells. Of course when they step outside their altitude house they re-enter an oxygen-rich environment which enables them to run harder, longer, and faster than they could if they were also training at altitude. The combination of low-altitude workouts bolstered by living at altitude, has led many European and American runners to adopt the motto, "Live high, train low."

But as Haile is quick to point out, altitude, hard work, and science are only some of the necessary conditions needed to produce great distance runners. "Most important of all," he says, "is self-belief, confidence, and inspiration. New stadiums, modern facilities, they are all good but they will never be a substitute for tradition and expectation. When one runs with the past, one never runs alone."

And Haile obviously knows what he's saying. For when he emerges from the forest his steps look lighter and faster than they did two hours earlier. He appears stronger and more secure. And what else could explain the glow in his eyes? Or why his skin is glistening and the ground beneath him is alight? Surely he's being led by a cast of spirits from another time. They must be in the trees, or in the air . . . the spirits that inhabit Entoto . . . Bikila, Wolde, Yifter. They're the ones, after all, who've made Haile's path possible: his trail to the top . . . his road to work.

5

On Track

Where Haile works extends beyond the forests of Entoto. To hone his sprint finish and to harden his midrace resolve demands a track's smooth surface. And in Ethiopia there is only one true, synthetic 400-meter track. It's in the capital, Addis Ababa, and to get there from the north of the city you drive west down Haile Gebrselassie Avenue through Meskel Square until you reach Ghion Street. The entire time you'll have to be careful to weave your way through the hundreds of taxis, people, and animals—dogs, goats, sheep, cows. No one, it seems, obeys crosswalks or acknowledges vehicles' right-of-way.

On Ghion Street, you turn right and drive through a small grassy area until you reach a parking lot the size of what you might find in any medium-sized strip mall in America. This is the entrance to Ethiopia's national stadium.

Today a dozen cars are parked out front—Toyotas, Nissans, Suzukis—all of them visibly used. There is one Mercedes, however, a silver four-door sedan, and it holds a reserved space next to the steps leading inside.

The sky stretches high above the stadium; it's deep blue, and the sun is temperate. The morning is new, just a few minutes past 8 o'clock. But not if you're a member of Ethiopia's national distance running squad. They've been at work inside the stadium for over an hour, running a tough series of 1200s, 800s, and 400s on the worn tartan track.

Over a bumpy soccer field that completes the track's interior, a local team repeats a series of passing and heading drills. Seating around the stadium is varied: backless concrete steps, fixed wooden chairs painted green with black vinyl seat cushions, and rows of folding blue plastic seats. A decaying roof covers the seats along the homestrech. The capacity is close to 30,000. But this morning only a handful of people are about. Cleaners outnumber spectators. But that's because nothing special is happening. Nothing special for Addis Ababa, that is, where it's normal on a Tuesday morning in January to find some of the world's best distance runners—Olympic champions, world record holders, world champions—all together in the same place.

Three sets of Olympic rings positioned like great billboards tower above the top row of seating along the backstretch of the track. A group of six runners occupy lane one. Up front and clearly in command is the smallest one, the best-dressed one—white spike shoes, blue shorts, and a matching silver short-sleeved shirt. Each set of Olympic rings signifies a podium position—gold, silver, bronze. And inside each respective set are portraits of the Ethiopian distance runners who have won an Olympic medal bearing that shade. It's a fitting backdrop considering the Olympic legend on the track below.

Set as it is in the center of a busy, cosmopolitan city of 3.2 million, all manner of noises reach the stadium: horns, screeches, ring tones, conversations. But that doesn't disturb the men and women at work here. They're oblivious to all things man-made except the large patch of red track that they fill with each new stride. This is running Ethiopian style: hard, fast, and firmly in the present.

Photographers, the press, and certainly any voyeurs aren't allowed in the stadium today. A pair of middle-aged men wearing faded black blazers patrol the central steps leading down to the track. They display the nerve of power-hungry Broadway ushers. But then this is a national troupe of sorts: international performers who represent the spirit of their country through the art of movement. And, oh, how easily they move. Particularly the one known throughout the world as "the Emperor."

Directing this morning's performance is Dr. Wolde-Meskel Kostre, Ethiopia's head track coach. From his position on the infield grass, just across from the finish line, Dr. Kostre barks commands, screams encouragement, and shouts out times. Called "Doctor," by his athletes, Dr. Kostre took his Ph.D. in physical education from a Hungarian university back in the 1960s when Ethiopia practiced sports education exchanges with the former Eastern Bloc. Doctor's voice is strong and youthful, easily reaching the back row of seating along the homestretch. His appearance, though, represents something very different. Following his recent hip replacement, the solid wooden cane he holds in his left hand is more for propping him up than just steadying him. Every step he takes exerts a heavy toll on his frame: a sudden twisting of his shoulders and back, an exaggerated and off balance weight shift. But his disposition seems unaffected by his disability. He never winces; he remains standing. Perhaps it's some form of sympathetic stoicism he's practicing? For like the athletes he's overseeing this morning, he knows that the reason for being here is not a matter of comfort.

It certainly has to be the discomfort of running such fast-paced intervals that contributes to the silence around the track: thirty runners—three men's groups, one women's—biting bullets in order to endure; turning out successive 400-meter laps near 60 seconds snuffs any idle chitchat. It's a quiet that resembles the hush inside a high-wire balancing act—each forward step carefully considered. Even the leader of the pack seems affected. Haile's chest heaves and his legs perform a broken jig at the beginning of each one of his recovery periods. He comes around slowly, like a boxer waiting out his standing eight count. But the moment his rest period expires, when it's time to run again, he's steady on the line, his feet and hands out front, his head poised anticipating Doctor's command.

Off the line Haile rises quickly and settles into the prescribed pace: 1200 meters in 2 minutes and 55 seconds. It will be his fourth such 1200 today, only to be followed by four 800s under two minutes, and four 400s in 55—there was also a 4-mile tempo run as part of the warm-up.

Finally the silence circling the track is broken with an explosion of high-fives and animated gasps. Doctor removes his stopwatch from around his neck; today's repetitions are done, and he stuffs it into his sweatpants pocket. Quickly relief spreads across everyone's face. The widest grin comes from the man whose smile lights up the world of international track and field. For Haile this is another satisfying morning's work.

Following a gentle cool-down jog, some light stretching, a quick shower, and a change of clothes, the squads' satisfaction reaches the parking lot. Mobile phones sound, departures are delayed, light chatter fills the air:

"You feeling good, man? You feeling good?"

"Nice work this morning, nice work."

Replies come forth rapidly, and they are all positive.

Soon small clusters of conversation form. Doctor leans against the stadium's outside wall discussing with Elshadai Negash, a sports reporter for the *Addis Ababa Tribune*, the results he's expecting at the world championships in Paris at the end of the summer. "At least three gold medals," he predicts. Million Wolde is speaking quietly with Derartu Tulu. And two of the "Young Guns" of Ethiopian distance running, Kenenisa Bekele and Gebre Gebremariam, are comparing the features on their new watches.

Getaneh Tessema, a former national champion over 10,000 meters, and now a manager as well as the husband of Olympic medalist and world cross-country champion Gete Wami, is explaining to Sileshi Sihine, another rising star, the European track races on offer when the outdoor season comes around—"There's Hengelo, June 1, and then the Golden League Series begins in Oslo . . ." Berhane Adere, another world champion among the group, rises onto her toes looking for her husband. "Start the car, start the car," she tells him when she finally catches his eye. And a minute later they're driving off in their red four-door Toyota.

When Haile finally emerges from the stadium he's moving slowly with his eyes cast down. He unlocks the trunk of his Mercedes and swings his gym bag off his shoulder and inside. He closes the trunk and then leans against his car's side. Fatigue, though, doesn't account for his lethargic pose. He's on the phone with his brother, Assefa, listening carefully. At inexact intervals, however, his head pops up followed by a barrage of speech. His hands move in coordinated waves with his words, his nostrils flare, and his voice sweeps across the parking lot. But no one turns and stares. The others' conversations are just as full—"Where are you off to now, man?" "Hey, show me what you got there." Besides, they all know it's just Haile being Haile: talking on the phone the second training is over, probably solving some problem at one of his buildings, going straight from one task to another, never resting, never taking a break. "That's just Haile, you know. That's just Haile . . ."

For any attempt Haile makes at a new world record, he carefully considers every split—400, 800, 1200 . . . —and then lap by lap mentally crosses them off as if they were items on a shopping list. He knows he must narrow his attention this way to succeed. And he's exactly the same with whatever he might be doing, like talking on the phone: lock into the job at hand, focus entirely on the moment. It's what helps to explain his incredible winning record: his ability to concentrate so wholly on whatever's before him. That and his boundless energy and remarkable powers of recovery. He'll even drive up to Entoto later this afternoon for two more hours of running. And before that he has a lunchtime meeting to chair, more than a dozen phone calls to return, and the opening of an art gallery to attend. Not what you'd call your typical elite athlete's self-absorbed schedule of training, eating, and sleeping. But whoever said Haile Gebrselassie is typical? In fact, it's the agenda for this afternoon's meeting that he's going over with Assefa.

". . . If it's a good idea to buy land there . . . make that our first matter of business."

Over lunch is where Haile generally oversees the running of his construction and real estate company. He might meet with his board of directors, his architect, or his accountant. Whoever's involved will arrive by one o'clock to assemble around the large wooden table in Haile's dining room. It's a much more relaxed setting than either of the boardrooms on the top floor of his buildings. He and his guests will first share some casual conversation—news, politics—as three servants quietly and efficiently serve all variety of foods—*injera*, an unleavened bread prepared from a locally grown grain, *tef*, *wat*, a fiery lamb or chicken stew, lasagne, steak, salad.

Haile is most at home here around the table, talking, eating, trading stories. "What's that?" he'll shout if someone says something he hasn't heard before. And he'll go on asking questions until he's satisfied. Or, if he needs to, he can be quiet. Listening is not one of his shortcomings.

By dessert the conversation will normally have turned to the business matters at hand—acquisitions, investments, marketing. There's freshly brewed coffee to accompany a five piece ripe fruit salad. For the most part all of Haile's associates are his relatives: uncles, cousins, siblings . . . And their meetings tend to last one hour. That usually leaves Haile some time to grab a nap before his afternoon workout begins at four o'clock. Unless he has a sick relative to visit, or a wedding or a funeral to attend. In Ethiopia a family's social life is extremely large and busy. It's something much more involved and compulsory than anything in Europe or America. And while it can be draining for Haile to satisfy his family's many obligations, it's also where he gathers much of his strength.

For Haile is a man who enjoys having people around. It's his nature to be social, whether on or off the track. It's one reason why he so strongly supports the squad system employed by the Ethiopian Athletics Federation (EAF): "I like to be together with other hard-working athletes when I train. They keep me honest. And that's something very special about Ethiopia's training system: We all have to train together here in Addis. In Kenya, for example, runners are spread across the country and train alone or in very small groups. Me, though, I like to be with people. Then the hard work is so much more enjoyable."

And in a year like this one, 2003, with the world championships scheduled for the end of the summer, support is even more vital for Haile as he contemplates his future on the track. If he does decide to compete at the world championships—a decision he plans to make in a month's time—every distance runner in the world will be out to stop him from collecting his fifth 10,000-meter title. Ironically, that challenge could come most directly from home. Young Kenenisa Bekele believes he might have a chance to win the 10,000 in Paris. But he's keeping that to himself—he has yet to ever even run a 10,000 on the track. Which is why Haile's not so worried about Kenenisa possibly upsetting his summer plans. At least for the moment, that is . . .

Compared to Haile's busy, bustling training environment of today, circumstances at the beginning of his career were much more solitary and straightforward: run alone, run long, run hard. His stride, too, so balanced and light, even failed to leave a trace in the dirt and scrub beneath his feet. It was as if he had never been where he just was: He was truly on his own. Through the endless hours he spent running around his home in his early teenage years, he had just his shadow to keep him company, and the wind rolling across the fields to race.

As he explains now, "My first days as a runner all took place in the countryside outside Asela, where I was born. I had no coaches or teammates. I would run late in the day when I finished my work around the farm. And the pleasure I felt was deep and satisfying. I knew it was my calling to be a runner. Certainly I never felt alone. Not when I could imagine Yifter and his Olympic gold medal, or dream about the world beyond Asela and the different possibilities before me."

For Haile life on the farm was hard, and leaving Asela and reinventing himself seemed to be an idea he was born with. There were no machines or tractors to do any of the work. Whatever got done got done by hand: plowing, digging, lifting, harvesting. It was backbreaking labor: "Today I could never do the work I did as a boy," Haile says. "I was much stronger then. Of course, not in terms of running, but I could dig a hole for five hours, or carry a heavy load for miles, like the jugs of water we had to fill at the river 3 miles away and transport back home. I could not do that today. As a boy, though, that was normal. But, of course, that wasn't my life to choose. It was my life by chance not choice. And I didn't like it. I never did. I always wanted something different: a life with more excitement, comfort, and new experiences."

At least there was always enough food around the Gebrselassie home, and young Haile never went to bed with an empty stomach: "But there was no variety, and little nutrition in what we ate," he explains. "Meat and vegetables weren't always available; week after week we might eat the same thing for every meal: corn, corn, and more corn. Our clothes, too, were only basic, and just enough to protect us from the weather. Life was a constant struggle. There were no comforts. Most days I worked 12 hours or more with only a short break for lunch. And even with so much hard work the profit we made from our farm was nothing. It was barely enough to feed ourselves. So I used to imagine some other life for myself, something, anything I could do besides farming and herding. Like becoming a pilot, I'd think, when I saw a plane fly overhead. Or if I noticed something curious it would spark an idea: *How is it possible for that animal to jump so far? Why can't I do that, too?* I thought about the future constantly: *Maybe I can be a carpenter? Maybe I can be an artist?* And while playing games with my friends like tag or hide-and-seek, I'd realize the pleasure of a challenge and the reward of doing well. I liked discovering what I was capable of, and what I could do better than others. Testing my limits was fun for me; that was always my quest."

Despite the hard times Haile endured growing up in the impoverished countryside of Ethiopia, he also experienced many moments of hope and joy like playing football with his friends, imagining a greater life for himself, racing donkeys, pitching pennies, and rolling boulders into gorges and watching them break apart. But fame—call it celebrity —intrigued young Haile the most.

As a boy Haile spent a great deal of time listening to his uncles and his older brothers talk about politics and current events. If one of them said something grand about someone, he would quickly ask, "Who is this guy?" Or if he heard a person's name on the radio, he would think, *He must be someone special. How can I be like that?* As such, Haile's understanding of the world and his own expectations far exceeded his age.

He tells a story that illustrates his precocious nature. "I remember one day in school we were learning about different ideologies around the world like feudalism, capitalism, and socialism. The teacher was explaining how feudalism is better than slavery, and capitalism is better than feudalism, but that the highest form of political development is socialism. Of course, this was the time when Ethiopia was under Mengistu and we were a socialist state. But I didn't quite understand this progression, so I asked the teacher which countries practiced capitalism and which countries practiced socialism. He said, 'Bulgaria, Hungary, Mongolia, China, they are socialist. And America, Britain, Germany, they are capitalist.' Then I asked, 'But Teacher, I have heard from my brothers that in those countries like America and Britain people have more than in those other countries. How is it possible then that socialism is better than capitalism?' And, oh, he was shocked that such a question came from one of his students. 'Haile,' he said, 'I want to talk to you after class.' When class ended I walked up to the front of the classroom and he told me to sit down. He took a big breath before he began to speak. I could see that he wasn't angry with me. His face was soft; his eyes were warm. So I wasn't afraid. 'Listen, Haile, what I'm teaching you in class, this is what it says in the book. Reality is not important here. According to my job I must teach you what the book says.' And it was from that moment on that I knew I must never automatically believe what people tell me. I should always ask why something is happening in such a way. Because there are always reasons for the way things are, and while sometimes those reasons are good, other times they may not be. And it's important to know the difference. For example, I could see that there was no better reason for me to become a farmer other than the fact that my father was one. But in my mind that was not a good enough reason for me to follow that plan. At least not without considering some other possibilities. If I wanted to do something different, then why not? If I wanted to be a runner, I should try. My father, though, couldn't understand this. He wasn't happy at all about my choice to keep running."

Gebrselassie Bekele, Haile's father, was a practical man concerned with the everyday realities of life on his farm: tending the fields, supporting the livestock, feeding his family. He wanted Haile to stop wasting his time: "How can running be anything else but something you might do for fun? How can a man make money running?"

Even when Haile explained to his father how special running was to him, and how he loved to test himself and experience his body in motion—the speed, the warmth, the freedom—he would refuse to understand. "I want you in the fields working, not out running," he would shout. And this became a big problem. Because like any boy, Haile wanted to please his father and make him proud. But even without his father's blessing, Haile always found a way to keep running.

"My brothers and sisters would sometimes do my work for me around the farm so I could go out running. And on Saturdays I would travel into the village to race against the other boys. It was so exciting, and such a relief from the fields. I had great support from my physical education teacher, too. He encouraged me and told me I could be a world-class runner. And I believed him. I could see, for example, how easily I beat the other boys. Also my oldest brother, Tekeye, was living in Addis and running marathons and he encouraged me, too. In fact, in June 1988, when I was 15 years old, I went to visit Tekeye in Addis to run the Abebe Bikila marathon. It was my first visit to the capital. My father didn't know why I was going there. I just told him I wanted to visit Tekeye."

In the city Haile couldn't believe his eyes: the big buildings, the rows of stores, the crowded streets packed with cars and people. It was his first experience with electricity and running water. All great curiosities. And the marathon was a shock as well. Haile's time of 2 hours 48 minutes wasn't bad for a 15-year-old boy, but the effort left his body bruised and battered with thick blisters across the inside of his thighs and on the top and bottom of his feet.

When Haile returned home and his father discovered why he had gone to Addis, his rage was immense. "How could marathon running ever be of use to anyone? Our country needs farmers, doctors, and teachers . . . not runners." But nothing could deter Haile at this point. He said to his father, "I must carry on training, Father. I am a runner, now. It's something I must do."

But to continue running Haile needed support. Fortunately the local police club coach in Asela recognized Haile's ability and spoke to his superior, a major in the police force, about Haile possibly receiving some funding. That decision wasn't the major's, though. It belonged to his boss, an old colonel, who eventually agreed to meet Haile.

"Take a seat," the colonel ordered when Haile and his coach entered his office.

"Thank you, sir," Haile's coach said after performing a special salute.

"Why are you here?"

And the coach replied, not Haile, who was shuddering in his chair. "Well, sir, I think you heard from the major about this young boy . . . this runner here, Haile Gebrselassie."

"Oh, that is him," the colonel barked without even looking up from his paperwork.

"Yes, sir, this is him."

Then, setting down his pen, the colonel glanced across the room at Haile. To make a good impression Haile sat up straight in his chair. "He's very young, and small," the colonel said. "Are you sure he can run?"

"Believe me, Colonel, he is so talented . . . and he'll keep improving, too."

"So what do you want from me now?"

"Well, Colonel, would it be possible for him to receive some support. Nothing too much, sir, just some pocket money to help him live while he trains."

And the colonel let out a scream: "Money, money, money. Everyone is always asking for money." This was followed by a long pause. And through the silence Haile sat still, holding his breath while wide streams of sweat ran down his back. "Okay, I'll fix it," the colonel finally said. "But you, boy," he added when Haile stood up to leave, "you keep going now and make me look like a smart man."

Now with a monthly income of $15, Haile could afford to leave the farm and his father to pursue his dream. He moved into a small one-bedroom apartment in Addis with Tekeye and Assefa. He was now a member of the police sports club, Omedla, and sworn in as Lieutenant Gebrselassie. It was from that moment on that Haile began to live the life of a full-time runner.

With no official police duties to perform besides his daily training, Haile's routine became constant and regular: He ran twice a day every day, once in the morning and again in the afternoon. His dedication was extreme; he found motivating himself second nature, like remembering the days of the week or the months in a year—"Training is very important; it is a must; I can never miss a day; nothing must stop me from following my program, otherwise my results will not be very good."

Between workouts Haile spent his time around the apartment listening to music on the radio, resting, or reading. Minus his transportation costs and his rent, his small wage afforded him little: perhaps an orange Fanta once or twice a month as a special treat. But thankfully, Assefa had a good job and could afford to buy the necessary food to fuel Haile's running. So it was that every day after work Assefa would come straight home to prepare dinner for Haile and Tekeye when they returned from their afternoon workout. After eating and washing up it would be time for Haile to go to sleep, after which he would wake up the next day at 6 A.M. and begin the whole cycle of training, eating, and sleeping once again.

Almost immediately after arriving in Addis, Haile began to impress his new coach and his police club teammates. Their long runs around Entoto were hard and exacting, and the new boy from the countryside was always near the front. Haile's strength was even more evident on the track. The sessions his coach designed were unforgiving—5 times 2000 meters, 15 times 400 meters—and run as they were in a large pack incredibly competitive, too.

As Haile continued to progress, lowering his times in practice by the day, his confidence soared. So hard and constant was his training that he actually came to see races as easy days. And in time he began to develop a unique combination of skills and abilities. He complemented his incredible resolve and endurance with the coordination and alacrity of a sprinter. Soon he was equipped to handle any tactical situation: In a race run at a sizzling pace he couldn't be dropped; in a slow race left to the homestretch he knew he could trust his kick.

Haile first recognized his "inner power," his ability "to challenge the best," when he was 19 and he completed a rare 5000/10,000 double victory at the 1992 world junior track and field championships in Seoul, South Korea. "After that competition I knew I was on my way. I felt confident that something special was inside me. And with more training and hard work I knew my success would continue. It was then that I started thinking seriously about Atlanta and the Olympics in 1996: *That's my chance to do what Yifter did,* I thought. *My chance to win the 10,000-meter gold medal.*"

Quite unexpectedly, however, Haile developed another obsession in 1992 that turned out to be just as strong as his desire to strike gold in Atlanta. It was an uncontrollable desire that came to him in a vision. One afternoon he saw the most beautiful girl selling sodas and juices behind a small makeshift stand in the middle of the city. "Who is that girl?" he asked his friends. And in time he had a name: Alem.

Almost immediately thereafter, in between his workouts on the track and her classes at school, Haile and Alem were spending every available moment of the day together. Initially, though, Haile found it difficult to start their relationship: "It was my first time wanting to get together with a woman . . . I had never had a girlfriend before.

And it was the same for Alem. Finally, my coach said he would help. But he wasn't sure because he wanted me to focus only on running and not be distracted by a girlfriend. 'No woman now,' he told me again and again. 'Now is for running. In a few years you will have everything you need following all your success and then you can date this woman.' But I kept bothering him about it until he eventually realized that because I am such a stubborn person and I will never stop thinking about possibly being with Alem unless I was to try, that not introducing us might actually cause a bigger distraction to my running than introducing us ever could."

So Haile and Alem had their first date, a quiet afternoon over two sodas. And before long they were seeing each other regularly, walking hand in hand through a park close to Alem's home. "While our first date was very difficult, and I had no idea how to start a conversation with a woman," Haile can say today, "things soon got better. Unlike anyone I had ever known, I could share with Alem my plans for becoming a runner and what I imagined would be our life together: 'We will have plenty of money and live in a good house and have all the food we want to eat,' I would tell her. Soon she became my everything. The one person in the world who accepted me completely. She kept me in balance with her strength and her ever-present calm. Then again, her name means 'world,' and for me that was what she was. She always told me that she just wanted a good man who was kind to her, and that being wealthy wasn't so important. But it was important to me. I wanted more. It's like when you make your first dollar you want to make a second, or when you win your first race you want to win another . . . and so on. Besides, how else was I going to make a life for myself away from Asela unless I could succeed as a runner?"

It wasn't long before Haile's grand designs began to come true. In 1993, when he won the 10,000 meters at the world championships in Stuttgart, his prize included a brand-new Mercedes Benz (the same car

75

he still drives today). And when his Mercedes was delivered to him in Addis his father finally realized, "Yes, Haile, I can see it's possible to make a living as a runner."

Alem also realized it. Except there was a problem. The more Haile ran, and the more races he won, the more time he needed to spend away from home. "After 1993 I was winning many races around the world and earning good money for the first time, but I was also very unhappy. I couldn't bear to be away from Alem. And in 1994, when my love for her was its deepest, I didn't know how I would manage. Going to sleep in different hotels across Europe all I could think about was Alem. I knew I was the one man for her and that she was the only woman for me. I would call her every day no matter where I was— Lausanne, Monte Carlo, Brussels—and we would talk for hours. Oh my, was my phone bill ever huge. Then came 1996 and the Olympics, and I knew that I had to do something about my love for her. So I said to her before I left for Atlanta, 'Alem, if I win the gold medal in Atlanta will you marry me?' That was my proposal. 'We can have our engagement party in the airport the minute I return.' And as I spoke those words to her I began to imagine the whole scene: me exiting the plane dressed in my Ethiopian colors with the gold medal hanging from my neck; Alem wearing a white engagement dress and surrounded by our two families. And all the Ethiopian media and thousands of people would be around the plane, too, everyone enjoying the great celebrations. And, of course, there would be a cake and champagne and a priest to bless the ceremony. And in my hand I'd be holding our engagement rings. Rings I would have bought before leaving Addis and taken with me to Atlanta. The rings that I hoped would come to symbolize the beginning of the rest of our life together—Alem and me. But I knew that two things stood in the way of my vision coming true: first Alem had to say yes, and second I had to win that Olympic gold medal."

6

Six Seconds High

The hotel suite is decorated in soft, neutral tones. The walls are painted a fresh magnolia, the floors carpeted in a sky-blue hue. Framed watercolors depicting mountains, coastlines, and meadows trace the room's rectangular dimensions. On a table there's a glass turned upside down and a pitcher filled with cold water. Also on the table there's a microphone and a small placard with HAILE GEBRSELASSIE spelled out in capital letters. This is where Haile will sit when he is eventually introduced.

As is normal for these events, Haile's clothes will be coordinated: an Adidas short-sleeved polo shirt buttoned to the top, an Adidas sweater vest. The pressed jeans he'll be wearing won't be Adidas, but his white socks and bright blue-and-white running shoes will be. And once the proceedings get under way more than one person will think to himself that Haile looks as neat as a schoolboy out to impress his teacher on the first day. Someone else will surely spot the plastic wristwatch that balloons off his left arm, and make a note of his bird-like bone structure.

The writers and other media personnel invited to this press conference—*Track and Field News*, *The Times*, *Athletics Weekly*, *Runner's World*, *The Guardian*, *L'Equipe*, NBC, ESPN, the BBC . . . —will file into the room at the appointed hour with cups of coffee in one hand and notepads, pens, and tape recorders in the other. They'll be men generally, and for the most part French, German, American, or

British. They'll know each other from past press conferences and so chat casually while they fill the evenly spaced rows of hard plastic seats that Haile will stare out to.

Photographers will erect their tripods and focus their lenses from the back of the room. The snapping steel and plastic parts, the clicking of shutters, and the winding of film will give the room a modern, clean feel. When they eventually have Haile in their sights, they'll be impressed by the possibilities: his wide smile, round cheekbones, and sharp jawline. Haile's face exudes depth and perspective, not to mention strength, stamina, and speed. A distance runner's body, though, is deceptive. After all, what's intimidating about Haile? Transporting oxygen is not brash. It travels silently through the blood; it's light and it moves invisibly inside the muscles. Haile is small and contained like a pocket watch or an egg. The power he generates off the ground and through the air is sublime, like a skipping stone as it crosses a lake. That's what these photographers will be trying to capture through their art: that hidden force within.

Everything about this scene could be taking shape anywhere in Europe or America. It's a routine that Haile has now come to expect: reporters assembling to ask him questions about running and his life in Ethiopia. And nothing about it makes him nervous anymore. He can easily turn a phrase, or cop some sort of reply: "What question can't I answer? I understand the sport language and what journalists ask very well. To be honest, it has been many of the same questions for over 10 years."

Most journalists take Haile's command of English for granted, and they expect him to know their ways. At the start of Haile's career, however, meeting such expectations was a challenge. He pleaded with reporters to use easy words and speak slowly. Yet they didn't listen, and after his first 10,000-meter world championship in 1993 he was forced to use a translator.

"I left those championships feeling ashamed and taken for a fool," he can admit 10 years later. "Why are so many journalists arrogant like that? In 1993 I was only young—20 years old. Everything was new to me, like press conferences and knowing English. When I returned home I immediately hired an English teacher and began reading books in English. I was determined never to use a translator again."

Now Haile sees preparing for interviews and press conferences as just another part of his training: "It's very important to be able to communicate with the rest of the world. Otherwise I'll remain isolated. And that's something I don't want. In Ethiopia we speak our own language, we have our own calendar, our own way of keeping time. But what good is any of that if I want to be an international athlete? I have to learn the European way. That's all right, though, because I'm happy to know new things."

Just as one might imagine, a press conference can't begin before a question has been asked; it's how the silence gets broken. Someone might ask for a comment, or a reaction to this or that. Or someone else might want to clarify one thing or another, or confirm a suspicion, or test a hunch. A press conference could even begin with a young Italian woman from a small radio station saying to her subject, "I'd like you to close your eyes and let your mind wander back to your childhood. It will help you get in touch with your true self." And if it was Haile she was speaking to, he would oblige her request and gently fold his hands across his lap and shut his eyes. The Italian reporter would be stunned. She'd be amazed that such an athletic legend had gone along with her new age psychological gimmick. She'd be so taken aback, in fact, that she'd forget to ask an actual question. And Haile would be left waiting, holding his tranquil pose until she was ready.

Finally the young woman would begin: "Now, Haile, I want you to relax and imagine you're a child again . . . Good. So, Haile, why did you become a runner?"

And what Haile would tell her would be a story of youthful ambition in search of an outlet. A story he has spoken many times before.

"I was seven years old when I first understood about running and racing. It was 1980, the Olympics from Moscow were being held. The Olympics in Ethiopia is always a big story. We expect some success from our running heroes. And 1980 was no different. It was Miruts Yifter who won the gold medal, first at 10,000 meters, and then later in the week at 5000 meters. I was so proud and inspired. I knew then what I wanted to do. I started running and won my first race at school. It was a 1500 meters, not Yifter's distance, but that was all right because I was too young to run longer. My physical education teacher also encouraged me. He said things like, 'You can be a real runner.' So I raced again, this time at a regional competition, and I won there, too. When I was 15 I followed my older brother to Addis Ababa to join a club and try to make the national team. And I suppose that's where everything really began."

When Haile opens his eyes and takes in the room full of silent but busy reporters, he smiles lightly and shrugs his shoulders, as if signaling for the next question. And in due course it comes.

"Haile," a middle-aged man with a British accent begins. "Are the rumors true that you have plans one day to become president of Ethiopia?"

Hearing this, Haile laughs. "Oh, come on." And then a wide smile breaches his face. "You know to become president is not an easy thing. But I am not saying it's impossible, either. I have traveled to many countries. I have very many interesting experiences. And if I am to share my experiences, and try to help people, I have to be in politics. But first let me finish my running. That's my work now. And then, who knows what can happen. Besides, I'll need a new job then, won't I?"

A wave of laughter sweeps through the room. Like parents at their child's school play who want to be enthralled and impressed, these journalists also want to believe in Haile. He represents what they think sport should be: fair, honest, sincere. There are no positive drug tests in his past, and he comes across as *loving to run*, with being paid a distant afterthought.

"Do you think you can be as successful as a politician as you have been as an athlete?" comes the British reporter's follow-up.

"No question people will be impatient and expect changes fast," Haile says. "But it takes time. Sport is different from politics. But you know, when I go to sleep at night I try to imagine how I would solve various problems as president. I imagine different scenarios with our neighboring nations, or other world leaders, and how I might deal with this or that. For example, what if Sudan gets nuclear weapons? Or what if the president of the United States wants to build an air base in Ethiopia? What would I do as Ethiopian president in that situation? That's what I try to figure out. Of course the most important thing a president must do is work for peace. A war is easy to begin, but I would never want to follow that path. Peace, you know, is much harder to forge."

More questions come forward; hands wave as frantically as a room of first-graders volunteering to feed the class bunny. Haile nods to a man in the front row. "Can one person solve the problems your country is facing?"

"Which problems do you mean?" Haile begins. "Drought, famine, disease, failed reforms and policies? I can tell you, though, it is very difficult to come from a country with so many poor people. Our current population is 65 million. Twenty years ago we were not more than 30 million. Imagine, in 20 years the population has more than doubled. So our problems are not only to do with nature and with drought—things no earthly man can control. There are human-made problems, too. Like overpopulation. And that's something we must manage. It's something we can perhaps solve."

Then from the back of the room: "What place do you see for foreign aid to Ethiopia, Haile?"

This question causes Haile to pause and lean back in his chair. He raises his eyebrows and rubs his hands over the top of his head. He knows that he needs to be careful here. What he thinks could so easily be misunderstood. "Sometimes I wonder why the West should worry about us in Ethiopia," he starts by saying. "We are not their problem. People like Mr. Blair and Mr. Bush should take care of their own people first, not us. Neither can we blame the West for all of our problems, and say that they haven't done enough. You know, we are behind some of our problems, too. We were the ones who spent one million dollars a day fighting Eritrea. That is why we must try to do more for ourselves and not just depend on aid."

"How long will the changes take, Haile?"

"Oh, probably not in my life. Change is a very slow thing, you know. Very slow. We have an old saying at home, 'As long as it rains in the United States and Canada, it doesn't matter if the rain is absent in Ethiopia.' That says something about the extent of our dependency syndrome. We are also still trying to erase the mistakes of the Dergue, and the impracticalness of socialism—the mass confiscation of private land, the lack of support for what few commercial farms remained. Then there is the problem of transporting food. Believe it or not, there are actually areas of Ethiopia with a food surplus. But then many of our roads are so bad we can't get that food to the people who need it. Although things are getting better. I really believe that. The government is committed to peace, development, and democracy. And there are plans for water containment projects, as well as agricultural reforms, and greater incentives for foreign investors. All of these things will make a huge difference to all Ethiopians' lives."

The next question comes from a German man, but Haile has

trouble understanding his accent and has to ask him to repeat himself. He says again slowly, "Haile . . . how is it to be so famous . . . and so loved by your people?"

"Well, thankfully, I understand the price of fame and celebrity, and I can accept it. Do you know that I have been unable to visit the Mercato, Ethiopia's largest outdoor market, for more than seven years because of how the people get when they see me. They just rush me. They want to shake my hand, they want to take a picture with me, or they want to touch me or just say, 'Thank you, Haile. Thank you.' And I can't pick up my daughter at school because the other children will run wild. Also, my daughter becomes very jealous when I receive more attention than she does. And if you have ever seen my daughter get mad, you would stop doing that thing, too."

Laughter again rises through the room.

"So, yes, all of this makes it hard for me to have a private life. When I drive my car people come up to me. They want money, and I always do my best to help people by giving some money here and there. You know at first, after my world championship in Stuttgart in 1993, I had the windows on my car tinted. I tried to hide from people and isolate myself. The attention and fame frightened me. But I soon realized that wasn't me. I like to be open about my life. I think I have a responsibility to be with people, and so now that's what I do. When I drive through Addis I leave my windows open. I'm happy to give out my mobile phone number and talk to anyone. People are generally respectful. Ethiopian people, especially. They don't want autographs, but just to shake my hand. And that, well, it's no problem. It's the Europeans and Americans who always want me to sign my name. I also have to be careful not to make a mistake because people are always watching me and looking up to me. Everyone in Addis knows my car. They know where I am all the time, and if I'm doing something not so good. That's one reason why I am always trying to do what's right, but, you know, people expect a lot. And it's not possible to please everyone. As if I can solve all of my country's problems? A few years ago our famine problem attracted world attention with celebrity concerts and fund-raising and Europeans and Americans giving us aid, and at that time the number of people in trouble was only one million. But that number is increasing. Some agencies say there are more than 15 million people with problems today. And that scares me. I think, *What will it be in the future? How many millions then?* Obviously I am grateful to all the people who have contributed aid to us, but that is not the solution. As long as we ignore a solution our problems will never go away."

"So what do you think should be done?"

"That's the same question I always ask myself, *What can I do to help my country? How can I contribute something to my people?* I know that just giving my money away isn't the answer. I cannot support 65 million people. So I decided from the beginning that if I had some success as an athlete I would invest in Ethiopia. And that's what I have done. And look at the benefits. When I built my first building in 1997 I started with 10 people working in the different businesses, and now after I have built my second building there are nearly 500 people with a job to go to every Monday morning. That's just fantastic, I think. And the schools I have built in different communities are doing so much to educate people and help them change their lives for the better."

An American screams out, "How big is your new building, Haile?"

"Well, I can tell you that exactly," Haile says, "because you see I have measured it very carefully. It's six seconds high."

"Excuse me," the American says, "six seconds high?"

"Yes, six seconds high. That's how long it takes for a stone dropped from the top floor to reach the ground."

And immediately the room goes silent as all the reporters scribble down that line . . . six seconds high—such an honest and earthy metaphor to portray the essence of Haile's beginnings and everything he has done for his country.

"Well, Haile, you must be proud of what you have done for Ethiopia?" a long-haired gentleman asks as the proceedings pick up again.

"Yes, it makes me very happy to help my people. On my company's payday, for example, I like to hand out the checks to my employees personally just to see how happy it makes them. Because although I can set up my businesses and do my best to run them, still the people must come and do their job. I'm not a charity handing out salaries to anyone who asks. People must work for their wage. If they do that then they will be provided for. Of course, some people say it's selfish. They say, 'Haile Gebrselassie is only trying to get rich: making business just to make money.' I don't blame them for thinking like that. But what do they expect me to do? Plus, don't they understand that I don't need so many headaches from running my businesses. I have enough money to take care of myself and my family and never work again. But Ethiopia is where I was born. It is where I will die. I am proud of my country. I am proud of my people. And I want to contribute to Ethiopia's development. For example, how can we mobilize local and external resources to raise our standard of living? How can we provide more effective social services? And how can we maintain an ecological balance while still ensuring our own agricultural self-sufficiency? These are the basic social and economic problems we face. Even more so in rural communities. And in cooperation with others I have helped raise money to build health clinics, primary schools, and roads, and to bring electricity to small villages. And it's working. Through these initiatives over three million people have seen positive improvements to their lives in the last 10 years."

"So, Haile, how do you want to be remembered," a man seated in the middle of the room begins to ask next, "as a sportsman or as a politician?"

Before answering Haile pours a glass of water. He fills it to the very top. Then he says, "I will say this." But he stops short to drain half of his glass. He begins again. "My involvement in politics is only something in my mind." He's still holding the half-full glass of water when his expression turns serious. "But, sport," he says carefully, "is something much more. Sport is in my blood." And he quickly empties his glass before pouring another.

But politics, or the fate of his people, hasn't always been on Haile's mind. Early in his life all of his energy needed to go to simple survival. His childhood was hard: no telephone, no electricity, no running water. His family's house was made of mud and straw, a type of hut in Ethiopia called a *tucal*.

Haile's father kept a small number of cattle and sheep that he fed from the few crops he grew. Blankets served as internal walls in the house, dividing the open space into a room for Haile's parents, another for his four sisters, and one for Haile and his five brothers.

It also took a great deal of energy for Haile to survive the death of his mother, Ayelech Degtu, when he was just seven years old: "My mother was a wonderful woman. Very caring and very warm. She developed cancer in 1979 and whenever she tried to do anything— fetch water, rake straw, clean the hut, cook—she became very weak and sick. Still, she was remarkable. And when she died I felt totally isolated and alone. More than anything she wanted her children to have a better life. My father was different that way: He didn't believe so much in pursuing dreams. He thought his children should work in the fields with him. Of course I don't blame him for this. He thought he was giving us his best advice. That was why my mother was so important. She influenced me to attend school and to get an education. She always told me to keep my opportunities open. It's because of her that I have the life I do today."

More energy as a boy was also needed for Haile to survive the regime of "Red Terror" that swept across Ethiopia. Although he was very young—just a couple of years old when the emperor, Haile Selassie, was overthrown in 1974—the wide-scale murders and other atrocities committed by the new communist leader, Mengistu Haile Mariam, established a specter of fear that lasted throughout Haile's childhood.

Every morning during the Red Terror, whether in city streets or quiet country villages, people across Ethiopia would open their doors to the sight of freshly killed bodies. Government ministers and military leaders loyal to Haile Selassie were lined up and machine-gunned down. The new regime was bloodthirsty and ruthless. Soldiers acted in unimaginable ways. Theft and torture became commonplace; thousands of families were thrown into turmoil as a thick pall hung low over the entire country. The morgues actually turned a profit. For to claim the body of a loved one, a family had to reimburse the government for the bullets used in the execution. More bullet holes meant more money. All of Mengistu's hitmen observed a two-bullet minimum. No one knew when the killing would end; everyone just waited and prayed and did their best to avoid trouble.

Haile's older brother Assefa was a high school student at the time of the Red Terror and also a member of the opposition party. One afternoon an official from Mengistu's government approached him. "Change your allegiance. Join the new government or face the consequences," he said. But Assefa refused and went into hiding. For a year he kept out of harm's way, deep in the countryside, surviving hand to mouth day to day, month to month.

Despite years of counterrevolutionary movements, it wasn't until 1991 that Mengistu's government came under serious threat. As just another satellite regime of the Soviet Union, Mengistu's forces couldn't withstand the breakdown of communism and the lost financial support that went with it. Mengistu's Provincial Military Administrative Council (the Dergue) was eventually deposed by the Ethiopian

People's Revolutionary Democratic Front. But this period, too, was a time of great uncertainty—definitely not the best conditions for a young and promising runner like Haile to begin thinking and acting politically. In fact, one of Ethiopia's running legends, the 1968 Olympic marathon gold medalist, Mamo Wolde, was accused by the new government of acting as a collaborator with Mengistu and murdering a young boy during the Red Terror campaign. For this, Wolde was put in jail and held without formal charges, or the possibility of a trial, for over 10 years.

Hardly a murderer, Wolde had actually been extremely lucky to survive the Red Terror campaign. As a captain in Haile Selassie's Imperial Guard, his life was in grave danger when the emperor was overthrown. But his Olympic gold medal saved his life. Mengistu gave Wolde a lowly coaching position in a rural outpost, and called on him for occasional propaganda purposes as a past Olympic hero. How ironic it was, then, when Wolde became a prisoner under the new post-Mengistu "democratic" regime.

But the report against Wolde was damning. He was said to have obeyed a Mengistu official's order to enter an Addis Ababa nightclub one evening in May 1978, dressed in uniform, and with his pistol loaded. He was given the command to shoot and kill a 15-year-old boy who allegedly belonged to an antirevolutionary youth group. Indeed, a 15-year-old boy was murdered that night. He was shot and left for dead in the street outside the nightclub, although there were no direct witnesses to the attack.

Wolde, as Kenny Moore later reported, tried to explain his innocence. "I didn't shoot anyone," he pleaded. "I was framed." He did admit to being at the scene, but said that another guard had killed the boy. "I was supposed to fire the second shot, to complete the two-bullet minimum. But the spirit had already left that poor boy's soul. I could see that he was dead on the ground. The shot the other guard fired killed him instantly. So I shot to the side of the boy's body and deliberately missed." But no one could corroborate Wolde's story.

That was how times were in Ethiopia through the mid-1970s and into the early 1990s: Trust was at a minumum, and danger was a constant presence. Everyone felt threatened. Regional governors were known as "the Butcher of Tigray" or "the Butcher of Gondar." It was impossible to break ranks as fear bound everyone together. But that's exactly what terror is: never knowing when the knock on the door might come. To fall out of step, to protest, or to challenge, might mean entering a world that's larger and more courageous mentally, but at the same time one risked extreme censure and the possibility of violence. It would have been foolish to underestimate the retaliation that could have been visited upon one for some profession of dissent. After all, we are only made of flesh. Swords do puncture us; bullets do tear us apart. Even runners had to be careful as they ran over the roads and through the hills and forests around Addis Ababa at this time. In certain places land mines littered the streets, and many runners lost their legs. Some still took risks, though. Like Getaneh Tessema, who as a promising 10,000 meter runner in the late 1980s walked 30 miles one day through enemy territory to reach Addis Ababa so that he could compete in the national championships. That was how much he loved sport: "Enough to sacrifice my life," he says today. For Haile, too, these were scary times.

"Soldiers and different rebels and revolutionaries who had been living in the forests for 17 years [from 1974, when Haile Selassie was overthrown, to 1991 when Mengistu was ousted] didn't understand anything about running or sport," he explains. "They only knew war and shooting and killing. They trusted no one. So to them a person running through the woods might be someone trying to attack them, or trying to escape, or maybe a spy. They were always very jumpy, and a wild look would come into their eyes when they saw you running. I remember many times them stopping me. 'What are you doing?' they'd shout. 'Why are you here?' Then thanks to Derartu [Tulu] winning the gold medal in 1992, even these soldiers began to understand sport, and soon running in the forests became safe again."

But as fantastic as Derartu Tulu's 10,000-meter victory at the Barcelona Olympics was, it wasn't going to bring back the good times for Ethiopia's elite athletes. With Mengistu's collapse, sport's role in Ethiopian society came under question. Direct sponsorship from the government ended. Under socialism athletes had been supported for the propaganda value their victories overseas afforded. But soon military clubs lost all of their funding, and long-standing civilian clubs associated with factories and other state-supported businesses had to close their doors. These changes weren't all bad, however. For someone on the cusp of international stardom, like Haile, the timing couldn't have been better.

"Now sport was free after 1991. Yes, the government's budget for athletes was gone, but so, too, were many restrictions. It became easier to travel, and to race, and to keep your prize money instead of giving it all back to the federation. Agents and promoters from Europe were also coming to Ethiopia and providing more opportunities for athletes to run anywhere in the world. You still needed an exit visa to leave the country, but even that process became much simpler."

Over time the nation's interest in sport resumed, and once again teams from Ethiopia were sent to compete overseas. A young French reporter speculates that events surrounding Haile's early trips abroad must have been the catalyst for his current political ambitions and humanitarian efforts: "Was it comparing other countries in the world to Ethiopia, Haile, that got you interested in politics and the cause of your country and your people?"

"When I saw other parts of the world like Europe and America," Haile begins in response as the press conference reaches the one-hour mark, "I couldn't stop myself from asking, 'Why does Ethiopia have so many problems compared to these places?' I couldn't understand it, especially since I knew that we had a better climate than most European countries, and millions of people willing to work hard and around the clock. I was amazed at almost everything I saw. My first flight was something else. I remember being surprised at the toilet. How could a toilet work in a plane? It has to go into the ground, doesn't it? I even asked the hostess if I could open the window for some air. And I couldn't believe the hotels. Televisions in every room, temperature controls, and at the entrance huge automatic doors. I had never imagined such things. It was all amazing to me. But frightening, too, as I realized in Europe you are judged not by who you are but by what you have, with money considered the most important thing of all to have. But money, as you know, is not everything."

It's quite typical at press conferences that Haile gives that questioning may run on for over an hour without anyone asking him a specific question about his training or his results. Journalists think they know the story of Haile Gebrselassie the runner—his Olympic and world titles, his world records. It's the new direction his life is taking as a businessman and a politician that interests the press now.

For example, a reporter will always ask him, "Haile, how can you combine serious training with business and politics? Isn't it too much? When do you rest?"

Haile's reply always brings a round of laughter. "I will rest when I die," he says. Then he continues by saying, "But since I am living, it's time for action. Remember, too, I have very good people running my businesses. It's entirely a family affair. They handle many of the day-to-day matters. Although I still like to be involved as much as I can."

"So how many more years before you retire, Haile?"

That's another question Haile has been asked before. It's because his looks are deceiving. His skin is rough and marked with varying shades of brown and deep red that prematurely add to his years. And everything he has achieved on the track speaks of a running body that must be nearing its end. "Well, Yifter was over 30 in Moscow wasn't he? By comparison, that makes me a young man."

Now more routine questions follow. Ones that Haile has answered hundreds of times. They have to do with his running, and how he has been able to dominate such competitive and grueling events as the 10,000 meters and the 5000 meters for so many years. Just the same, he answers each one with plenty of enthusiasm, never letting on that he's simply rephrasing the past: "When I miss a day's running? Oh, that is not good. Then I can't sleep at night. I feel restless and jittery . . . I don't like that." "Of course training isn't boring to me." "What do I think about when I run? I think about my family, and I go over each one of their faces in my mind . . ." "Yes, running is private and personal and something soothing to me." "No, I never think about business when I run. Business is about problems and worries over money. I want to enjoy running." "My training program? I run twice a day, every day." "More specifically? Okay. I run hard on the track three days a week during the competitive season and I go to the gym three days a week, too." "Well, I'd be lying to you if I said losing isn't something I think about. But then no one can be at the top forever." "Oh, yes, I believe the mind is very important in sport. That's why I'm more afraid of myself than my competitors. Because I'm the only one capable of making a mental mistake that might result in a loss or some other problem." And when a Japanese reporter who is obviously unsatisfied with Haile's earlier account of his training asks his third follow-up question, Haile finally invites him to come to Ethiopia. "You need to come and see for yourself how I train. Please visit anytime. You are very welcome. Ethiopia is a great country, you will love it there."

Occasionally Haile does get asked a question that he hasn't heard before. For example, a woman in the audience asks, "Haile, do you attribute your success to luck or to fate?"

"Well, for me the important matter is not to believe in luck, but to ask myself, *How can I get more luck?* Because you know, it's not only by training hard that luck happens, or that good things happen. What I believe, and what I trust, is to do what God says. That means: Don't do wrong things, don't do bad things that hurt other people, be honest and helpful to all people, and work hard, and pray, and then luck will come to you. That is what my faith teaches me. Prayer, though, is not about asking for things from God without giving anything back. Like more money, or a new car, or a big house. Hard work must always come first. What I pray to God for is that my hard work will be rewarded."

"Do you pray when you are out running?" comes another original question.

"First of all, prayer is a habit. It's a way of being respectful to God. It's something I do always. And, yes, even sometimes when I run. For example, I'm always saying to God when I run, 'Thanks, God, for letting me be here now, healthy and running.' And I say to him, too, 'Please, God, give me a fair price back for my work.'"

This piques the interest of an Amercian reporter sitting in the front row. "But I read, Haile, that following the Atlanta and Sydney Olympics you gave that price, the result of all your hard work, your gold medals in other words, away to the church."

"Actually, I believe that there is no better place for my two Olympic gold medals than a church. I am so happy I put them there because then more people can enjoy them. Even you can come to Ethiopia and I will show you them. But you know, a medal isn't the true price or reward for hard work. That is not what I am talking about. The most important thing in this life is happiness. And when I ask God for happiness I am not talking about medals or money. I'm talking about feeling satisfied. That feeling inside when you know that your life is doing something good not just for yourself but for other people, too. That is the price I ask for my hard work: to make a difference in many people's lives. Not just my own. And I can see when I return from the Olympics with a gold medal and everyone is so happy that I have succeeded through my work. This is what gives me the greatest happiness. That is why I must keep running. I must keep making people happy with the talent that God has given me."

To follow up, the American reporter asks, "Haile, are runners artists?"

"Of course runners are artists," Haile says almost defensively. "Because you know, what you are showing to the people is a kind of performance. I always try to be beautiful when I run. For example, by finishing fast and with a good stride, or maybe with a new record. That is what pleases people. Also, I always wear nice clothes for competition, and attractive colors. That is my costume. Not like when I am alone in the forest wearing my workout clothes. Then I will spit or blow my nose as I run. But the time when I run in a stadium, before a crowd, that's the time for action. Like Hollywood. And for me training is like some kind of rehearsal. I'm forever thinking as I run, *How is my step? My form? Am I running tall and moving easily?* I'm also trying to judge whether I'm ready to show my ability—my work of art—to an audience. Maybe I'm a little bit like a painter who doesn't want anyone to see his first draft. It's only when I'm finished, not before, that I reveal myself to the people. That's when I say, 'Jos, I'm ready to race.'"

A puzzled look comes over the American's face. "Jos, who is that?"

"Who is Jos?" Haile screams. "Oh, come on, everyone knows about Jos."

Indeed almost everyone in the room nods. And as they do, Haile lifts his eyes to the back of the room. "Next question?"

7

Jos Hermens

Jos Hermens always imagined a future in coaching. Coaching long-distance runners. His motives were more than genuine, too. It wasn't that he fancied becoming wealthy or famous, a sycophant of athletic stars. He didn't crave the limelight, or need to read his name in the newspaper. A coach's rightful place, he believed, was offstage, in the background. The attraction had to be the athlete, the runner. That's who people want to see, he felt. That's the name that should be spoken and remembered, not the coach's.

It was arranging the details of a season and developing a yearlong plan—how to train, when to race—that intrigued Jos. And most importantly, doing it wisely. After all, consider the myriad variables: the optimal combination of speed and endurance work, a proper diet, strength training, rest, and of course always the psychology.

Jos understood what a delicate balance it was to get an athlete to peak on cue—an Olympic games, a world championship, a world record attempt. How the science of running was something akin to cooking or architecture—combining ingredients, mixing materials, establishing a foundation, considering the finish. Except sport isn't grounded in anything so exact as food chemistry or engineering. Besides some general physiological truths—the overload principle, the supercompensation curve—coaching is more art than science, a business of case studies. The right decisions have to be made one individual at a time.

A coach's satisfaction, however, doesn't derive so much from getting everything right as it does from not screwing up. To experience the promise of a top runner—his effortless stride, his winning touch—so much so that you can't sleep at night for dreaming of the fast times he'll post, the records he'll claim, or the prizes he'll acquire, is to eventually have your excitement turn to anxiety as you begin to realize that all you're visioning is yours to prevent: a stress fracture following too many long runs, a virus from not getting enough rest. More than developing talent, coaches steer potential; they direct promise away from disaster; they help their charges avoid costly, career-threatening mistakes. To do this they'll create diversions, or set up roadblocks. Whatever it takes to prevent an athlete from crossing the line between performance and absence. They're a cautious lot, coaches, always searching for the safest route forward. The road to the top, after all, is fraught with danger. Mistakes are just that easy to make.

Mistakes are one thing Jos knows about. For a time he had his own successful long-distance running career to manage—an Olympian in 1972 (5000 meters) and 1976 (10,000 meters) for his native Holland, a European championship finalist in 1974 (5000 meters) and 1978 (10,000 meters), and the world record holder from 1976 to 1991 for the one-hour run. Then came an injury, his Achilles tendon. It flared up following the '76 Olympics. Jos did everything he could to extend his career. He was planning on running the New York City marathon in the fall of 1978. It was going to be his marathon debut. And all the work he had put in that winter and spring indicated that he was on course to run a very good time. But Jos never made it to New York. With seven laps remaining in the 1978 European championship 10,000-meter final his Achilles tendon snapped in half. He hit the ground hard; he watched helpless as the pack he had moments before been part of drifted out of touch. The pain in Jos's leg couldn't begin to match his disappointment. Still 25 years on he mulls over the mistakes: *Too many miles a week . . . not enough planning . . . not enough rest.* Not to mention what could've been: *Maybe the marathon world record holder . . . maybe Olympic champion?*

As a young runner Jos believed he had to post more impressive numbers in training by the week, by the month, by the year. His best times for 5000 meters and 10,000 meters kept dropping the more miles he ran. In a world record run over 10,000 meters by Samson Kimobwa in Helsinki on June 30, 1977 (27:30.47), Jos was just seven seconds back. Only seven seconds away from setting a new world record. The correlation between high weekly mileage and fast times became cause and effect for Jos, and just too delicious to ignore. He scoffed at limits. He ignored common sense. He was young; he thought he was indestructible. And without any experienced coaches in Holland, he had no one to turn to for advice. He was totally on his own. Besides, he just loved to run.

Two- and three-hour runs through the forests near his home were routine for Jos. They were as much about adventure as they were training. He was curious about the natural world and his place in it. Running long distances over trails and past streams helped satisfy that curiosity. Following one seven-day stretch in the early 1970s, when Jos logged 150 miles in training, he immediately wanted to know what it would feel like to run 200 miles in a week—*Surely running 200 miles will make me stronger than running 150?* Jos wasn't particularly patient in this regard, but he wasn't greedy, either. Just tireless. "Hard work was all I knew," he explains. "My father was a gardener and he began work every day at 6 A.M. He also had a small farm of his own that he worked on when he came home. When I was born in 1950, after the war, the economy in Holland and across Europe was very unstable and my father was doing all he could to make ends meet. The only time he relaxed was on Sunday afternoons when he would sit down next to the radio and listen to an hour of opera."

But Jos's home-grown work ethic wasn't entirely to blame for his unguarded zealousness. High weekly mileage was also a sign of the times. The 1960s and 1970s were experimental days for distance runners. Coaches and athletes around the world were constantly testing the limits of human tolerance and endurance.

Out of New Zealand came Arthur Lydiard, a charismatic coach who encouraged a band of local boys from his neighborhood in Auckland to follow him into the Waitakeri Ranges on the outskirts of the city center and thrash themselves over his self-fashioned 22-mile training loop designed to build the stamina needed to collect world records and Olympic gold medals. Lydiard's "marathon training" produced numerous champions, the best among them Peter Snell, who won Olympic gold medals in middle-distance running in 1960 and 1964, and broke the world record for the mile twice. Lydiard's system sparked a high-mileage revolution throughout Europe and America. And Jos quickly became a Lydiard disciple, taking into his own hands Lydiard's ideas and enthusiastically following them.

Prior to such a hard, workaday approach to training, running's ethos had been largely fashioned by the Oxbridge group out of England, who trained part-time and even viewed trying too hard as distasteful and crass. This was the old amateur ideal, whereby an athlete merely strided out in training or covered a few laps of the track briskly. This sporting ethic was epitomized most wholly by Roger Bannister and his chums Chris Brasher and Chris Chataway, who eventually teamed up to run the world's first sub four-minute mile in 1954.

Bannister condemned the pioneers of serious sport, such as the Czechoslovakian Emil Zatopek, who won three distance running gold medals at the Helsinki Olympics in 1952—5000 meters, 10,000 meters, the marathon. Bannister, who placed fourth in the 1500 meters at those same Olympics, referred to Zatopek's achievements as subhuman, and ostensibly accused him of cheating and being unsportsmanlike for running 100 miles a week in training. Unlike Bannister, who limited his practice time on the track to one hour, Zatopek ran across the day through the forests around his home in Prague. He would even wear heavy army boots to increase the difficulty. Running was not just an avocation for Zatopek, like it was for the Oxbridge boys. He was a new breed of athlete: goal-oriented and fiercely competitive.

Another early advocate of serious and hard training came from America. Jim Ryun, the 1960s miler who under his coach Bob Timmons tried new methods of high-volume speed work, greatly extended the barriers of "normal" training. As did Lasse Viren from Finland, who logged hours a day over wood-chipped trails. A new generation was also emerging from England in the early 1970s, bypassing the conservative approach so representative of Bannister. Dave Bedford, Ron Hill, Ian Stewart, and Brendan Foster put it all on the line—their health, their personal lives—by regularly running 200 miles a week. And their ideas and approaches inspired Jos: "I was reading in different magazines what Bedford and Foster were doing and it was all about running more, more, more. So obviously I thought I was on the right path with my superhigh-mileage plan."

This was hands-on science these young runners and coaches across the world were practicing. They were stubborn idealists and ambitious fanatics who redefined the boundaries of human work long before the scientific community became interested. Physiology labs were for rats in most scientists' minds. Researchers were out to solve larger problems in nature than how fast or how long a man could run, or exactly what factors of blood, muscle, and bone enabled one human being to become an Olympic marathon champion, for example, when another became exhausted walking up a single flight of stairs.

New approaches to training, therefore, largely evolved by trial and error. Fitness wasn't a fad in the 1960s; sport wasn't a billion-dollar industry; and the Olympics were 20 years away from becoming the greatest show on earth. Distance runners were more akin to explorers, curious to know what lay on the other side of a four-hour run or a 200-mile week. They were highly self-motivated, and the compensation for their efforts was minimal. They were, quite honestly, a bit mad. But then one had to be to run 200 miles in a week.

To manage his 28-mile-a-day, 200-mile-a-week habit, Jos trained three times a day. In between he would shower, sleep, and eat. That was about it. That was how he lived from 1971 to 1978, between the ages of 21 and 28.

Naturally there were days when Jos's runs would be pure joy and pass effortlessly. The earth would feel soft and light on what could only be tired and heavy legs, and time would spin past in great swathes instead of fractions. Other days, though, with the wind howling, or the temperature in triple digits, it might take Jos a half hour or more to shake off his stiffness and work through the effects of a previous session. There was precious little time left in Jos's life for other pursuits or diversions—romance, education, hobbies: Run 200 miles a week and it's almost impossible to think of yourself as anything but a runner. Jos never became bored with his life's work, though; he always had one thing or another to occupy his mind.

"I'd think about my future and the way of the world out running. My father had always felt oppressed in his life. As a boy he'd tell me to be careful of authority figures and to always watch my back. He was absolutely frustrated by his powerlessness as a worker. As a result, he developed a real inferiority complex. He'd warn me, 'Never rock the boat, son. Don't upset the bosses.' He was terribly afraid of these people. He thought they controlled his life, and that there wasn't anything he could do to assert his own will over the future. But I ignored his warnings. Instead of submitting to authority, I rebelled against it. For example, I challenged the Dutch track and field federation and their ridiculous amateur rules regarding money, sponsorship, and marketing. They expected the best from me as an athlete but they weren't willing to pay for it. My father, of course, told me to keep quiet. He thought someone might hurt me for being critical. But then he never really understood how important running was to me . . . that my criticisms also reflected my values. Maybe that's why he never came to see me run? Or, I don't know, maybe he was just trying to protect me. Still, I'm sure he was proud of what I achieved, although he probably would have been happier if I had just become a normal worker like him."

Jos's outspokenness extended beyond the track. He grew his hair long and read Marx, Engels, Bakunin, and other socialist philosophers. He became interested in politics and protested against the Vietnam War and joined the socialist party in Holland. He was going to change the world. At the very least, he was going to change himself. "While out running I'd try to imagine the future, and how the world could be a better place if people weren't so greedy and selfish. But my father thought it was impossible to change other people or even yourself. 'Born a penny, never a dollar,' he used to say. But I wouldn't accept that. I was out to prove him wrong. And the way to do that, I realized, was through running."

Where Jos grew up, in Nijmegen, the oldest city in the Netherlands, wide-open forests that crossed the border into nearby Germany defined the landscape. Jos's family had little, and running was an inexpensive hobby. Originally, Jos wanted to be a cyclist like his older brother, who was a professional racer in Belgium. But his father had to explain to him that it was too expensive. "Buying a good bike, Jos," he said, "and having a car to travel to all the races is just unrealistic for our family." So Jos followed another brother to the local track club when he was 12. By 14 he had discovered distance running.

He saw immediately that compared to the other kids he had talent. He could run on and on and not get tired. Then he began winning junior races all across Holland and Europe. And he saw that running was a sport where he could prove his ability and exert his influence over the future.

"There were no bosses watching me in the forest. It was my decision how hard I was willing to work. No one could prevent me from training all day if I wanted to. And I liked that freedom."

Wicked speed sessions, steep hill repeats, hours of running a day, Jos pushed himself hard: "I desensitized myself to pain. I even used to refuse Novocain when I went to the dentist. I didn't need it. Nothing could hurt me. But this was part of my problem, too: I could withstand so much pain that injuries would slowly creep in without me noticing . . . like that damn Achilles tendon. Until it was too late, of course."

For Jos, as the youngest of 10 children, running quickly became his salvation. His steps over the forest floor triggered a symphony of color and sound in his head. Running was a means of escape. With 12 people sharing a small house, privacy was precious. But in the fresh air of the forest the world was silent and open for Jos, and filled with nothing but pleasure, sky, and trees.

"I experienced such intense moments of freedom and exhilaration when I ran. In fact, it was the training I liked more than the competition. I wasn't such a hard-nosed competitive guy. The idea of top sport even disturbed me a little bit because it was based so heavily on a capitalistic model: the best people thrive and get more money and medals while everyone else gets less. That's what leads to hierarchies and a privileged class forming. And I had a real problem with that kind of thinking. It violated my socialist ideals. I also had trouble justifying how I could spend so many hours a day doing something so unproductive as running. I thought I should be working harder for the people, or for my community. I was always studying pedagogy, or reading writers like Erich Fromm who preached love, freedom, cooperation, and responsibility. And to me a lot of those ideas didn't seem to go hand in hand with being an athlete. For example, following the terrorist attacks at the 1972 Munich Olympics, when 11 Israeli athletes were murdered in the athletes' village, I chose to go home and not compete. In the buildup to the games the Germans were referring to them as the "Happy Games." It was supposed to be a party. And I couldn't get that analogy out of my head. I mean, if you're at a party, say a friend's birthday, and a gunman storms in and shoots someone are you going to go on with the party? Of course not. You're going to go home. And that's how I saw what happened in Munich. That's not to say I didn't want to be an Olympic champion, because I did. Quite badly, in fact. I wanted to show my father and everyone else that I could make something out of myself. And that kind of contradictory thinking, on the one hand wanting to win, but on the other hand trying to be ethical, presented a real dilemma for me: how to compete in a fair and just way. Because really, running is about so much more than sport. It's a vehicle for change and self-improvement. At least for me it was. I saw it as a form of meditation or art: to train every day . . . to try so hard to perfect this one simple thing . . . running fast around a track. I loved that. I really did."

Jos still speaks this way about running. Go to a track meet with him today, for example, and you'll notice his skin begin to glow and his eyes widen—"Running is something I love so much, and it's especially beautiful to watch someone do it well." Go to a track meet with Jos today and it's obvious that he still thinks like a coach. He's always willing to lend his support to the athletes at work. He resembles a helicopter: taking off and landing, maneuvering, excited, jumpy. He brings a polished appearance with him, too: wire-rimmed glasses that rest across the middle of his long face, smart Italian shoes, tailored pants, and always a matching shirt and sport coat. He carefully selects the best position trackside to yell out encouragement. And he considers at length what particular individuals need to hear—"Some athletes prefer quiet praise, others like shouting; for everyone it's different." But always it's faster that Jos wants athletes to run. "Faster, Faster, Faster," he screams. Seeing runners produce fast times excites him. Especially new world records. And in the past 10 years Jos has witnessed his fair share of records, including every world record that's been set over 5000 and 10,000 meters. That's because Haile has set most of them. And wherever you find Haile racing you don't have to look very far to find Jos.

The sport of track and field has undergone some dramatic transformations since Jos was a promising athlete in the 1970s. It's no longer the innocent extension of simple playground games that children everywhere play—running, jumping, throwing. Instead it's become a multinational, multimillion dollar business following some spectacular rule changes brought about in the 1980s.

In 1985 a set of new eligibility requirements was drawn up by the world governing body of track and field, the International Association of Athletics Federations (IAAF). Most dramatically, runners could now be paid for competing. This was a drastic departure from the origins of the sport as laid out by the Amateur Athletic Association of England (AAA), whose members, when they met in London in 1880, were determined that track and field remain an amateur sport.

In their charter, the Victorian men who founded the AAA banned prize money and other forms of gift giving. They believed this would protect their sport from betting and bribery, conditions they argued were contaminating other sports like boxing and horse racing. As a result, track and field developed as a "gentlemen's" game, with limited participation coming from outside groups or social classes.

According to the AAA, bettering one's previous personal best, not earning a wage, was certainly compensation enough for time spent training—with the ultimate reward being the opportunity to represent one's country at an Olympic Games. For the first 100 years of organized athletics this exclusive perspective was largely adhered to by athletes, coaches, and administrators around the world.

However, with the increased professionalization of sports such as tennis and golf in the 1980s, and the profits turned at the 1984 Los Angeles Olympics, many in track and field began to question the relevance of the old amateur rules. Television was now interested in throwing a bundle of money at the sport, as were large corporations such as Mobil Oil and Coca-Cola. Road racing was taking off and becoming part of the wider global entertainment industry with the advent of the big-city marathon. Drawing cards in track and field were emerging, too. Carl Lewis, Mary Decker-Slaney, Sebastian Coe, and Edwin Moses all commanded large appearance fees and received spectacular bonuses for world records. Track and field stars were now becoming full-time athletes.

In the summer of 1995 alone, Steven Downes and Duncan MacKay report in their book, *Running Scared*, the organizers of the top 15 meets on the international Grand Prix circuit paid a total of $15 million in appearance fees for athletes. And with these financial incentives came a widening of participation, especially from North and East Africa, where many young men saw the chance to turn their lives around by doing something as simple as running around a track or down a road.

At the outset of this professional boom, Jos was a newly retired athlete. His Achilles tendon rupture in 1978 had been irreparable, forcing him to consider his future after athletics. His instincts directed him toward a career in coaching. It was what he always imagined he'd do when his own running career ended: "I wanted to help the next generation of Dutch runners avoid the same mistakes I had made: too many miles a week . . . not enough planning . . . not enough rest." So Jos enrolled in a coaching course and began advising an impressive group of top runners. But what concerned the athletes Jos was working with had little to do with how to mix speed work with endurance work, or how to achieve a peak performance at precisely the right time—exactly the questions that had troubled him as a runner, and that had inspired him to study coaching. Instead, their concerns were to do with appearance fees, shoe contracts, sponsors, and healthcare. Everything, in other words, to do with the new business of track and field. And Jos caught on quickly.

"I realized that guys needed more help managing their careers than structuring their training. There were so many races on offer, and all of them with good prize money, that one could easily overrace, get injured, and then miss the Olympics or some other important event. In my day that wasn't a concern. There were just a handful of meets across Scandinavia, Britain, and Europe, and the prize money was meager, maybe $1,000, that's all. All the promoters knew you, too. If they needed runners for a race they'd just phone you up. But with money coming in, and meets appearing everywhere, the whole sport was growing incredibly fast. Take the advent of the African runner, for example. Who saw Africans running in Europe in the '60s and '70s? It was very rare. How were they going to get here? Who was going to pay to bring them over? With professionalization, however, this suddenly became possible. In saying that though, the first African athletes who came over to Europe in the '80s were totally exploited. There was no way they could strike a fair deal for themselves. Either they didn't speak English very well, or they didn't know what to demand, or their national federations arranged everything for them and then kept the money themselves. A lot of these guys ended up competing for free, totally unaware that a host of other people were profiting from them.

They'd get a plane ticket, a room in a hotel, some meal money, and think they were doing well. What they needed was an advocate, a mouthpiece to represent their interests. And that was what I decided to do. I stopped coaching and became an agent."

By the mid-1980s Jos was arranging races for dozens of athletes and setting up contracts with sponsors around the world. He became one of the first professional managers in track and field, and he formed his own company, Global Sports Communications, which he operated out of his one-bedroom apartment in his hometown, Nijmegen. He was on the phone with athletes and journalists for hours at a time. He was constantly promoting the sport and pitching new ideas to anyone who would listen. He was flying across Europe and over to America to propose deals, negotiate appearance fees and bonus structures, and meet with representatives from Adidas and Nike. He was at the cusp of track and field's modern development and expansion. In 1983 Jos visited Ethiopia to watch the Abebe Bikila marathon and recruit runners for the Rotterdam marathon. He was the first Western coach or manager to go there. Soon he was traveling to Ethiopia regularly, building up contacts, making friends, and supplying Ethiopian runners for track meets and marathons all around the world. And he believed what he saw in Ethiopia was the future of long-distance running.

What impressed Jos the most about Ethiopia's runners was their vast talent and fearless commitment. "Ethiopians raced with true spirit and desire. They were hardworking, intense, and light and smooth in full stride, as well as fiercely competitive." These discoveries, however, weren't a total surprise for Jos. As a young boy he had been struck by the courage of Ethiopia's runners at the 1960 Rome Olympics. In particular, the marathon gold medalist, Abebe Bikila: "I remember watching this skinny black man from this faraway country called Ethiopia running with bare feet over the cobblestones of Rome. The race was at night, too, and large shadows covered the ground of the marathon course. It was all very mysterious looking. Something about Ethiopia filled a space in my soul. *What a magical place it must be,* I thought. *What amazing people must come from there.* I started to read about Ethiopia, too, and I was impressed that they had never been colonized and that they always kept their own culture. Over time I began to develop a real sympathy or shared understanding for the place and its people. Maybe it was my own impoverished background and crowded house of 10 brothers and sisters? Or their amazing tradition of runners? I don't know exactly. But something definitely clicked inside me, and I knew even as a boy that one day I would go there."

While Jos continued to be impressed by the runners he saw in Ethiopia on subsequent visits, other aspects of the country shocked him. "It was so gray there. You'd notice police on every corner, too. Old posters of Marx and Lenin hung from buildings . . . It could've been sunny outside but there was a real feeling of depression or hopelessness in the air. Mengistu's policies just weren't working. The poverty was shocking; I couldn't believe the state of basic services like roads and sanitation. As an idealist, a child of the '60s, I found facing the abject failure of socialism in practice extremely disheartening."

But instead of succumbing to his despair, Jos drew on the spirit of his idealism and began to offer free medical care in Europe to family members of the Ethiopian runners he was representing. He shipped over cars and tractors and helped his athletes set up their own businesses once their running careers ended. He sponsored education grants, arranged visas, and bought plane tickets to help any number of people being persecuted by Mengistu to flee the country. Moreover, the athletes Jos was introducing to Europe and America—Wodajo Bulti, Abebe Mekkonen, Addis Abebe, Fita Bayesa, Worku Bikila—were lighting up the running world, winning races, and setting records over distances from 5000 meters to the marathon. Business was good. But it was about to get even better following a trip to Ethiopia that Jos made in February 1991. Little did he know that at the junior cross-country selection race he had traveled over to see, held annually at Jan Meda, the former imperial racetrack for Haile Selassie's stable of imported Arabian horses and the site of thousands of Ethiopians' baptism in the pool at the race course's center, a vision would appear before him of how incredible the future of the sport he loved so much could be.

"I was scouting this junior cross-country race with an eye towards spotting some young talent. As usual, I was looking up front and watching the first two or three. Then I noticed this kid back in fifth place. He had style, I could see that right away. He was compact and fluid; he had a big chest and ran up tall and on his toes. I loved that look. It said one thing to me: speed. That was different from most Ethiopian runners, who normally have a long, rangy stride. Anyway, I thought I'd go up to this kid after the race and introduce myself. But before I could say anything, he reached out and grabbed my arm and told me his name. Then in broken English he began shouting, 'Me Europe. Me Europe.' He kept repeating this. It was obvious that he was desperate to get out of Ethiopia and change his life through running. And as he spoke those words, 'Me Europe,' this huge smile hung from his face that you just couldn't ignore. Eventually when I got to talk to him some more through my translator I realized how focused his goals were. And that's unusual for a young Ethiopian boy from the countryside, to have his future mapped out so clearly in his mind. In addition, I could see that this kid had a soul. His personality just leapt out at you, and he was so eager to learn. He was already saying things like, he wanted to study English and then go on to help his people once he was through running. He had a vision of the future, both for his country and for his running, that was incredibly exciting. I mean, he actually told me that he wanted to become the greatest distance runner of all time. Now, as a manager that's exactly the kind of thing you want to hear a young athlete say. But I thought to myself, *Who is this skinny kid named Haile Gebrselassie to say that?*—'I want to become the greatest distance runner of all time.' It was ridiculous, but I half believed him, too. That was the kind of passion and conviction he conveyed. The real truth of the matter was, he just wanted to change his life through running. And I could certainly sympathize with that."

8

The Greatest

Over the course of two Olympic gold medals, four outdoor track world championships, four indoor track world championships, one half-marathon world championship, eight outdoor track world records, eight indoor track world records, one world record on the road, a lifetime winning percentage of .750, including a 54-race unbeaten streak above 800 meters between February 14, 1997 and August 8, 2001, Jos and Haile are still traveling to races around the world together not only as business partners—athlete-manager—but as best friends, too.

In the hotel lobby the day before some race in one big city or another—maybe Paris, maybe Berlin, maybe London—you might see Jos and Haile sitting at a corner table with two cups of coffee in front of them speaking in warm, respectful tones—"You know, Jos, it's the marathon that's ultimately the most important for me."

Or following dinner together in some other city, before some other race, they might duck into Haile's room to talk more openly—"How are you really feeling, Haile?"

"I'm a bit tired, Jos. That's all."

"What do you think about tomorrow's race?"

"I think I have to forget about myself and just run hard."

"Haile, if you don't feel well I can tell the promoter right now that you're not running."

"But, Jos, he expects me to run . . . the people expect me to run."

"Not if you're not right, Haile."

"That's okay, Jos. Thank you. Let me just take some sleep now. I'll feel better in the morning."

It's a true partnership these two have; their concern for one another runs deep. After all, they've built their careers together; they've revolutionized distance running together. And sitting next to each other on a flight to some promotional event here or there—a photo shoot for Adidas in Germany, the premiere of Haile's biopic, *Endurance*, in New York City—gives them the opportunity to catch up on other news—"Jos, you should see Eden now."

"She's getting big?"

"She's growing into a little lady, Jos. And her English, soon it will be better than mine."

"That's good, Haile. Then she can teach you."

"I know, Jos. That's my plan."

Or with some time on their hands they might begin to wonder if anything good is coming from their work—"But how will that help, Jos?"

"I'm not sure, exactly, but it's something."

"To sell your house and car and give the money to someone in Ethiopia isn't the answer. We need education and jobs, not handouts. We need to learn about self-responsibility."

"But, Haile, when are things going to change?"

"Not in our lifetime, Jos. But some good is already happening: the money to build schools and offices, the awareness campaigns around AIDS, the Great Ethiopian Run . . ."

"You really think so?"

"Trust me, Jos. Ethiopia is becoming a better place."

It can be difficult for Jos and Haile to move past the business of track and field. That's just how consuming their life around running is: the racing, the training, the traveling, the media commitments, the sponsors to please. Time for them is so often hurried and rushed—in and out of one city, onto the next. That's the high-stakes global game that track and field has become. But in the end it's always Haile's and Jos's shared upbringing—cramped houses with nine siblings and little money to spare, fathers who didn't understand their dreams, and punishing workouts designed to change their lives—that keeps them in sync and well on track into the future.

But of course it wasn't always that way.

Early in their relationship, Haile's English was poor, and Jos struggled to understand the Ethiopian mindset. For Haile, too, everything European was so foreign. And the Ethiopian Athletics Federation (EAF) was constantly interfering, making it difficult at times for Haile to run his best.

On July 23, 1993, for example, after he'd finished third in the 5000 meters at the London Grand Prix (13:15.10), the EAF insisted that Haile return home to join the rest of the Ethiopian squad as they prepared for the world championships a few weeks away in Stuttgart. Jos, though, had already arranged for Haile to run in Zurich the following week.

"But the federation wants me home, not in Zurich, Jos," Haile said.

"Yes, but, Haile, the race in Zurich will be fast. I think you can break Bulti's national 5000-meter record. That's much better preparation for Stuttgart than going to some training camp in Addis."

"But, Jos, it's my first world championships . . . you know they can prevent me from going if I don't do what they say."

"But, Haile . . . the record."

"Honestly, Jos, you think I can do it? That's very fast, 13:07."

"Trust me, Haile, I know you can."

Using contacts he had with the Dutch airline company KLM, Jos managed to get Haile on a flight to Holland without the necessary visas or travel documents. From Amsterdam it was a one-and-a-half hour drive through the night to Jos's home in Nijmegen. These two were on their own now, outlaws risking severe sanctions.

Despite the change of government in Ethiopia in 1991, and the overthrow of Mengistu, many aspects of Ethiopian society still remained under tight control, among them immigration, customs, and the freedom to travel. For this transgression, Haile would certainly be made an example of.

From his office in Nijmegen, Jos fended off threats from the Ethiopian embassy in Amsterdam. He was told to put Haile on the very next plane to Ethiopia. Meanwhile, Haile tried to stay focused on Zurich. He went out for long runs over the same forest trails that Jos had once trained on. He was 20 years old, just as Jos had been, and he, too, was hoping to change his life through running and prove to his father that he could be a success.

By now Jos was convinced that this skinny kid from rural Ethiopia he had met two years earlier at a junior cross-country race, and who had told him that he wanted to become the greatest distance runner of all time, actually knew what he was saying. Jos could see the talent and the potential. That was why he was willing to risk so much to make sure Haile ran in Zurich.

"You have to begin testing yourself against the best," he told Haile all week. "You need a confidence boost before your first world championships."

Haile knew Jos was right. He could hear Jos's voice over and over in his head as the race in Zurich approached . . . *You can break Bulti's record . . . that's much better preparation for Stuttgart than going to some training camp . . .* No way was Haile going to let this opportunity slip past.

In the end, it was a hard race and Haile finished fourth in 13:05.39, a new Ethiopian record. But any celebrations were short lived as Haile immediately jumped onto a plane back to Addis Ababa.

The Ethiopian officials dispatched to the airport, including a representative from the EAF, were actually surprised to see Haile walk off the plane. They thought he would remain in Holland permanently, where it would be easier for him to pursue his running career. Regardless, talk quickly turned to an appropriate punishment: a future travel ban, and removal from the Ethiopian team competing at the world championships, now just 10 days away. Then again, Haile's performance in Zurich couldn't be ignored: a new national record, his emergence as a real medal contender in Stuttgart. This was the card Haile played in his defense.

"Zurich was my breakthrough," he explained to the panel of men judging him. "I know I can win a medal in Stuttgart now. I have the confidence. It's my dream to win a gold medal for Ethiopia. Please, you must let me run."

Eventually a compromise was reached: Haile could compete in Stuttgart with the understanding that his case would be reviewed at a later date.

It's amazing the color gold's effect. The luster, the shine . . . The effect especially of gold hardened into metal, a gold medal. Its value and return are so real and tangible that it affects people in magical ways. That was what Jos had explained to Haile. "A gold medal will make them forget everything. Sanctions, travel bans, all of that will disappear. Trust me, Haile, win a gold medal in Stuttgart and what happened in Zurich will be ancient history. You'll be a hero."

Haile did trust Jos. And just as he had been right about the national record in Zurich, Jos was right about this: On August 22, 1993, the night of the 10,000-meter final, Haile won Ethiopia's first world championship gold medal (27:46.02), setting off wild celebrations in Addis Ababa as ordinary people, ministers, and all sorts of officials congratulated themselves for developing such a faithful son as Haile Gebrselassie. While for Jos and Haile back in Stuttgart, it was the beginning of an incredible ride. And what followed absolutely stunned the world.

1994 . . . First World Record

June 4, 1994, and despite winning the world 10,000-meter title the year before Haile was still relatively unknown across wider track and field circles. But that's to be expected. Distance runners tend to come and go, their life span at the top usually cut short by injury or burnout. So names fade and personalities rarely leave a mark. That was why to the majority of the crowd in Hengelo, Holland, that early-summer afternoon in June, Haile was just another African runner standing on the 5000-meter starting line. Moreover, following his world championship in Stuttgart, Haile had largely raced on the road or over the country, including a third-place finish at the world cross-country championships in Budapest on March 26. Hengelo was his first track race of the year.

The men's 5000 meters in Hengelo was the final event on the program. And many in the crowd were satisfied that they had already witnessed a great day of track and field, and so decided to make an early start for home. That didn't trouble Haile, though: "The only thing on my mind as I waited for the gun that afternoon was the splits I wanted to hit." And the average time per lap Haile needed to run to break Said Aouita's seven-year-old 5000-meter record of 12:58.39 was 62.3 seconds. To succeed would mean a seven-second personal best for Haile. But he wasn't concerned: "I knew I could break Aouita's record. My training had been going so well in 1994. That was what I had told Jos. I said, 'Jos, I'm sure I can break Aouita's 5000-meter world record. What do you think?' But Jos was cautious. 'I don't know, Haile,' he told me. But I said to him, 'Come on, Jos, believe me when I tell you, I'm ready.'"

When the pacemaker with Haile in tow passed 3000 meters in 7:52, Jos quickly calculated what Haile needed to run for his last five laps to break Aouita's record: near enough to a four-minute mile plus another lap. He began to shout from his position on the backstretch. "Sixty-ones, Haile. You need to keep running 61s."

With two of those five laps left, Haile was still turning out 61s. He was alone at the front now, and beginning to lap the other runners. That was when the Dutch stadium announcer realized what was happening and launched into a frenzied call. He repeated Haile's name three times before delivering the news. "Haile Gebrselassie, Haile Gebrselassie, Haile Gebrselassie, ladies and gentlemen, is on world-record pace." His excitement reached the streets and sidewalks outside the stadium. Scores of people just about to open their car doors or step into buses froze in their tracks. "Haile Gebrselassie? Haile Gebrselassie? Who's Haile Gebrselassie?" But only the swiftest made it back to their seats in time to see Haile stop the clock at 12:56.96: his first world record, and the beginning of Haile's very special relationship with the Hengelo crowd.

Despite being a world record holder, Haile was still a novice on the international track circuit. The travel, the hard-fought races—there was a lot to learn yet. After Hengelo he suffered defeats over 5000 meters (June 10 in St. Denis, 13:10.79, and July 15 in London, 13:11.87), 1500 meters (July 30 in Hechtel, 3:37.04), and 3000 meters (August 2 in Monte Carlo, 7:37.49). But over 10,000 meters Haile remained secure. He notched up wins at the highly competitive Athletissma track meet in Lausanne on July 6 (27:15.00), and the prestigious Ivo Van Damme Memorial in Brussels on August 19 (27:20.39). The wider track world was now beginning to take notice of this diminutive Ethiopian with the wide smile. Was a new distance running phenom on the rise? Judging by the year to come, apparently so.

1995 . . . Three World Records in 71 Days
and a Second World Championship

The annual track meet in Hengelo is always one of the opening events on the European track and field calendar, and in effect it's Jos's meet. As race director he creates the fields and sets the stage. The year after Haile's 5000-meter world record, Jos arranged for Haile to attempt another world record in Hengelo. He scheduled it for the last event on the program, too. Only this time Haile would be running 10,000 meters, and not a single person would leave his seat early.

To prepare for his Hengelo 10,000-meter world record attempt, Haile opened his outdoor season in Kerkrade, Germany on May 27 with a new world record for 2 miles (8:07.46). Nine days later (June 5) he was on the starting line in Hengelo.

As the first of the 25 laps Haile needed to run began to unwind, the stadium announcer launched into his call. "Ladies and gentlemen, you know who he is. He's back in Hengelo to try to break William Sigei's 10,000 meter world record of 26:52.23. Show him your appreciation, everyone—he's just passed the 1-kilometer mark on record pace. He's the Emperor from Ethiopia, the current 5000-meter world record holder and 10,000-meter world champion, ladies and gentleman this is Haileeeeeeee Gebrselassie."

The audience rose and screamed; they stomped the ground in delight. And as the clock ticked on the stadium announcer provided regular updates—"Four kilometers down, ladies and gentlemen . . . still on record pace." No one stopped clapping as Haile kept pouring it on. He appeared tireless. His legs resembled steel wheels tempered to strike the ground without a single shimmy, effectively rolling ahead frictionless as if the lane he was running in was downhill.

By halfway—5000 meters—just one of the three designated rabbits remained, Worku Bikila, Haile's good friend and countryman. For every lap Jos was out in lane three yelling splits into Haile's face, "Another 64, Haile, good, good." But the noise around the stadium made it difficult for Haile to hear. Luckily he knew the tempo to keep: "All the hard training, all the repetitions I'd run around the track back home to prepare for that record had synchronized my mind and legs to the exact pace."

Haile was precision in motion, as efficient in his steps as a surgeon is with his hands.

Seventeen minutes and Haile was alone. Worku was finished. That left roughly 10 minutes of hard running for Haile to get under the Kenyan Sigei's record.

At 21 minutes shadows began to cover the outer lanes of the track. Haile, though, ran in the sun in lane one. His eyes were sharp and focused like a bull's-eye; his body remained perfectly still with the exception of his arms and legs, which swung hypnotically in light, parallel harmony.

With just under a mile's worth of running to go, Haile's efforts became pronounced. He was biting the air in front of him, literally chewing on his breaths in an attempt to swallow all the oxygen he could digest. His lips tightened through the struggle, but he was holding on. And he managed to stabilize his form through the line, stopping the clock at 26:43.53. It was a massive nine-second improvement on the world record, and the capacity crowd in Hengelo was jubilant.

Immediately a mad rush of Ethiopian supporters hoisted Haile onto their shoulders. His victory parade around the track ensued. The runners who had been lapped—the entire rest of the field—had to break through the joyous mob to proceed with their race. Ethiopian flags flew from every vantage point; Haile's smile beamed like a heart in love. And tremors and tingles rippled through the stadium as Jos went on hugging anyone he could find. This was Haile's great reward, holding two of distance running's most treasured prizes: the world records for both the 5 and the 10. His celebrity around the world and throughout Ethiopia was now guaranteed. Simultaneously possessing these two records was something that not even Yifter had done. However, Haile's double-record reign would be short lived: The very next day in Rome (June 6), Moses Kiptanui from Kenya took a second and a half (12:55.30) off Haile's 5000 meter record. Although it wouldn't be long before Haile had both records back in his hands.

Two 5000-meter victories followed for Haile after Hengelo—June 17 in Lille, France (13:04.20), and July 3 in Paris (13:07.81). Then in Gothenburg, Sweden, on August 8 he defended his 10,000-meter world championship. Steady laps of 65 seconds were on order from the three Kenyans who headed the field—Josephat Machuka, Joseph Kimani, Paul Tergat—as they tried to snuff out Haile's kick. With four laps remaining Tergat hit the front with a hard, solitary push for home. But his efforts were to no avail. Haile simply attached himself to Tergat's backside and then ran the final 200 meters in a blazing 25 seconds. Such speed was unheard of in distance running. And now Haile had his second world 10,000-meter championship (27:12.95).

Never one to leave a job waiting, a week after Gothenburg, Haile traveled to Zurich (August 16) where he took a gargantuan 11 second chunk out of the 5000-meter world record recently set by Kiptanui. He crossed the line in an incredible 12:44.39. To Haile's delight he was again the proud holder of distance running's two jewels: the world records for 5000 and 10,000 meters.

1996 . . . Olympic Gold

The year opened for Haile on a grand scale as he made his debut on the European indoor circuit by setting his fifth and sixth world records—13:10.98 for 5000 meters in Sindelfingen, Germany on January 27, and 7:30.72 for 3000 meters in Stuttgart on February 4.

By now Haile's reputation was well established: He was becoming one of the greatest long-distance runners ever. But his most important athletic goal still remained: winning an Olympic gold medal. "The Olympics are what people remember," he commented as the Atlanta games approached. "Without an Olympic gold medal your career is nothing. People will ask me when I'm older, 'Which Olympics did you win?' So you see, I must win in Atlanta."

Heading into Atlanta, Haile felt extremely secure in his fitness and his tactics. He had prepared for his first Olympics by running two underdistance races, a 1500 meters in Chemnitz, Germany on May 19 (3:34.64), and a 3000 meters in the familiar confines of Hengelo on May 27 (7:34.66). Victory came easily for him in both cases, and in Atlanta he knew his rivals would find it difficult to sustain a hard enough pace to tire him out, or sprint fast enough over the final lap to outkick him. He thus announced his intention to attempt the 10,000/5000 double, just as his hero Miruts Yifter had done at the 1980 Olympics.

In Atlanta, the 10,000-meter final was held first (July 29), and Haile followed Paul Tergat until the last lap. He then passed Tergat and sprinted away to claim his first Olympic gold medal in an Olympic record time of 27:07.34, leaving the silver medal to Tergat. Haile had run his second 5000 meters in 13:11.4, which was faster than all the Olympic 5000-meter winning times except one (Said Aouita in 1984). However, serious blisters Haile acquired from the extremely hard track forced him to abandon his plans to double. It didn't matter, though. He was still a hero in Ethiopia and he returned home to a joyous reception, only to have to get back on a plane eight hours later and fly to Zurich for a head-to-head meeting over 5000 meters with Kenyan star Daniel Komen.

Entering his hotel room in Zurich, Haile collapsed into bed exhausted from all the travel and fanfare of the previous 24 hours. Moreover, his blisters were still tender and raw. His race the next day

(August 14) proved too difficult in the end, and Komen won in 12:45.09 to Haile's second place finish of 12:52.70. His season was over. To make matters worse, nine days later in Brussels (August 23) Salah Hissou from Morocco, who had finished third behind Haile in Atlanta, took five seconds off Haile's incredible 10,000-meter world record, running 26:38.08. But Haile was determined to strike back. Six months later he would begin a winning streak over 5000 and 10,000 meters that would stretch across the next four years!

1997 . . . Four More World Records, Two More World Championships

Haile claimed his first world record of the year (number seven in total) by lowering his already impressive indoor 5000-meter record an incredible 11.94 seconds to 12:59.04 in Stockholm on February 20. He capped off the indoor season by winning his first indoor world championship, running comfortably away from the field in Paris on March 9 in 7:34.71 for 3000 meters.

As was now becoming his custom, Haile began his outdoor season in Hengelo on May 31 with another world record. The distance was 2 miles in what was billed as a match race between the 1500-meter and mile world record holder Noureddine Morceli (Algeria), with a bonus of one million dollars for a sub-eight-minute performance. Morceli, however, dropped out after four laps, and Haile was left to go for the record and the bonus on his own. He was able to secure the former, and he came within just one second of the latter, posting a time of 8:01.08.

Haile's outing in Hengelo proved the perfect warm-up for him to attempt to reclaim the 10,000-meter world record from Hissou. Following comfortable 5000-meter victories in Nürnberg (June 13, 12:54.60) and Paris (June 25, 13:01.51), Haile arrived in Oslo on July 4 in fine record-breaking form.

A world-class field had been assembled by the meet director, Arne Haukvik, but Haile wasn't interested in racing. He only wanted his record back from Hissou. He amassed a huge lead within the space of a few kilometers, and in no time he had lapped the rest of the field. Haile went on to obliterate Hissou's record by seven seconds, bringing the 10,000 meter world record down to an unimaginable 26:31.32.

A month later in Athens (August 6), Haile retained his world 10,000-meter title in 27:24.58, with Paul Tergat again finishing as runner-up. And the next week Haile returned to Zurich (August 13) determined to make up for his loss there the previous year to the now newly crowned 5000-meter world champion, Komen.

Together Komen and Haile went after Haile's 5000-meter world record. And once the rabbits dropped out it was Komen who was left to lead as Haile craftily avoided doing any of the work. With 150 meters remaining, however, Haile released a ferocious sprint to pass Komen on the homestretch and dip inside his world record by three seconds (12:41.86). In Haile's mind his score with Komen was now settled. Komen, however, had ideas of his own on this matter.

On August 22 at the Ivo Van Damme Memorial track meet in Brussels, Haile had to watch from the stands as first Komen and then Paul Tergat broke his 5000- and 10,000-meter world records. It was a night of fabulous Kenyan revenge, and for Haile extremely frustrating.

"Halfway through the 5000 I could see that my record would go. The conditions were perfect and the Kenyans were working so well together. Komen looked relaxed and in control; the atmosphere was fantastic. A band of African drummers kept the whole stadium charged. Occasionally I felt the television cameras on my face trying to catch my reaction. But I didn't give anything away. Inside, though, I was furious for running the 3000 that night and giving up the opportunity to defend one of my records. But at that point, what could I do? And once Komen broke my record [12:39.74], I knew the

10,000 would go as well. What Tergat ran was impressive [26:27.85]. It was the Kenyans' night all right, and they were determined to get back at me for all the times I had defeated them, or sat behind them as they did the pacing. I knew, though, what needed to happen next. Back at the hotel when I saw Jos, I said, 'Jos, start getting ready for Hengelo next year. Because that's where I'm going to take back the first of my records. And I want to begin with the 10,000.'"

1998 . . . Back on Top

Just as he had done the previous two years, Haile opened 1998 with more world records indoors—on January 25 in Karlsruhe, Germany he ran 7:26.15 for 3000 meters, and on February 15 in Birmingham, England, he ran 4:52.86 for 2000 meters (world records number 11 and 12 in total). This was merely a prelude, however, to the summer ahead and Haile's main course of business: He was anxious to go hunting for records.

"All that winter [1998] I felt so empty without my 5000 and 10,000 records. People were referring to me as the *former* world record holder, and treating me as if my career was over. I didn't like that much; I wanted to show everyone that Haile Gebrselassie was not through. When I'd check the all-time lists on the internet and see my name off the top I'd get angry. But as spring came, and the Hengelo 10,000 meters approached [June 1], I knew from the workouts I was doing that the coming summer season was going to be a good one, probably my best ever. Of course, I never could have done what I did in Hengelo without help from Assefa Mezgebu, who did a great job with the pacing, lasting a full 15 laps, and leaving me with only 10 to do on my own. I knew that wasn't going to be a problem, either. I simply concentrated on one lap, and then another, one at a time, just like that. And Jos had arranged for my favorite song, 'Scatman,' to play over the PA, which helped keep my legs turning over as I tried to match the song's beat. And then before I knew it I was done. Job complete: 26:22.75. I had my most precious record back [a staggering five second improvement], and in front of my 'home' crowd in Hengelo. That just left me with the 5000 meter record to regain, which I did 12 days later in Helsinki [June 13] when I ran 12:39.36. I knew the Kenyans would be furious with me for taking back both records so early in the season. But I didn't care. That had been my intention since Brussels. That had been my motivation for almost a year."

The 1998 season continued with more victories for Haile—Oslo, July 9 (7:27.42 for 3000 meters); Rome, July 14 (13:02.63 for 5000 meters); Monte Carlo, August 8 (7:25.54 for 3000 meters); Zurich, August 12 (12:54.08 for 5000 meters); Brussels, August 28 (7:25.09 for 3000 meters); Berlin, September 1 (12:56.52 for 5000 meters); and Moscow, September 5 (7:50.00 for 3000 meters)—as he strengthened his hold on the title Greatest Distance Runner Ever.

1999 . . . An Indoor Spectacle

Not surprisingly Haile opened 1999 with an indoor world record. The previous winter (February 19, 1998), Daniel Komen had again claimed one of Haile's records, running 12:51.48 for 5000 meters indoors in Stockholm. It was a massive eight-second improvement. But Haile found a way to knock it down farther still. And on Valentine's Day, in Birmingham, England, he ran 12:50.38 to increase his tally of world records to a staggering 15.

Finding the tight confines of indoor track more to his liking with each passing year, Haile headed to the indoor world championships in Maebashi, Japan, with an incredible double in mind: He would attempt both the 1500 meters and 3000 meters, which meant running a race on every day of the three-day championship.

Haile earned title number one on March 5, winning the 3000 in 7:53.57. The next day he won his 1500 meter heat in 3:41.22. And 24 hours later, on the final day of the competition, he claimed his second gold medal with a fine 3:33.77 performance in the 1500 meter final. This showing highlighted Haile's tremendous range, and sent a strong warning to anyone thinking of preventing him from claiming his fourth 10,000 meter world championship at the end of August in Seville.

Haile's pre-world-championship string of victories again showcased his incredible versatility and depth of talent. Among his series of eight wins, which for the first time in a world championship year didn't include a 10,000 meters, were a 3:33.73 for 1500 meters in Stuttgart on June 6, a mile in 3:52.39 in Gateshead on June 27, and a 12:49.64 5000 meters in Zurich on August 11. By the time Haile reached Seville on August 24 for the last race of his season, he was in perfect form.

Any fast-paced front-running ideas in this 10,000 meter world championship final were knocked on the head early due to the extremely hard track surface and temperatures well into triple figures. A tightly bunched pack, including three Kenyans and four Ethiopians, passed the halfway mark in 14:17. This was a jog for athletes of this caliber. Clearly someone needed to act if he had any designs on preventing Haile from simply sprinting clear on the final lap. But the field proved hesitant, and with one lap to go five athletes answered the bell. Left to play his strongest card—speed—Haile sprinted away from the field with a 55-second final lap to claim his fourth world 10,000-meter championship. Once again Paul Tergat was left to settle for silver (his third behind Haile in championship 10,000-meter races). But Tergat left Seville determined to reverse his fortunes the next year at the Olympics in Sydney. And he very nearly did.

2000 . . . Olympic Gold Again

Just like 1996, 2000 was also about only one thing for Haile: winning the 10,000-meter Olympic gold medal. He used four early summer 5000-meter races (all victories) to sharpen his fitness and get his mind race ready. At these Olympics he'd be the defending champion, and the challenge would be just as difficult as it had been four years earlier in Atlanta.

Paul Tergat was desperate to upset his Ethiopian neighbor's plans for a second Olympic gold medal, and his hopes couldn't have been dashed in a more frustrating manner. In what has come to be regarded as one of the greatest long distance races of all time, these two old rivals battled each other to the wire, with Haile emerging victorious by a mere 0.09 second in 27:18.20.

Haile's season ended in Sydney, however, as he was forced to take time off to rest his suffering Achilles tendon. Later in the year he would have surgery on his Achilles, and as 2001 dawned with Haile yet to run a race, his chances of winning a fifth world championship were beginning to look remote.

2001 . . . The End of an Era?

Haile's injury troubles forced him to delay the opening of his season all the way up to the world championship 10,000-meter final on August 8 in Edmonton, Canada. As defending champion he received a bye to the final, and it turned out that he needed every last day to get himself race-fit.

As he explains, "Three days before the final in Edmonton, which was going to be my first race since Sydney, I came down with a very serious fever. I couldn't stop sweating; my temperature reached 103 degrees; I was burning up. Finally, my friend Getaneh Tessema thought he'd better call an ambulance. At the hospital they gave me shots and pills to bring the fever down, and I spent the night there under close watch. The next day my fever was gone, but I had terrible diarrhea that lasted the whole night. When I woke up on the morning of my race I felt a little better. Although no one thought I would be able to run. But I said, 'Yes, I can run.' And even with so many problems I almost won. My mistake was to wait too long to attack the Kenyan, Charles Kamathi. If I had sprinted from farther out, with 400 meters left not just 200, I'm sure I would have beaten him. And I would've had my fifth world championship. Enough to fill one whole hand."

Haile was left to claim the bronze medal in Edmonton as his teammate Assefa Mezgebu passed him at the line to take the silver medal. But the possibility of a fifth world 10,000 meter title still loomed for Haile. After just a handful of races following the world championships in Edmonton, and a shortened 2002 season because of a number of persistent injuries, Haile was healthy again and his 2003 season was about to begin—and with it the possibility to run the 10,000 at summer's end in Paris at the world championships. Victory in Paris would make 2003 the year that truly defined Haile's greatness: the exclamation point in what had already been the most consistent and dominant career of any distance runner in history. For no other athlete from any other era had so single-handedly set the course for the future of distance running as Haile Gebrselassie.

Boston, 1992, Haile at the World Junior Cross Country Championships.
Photo by Mark Shearman

Stuttgart, 1993. Haile leads the 10,000m World Championship final.
Photo by Mark Shearman

Gothenburg, 1995. Haile celebrates his second World Championship 10,000m title.
Photo by Mark Shearman

Atlanta, 1996: the Olympic 10,000m final.   Photo by Mark Shearman

Atlanta, 1996. Haile wins the Olympic 10,000m ahead of Paul Tergat.
Photo by Mark Shearman

Oslo, July 4, 1997. Haile on the way to his second 10,000m world record, 26:31.32.

Photo by Mark Shearman

Athens, 1997. Haile in the World Championships 10,000m.

Photo by Mark Shearman

Seville, August 1999. Haile leads at the World Championships 10,000m.
Photo by Mark Shearman

Sydney, 2000. Haile wins his second Olympic 10,000m gold medal ahead of Paul Tergat.
Photo by Mark Shearman

Sydney, 2000.
Photo by Mark Shearman

Sydney, 2000.
Photo by Mark Shearman

Bristol, October 2001, World Half Marathon Championships.   Photo by Mark Shearman

London Marathon, April 2002. Haile, Khalid Khannouchi, and Paul Tergat.
Photo by Mark Shearman

Birmingham, February 2003, after Haile's indoor 2-mle world record.

Photo by Mark Shearman

Birmingham, March 2003. Winning the World Indoor Championships 3000m.

Photo by Mark Shearman

Paris, August 2003. Haile leads Kenenisa Bekele and Sileshi Sihine
in the 10,000m at the World Championships.

Photo by Mark Shearman

A scene from rural Ethiopia.

On the streets of Addis Ababa

Haile training at Entoto.

Running the steps at Meskel Square, Ethiopia's "Field of Dreams."

Haile and Alem on their wedding day.

The birth of Haile's first daughter, Eden.

Haile in his office.

A view of the Addis skyline.

The Gebrselassie family at home. Photo by Anton Engels

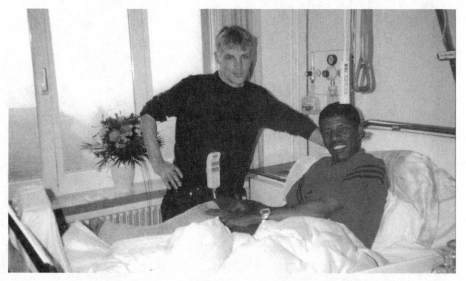

With Anton after Achilles surgery in 2000 after the Olympics.

Parade for a national hero, after returning from Sydney in 2000.

Some of Haile's medals and trophies at home.

Haile and Jos at the London Grand Prix, August 2003.

Doctor Wolde-Meskel Kostre, Haile's coach.

Haile doing some shopping in Addis Ababa.

Street sign for Haile Gebrselassie Avenue in downtown Addis Ababa.

Haile with his friends Yasin and Girma at a May 1 celebration, 2003.

Haile and teammates enjoying some free time.

Haile during the filming of *Endurance*.

Jim Denison and Haile.

Part Two

INTO THE LEAD

Experience is not what happens to a man;
it is what a man does with what happens to him.
—Aldous Huxley

9

Birmingham, February 21, 2003

It's only a few hours before Haile has to begin warming up for his attempt at a new indoor 2-mile world record at the 2003 Grand Prix track meet in Birmingham, England, and not surprisingly he's talking politics. Over lunch on the second-floor restaurant of the Crowne Plaza Hotel in downtown Birmingham, the meet's official headquarters, the mood around Haile's table is relaxed, despite some obvious concerns that remain unspoken.

"The situation with Saddam Hussein is very tricky," Haile says.

The impending conflict in Iraq touches everyone's mind.

"That's true, Haile, it is," Anton Engels, Haile's Dutch physiotherapist, responds.

Also around the table are Ellen van Langen, the 1992 800-meter Olympic champion from Holland who's now an integral member of Jos's ever-expanding management team, and Hailu Mekkonen and Abiyote Abate, Haile's Ethiopian teammates, who are also running the 2-mile here tonight. Mekkonen, in fact, holds the current world record of 8:09.66, but his posture almost suggests that he'd be relieved if Haile succeeded tonight and took his record away. His shoulders fold in on themselves, cutting his size in half. Between careful bites of pasta and sips of water he adds nothing to the conversation, keeping his eyes fixed on Haile, listening.

"George Bush and Tony Blair have a lot to consider before they take action." Haile carries on speculating this way all through dessert and over his second cup of tea. At the same time, he's frequently interrupted by well-wishers glad to see him back on tour. Linford Christie, the British Olympic 100-meter champion from 1992, shakes Haile's hand. Wilson Kipketer, the world record holder indoors and outdoors for 800 meters, slaps Haile on the back and gives him a friendly thumbs-up sign.

These are all quick exchanges: "Hello," "How you doing," "Good to see you." After all, Haile is among his peers here in the hotel restaurant, which has largely been taken over by tonight's event. It's downstairs in the hotel lobby, or outside in the street, where the public congregates, that Haile has to manage the autograph requests and pose for pictures. But these demands he obliges with a wide smile and a warm embrace. As anyone who knows Haile well will tell you, he is always willing to accommodate others.

Getaneh Reta, one of the best men at Haile's wedding (he had five in total), and the architect of his two office buildings and his future house, explains that there is an Amharic word that describes Haile perfectly . . . *yilugnta*. It means the inability to say no. "You see," Getaneh says, "Haile always wants to please everyone. For example, the Ethiopian people want to see Haile Gebrselassie win so he keeps running even though he has won everything there is to win. And when he loses he's not necessarily upset because he didn't achieve something he wanted, but because he didn't achieve what others wanted. Take the house I've just designed for him. It's a classic villa, and therefore highly symmetrical and spacious. Such a house reflects a man who likes order. But Haile's spontaneous and impulsive, someone who can multitask extremely well. For such a person I would expect to build a modern, iconoclastic house. But Haile has put the function he believes his house needs to serve—entertaining and accommodating others—above his own needs. He is a completely selfless person. And the little I know about world-class athletes apparently that's very unusual."

Richard Nerurkar, another one of Haile's close friends and a former world-class marathoner, also uses the word *selfless* to describe Haile. "Most people only know 'Haile the runner,' not 'Haile the person.' And as extraordinary as he is as a runner, he is even more so as a person. His sincerity and generosity are incredible. He is a leader of people with incredible drive, energy, and confidence. Let's face it, being a world-class athlete means putting your own needs first in most situations. I know that's what I did when I was competing. But Haile never does that. He's completely selfless. He's always thinking, *What can I do to help my people? What can I do to make Ethiopia a better place?* And his actions reflect this. He raises millions for various charities, he supports all manner of local causes, he employs hundreds of people, and he interacts with politicians and diplomats on a regular basis. There is no other athlete today who could lead that sort of life and still dominate his sport like Haile does. He is a very, very, very special man."

But as dominant as Haile has been for the last 10 seasons on the international track and field circuit, his race here tonight in Birmingham actually marks an important beginning: the official launch of his campaign to win back his world 10,000-meter title later in the summer in Paris that he lost in Edmonton in 2001 to an unexpectant but jubilant Kenyan, Charles Kamathi.

Haile's bronze medal at those championships is one of the few blemishes in his career, and he is anxious to put it right. Attempting to win that elusive fifth world championship in Paris, however, is only the prelude for Haile's return to action tonight. His sights are set more squarely on Athens 2004, the next Olympic Games, where he hopes to win an unprecedented third gold medal in the 10,000 meters. "My Olympic hat trick," he told the media yesterday in announcing his plans for 2003 and 2004. And tonight in Birmingham that campaign opens. Tonight Haile will get to answer the question that has been troubling him since Edmonton, *Do I still have what it takes to run at the top?* Tonight's race, then, marks one of the few times that Haile has harbored doubts about his ability to succeed. But he's keeping those concerns to himself. Anton and Ellen, however, suspect as much, which is why they steer the lunchtime conversation away from track talk and prompt Haile for further political conjectures—"So, Haile, what's Ethiopia's stance on war against Iraq?"

"Well, I can't even begin to answer that question," Haile starts, "until I first explain to you . . ." And away he goes.

Certainly Haile didn't exhibit any signs of doubt or anxiety about his return to the track last night. As he relaxed facedown on his bed, stripped bare bar a black T-shirt and red briefs, and Anton's oil-drenched fingers sunk deep into his hamstring muscles, he laughed, questioned, and commented on all sorts of images coming across his hotel room's television. Here was more news of the unfolding Iraq crisis, scores from the English Premier Football league, the Cricket World Cup, and recycled weather reports and car and toothpaste commercials. With each passing topic, Haile had a remark.

Again, Saddam: "Oh, there he is. He must be wondering what to do."

Or on football: "What, Arsenal lost? Impossible."

And concerning one new product or another: "Look, my favorite car commercial. It's on my television in Ethiopia all the time."

Haile's chatter continues uninterrupted until the phone rings and he quickly switches from English to Amharic. It will be Hailu or Abiyote calling from their room across the hall. And while Haile talks, Anton continues his massage, moving down Haile's hamstrings until he reaches his calves.

Anton shouts above the television and Haile's phone conversation.

"Everything, it's all right, Haile?"

"I don't know, Anton, what do you think?"

"I think it's good, Haile. I think it's very good."

Haile smiles in agreement, realizing perhaps that another world record will soon be his—number 17. Or that after two lean years following his troubles in Edmonton, his chances of striking world championship gold and later Olympic gold are looking up.

Almost immediately after Haile hangs up the phone there's a knock on the door. He bounds off the bed and lets in Abiyote and Hailu. They each find a seat in the corner of the room and immediately fix their gaze on the television. Their English is in its early stages, so they only speak to Haile—and even then, only after they've been spoken to first.

So the night carries on—conversation mixed with questions, laughter, and discussion. Pretty much what you'd expect to find in any hotel room full of teammates who have traveled to an away competition. Maybe a high school basketball team on the eve of an invitational tournament, or a track club on the road for a league championship meet. Time isn't spent analyzing the field or preparing tactics. There's ample opportunity for that tomorrow. Nothing magical or secretive happens, either: Haile applying some special balm to his legs, or fixing tiny electrodes to his skull. Forget that he's the most gifted distance runner in the history of the world and what you're really left with is just another guy in a hotel room channel-surfing before going to bed. Moreover, from Haile's point of view this whole weekend away from home is more like a holiday than work: "When I'm in Europe no one can call me on my mobile phone because it doesn't work outside Ethiopia. So I don't have to worry about my businesses and what might be going wrong. I have to leave those problems behind for the others. When I go abroad for races I have so much free time around the hotel to relax. It's actually a very easy time for me. The only thing

I need to do is run well."

But as relaxed as Haile is tonight, he still knows that his race tomorrow will be demanding. Not necessarily because the field is so tough, but because he hasn't run a single race on the track since early last summer—eight months ago. And that race he couldn't even finish.

On June 1, 2002, in Hengelo, Haile had to abort his attempt at a new one-hour world record because of a calf injury he'd sustained that spring. His pacemaker that day, his good friend Worku Bikila, sensed that something was wrong as he watched Haile from the side of the track after he completed his pacemaking duties. "I detected some signs that Haile was running with pain: I saw a kind of cringing reaction about 200 meters before he stopped. I could see the tension in his movement, in his body, on his face. I could tell he wasn't extending his leg as much as he should. Prior to that his stride had been fine, but then I could see that he was unable to stretch his leg."

"Actually, after Hengelo I thought my career might be over," Haile says now. "It was the first time in my life I had to drop out of a race. The pain was very bad. I had to cancel the remainder of my season. The doctors told me to take complete rest, not even any type of cross-training. And, oh my goodness, what a terrible time that was for me, not to be able to exercise at all. Maybe the hardest part of my life so far. I was incredibly bored and becoming depressed. There was nothing to do; I was spending more and more time in bed each morning unable to get up. What was the point, I thought, if I couldn't run? I was angry all the time, too, and jealous toward other runners, *Why can they run and I can't?* I wasn't very pleasant to be around. Imagine, the most time off training I had ever had was four days, and now I was being told not to do anything for six weeks. In the end, I couldn't do it. I began some light training after two weeks. And thanks to God I was able to keep going. My goal the whole time I was training was to get ready for the 2003 indoor season. And if that went well I wanted to try to win back my world 10,000-meter title in August in Paris. And if I succeeded in Paris, well, then I'd know that another Olympic title in 2004 was possible."

Despite making excellent progress since his return from injury post-Hengelo, the fact still can't be ignored that Haile is heading into tonight's race short on competition. "Please don't forget," he cautioned the media at yesterday's press conference, "my last indoor race was four years ago"—the 1999 winter season when Haile ran an indoor world record for 5000 meters and won both the 1500 meters and 3000 meters at the indoor world championships in Japan. Which is why it isn't only sensationalistic reporting that the British press have labeled Haile's race tonight "the Comeback." Or asked in various feature pieces and pre-meet analyses, "Does Gebrselassie still have what it takes?" "Is the Emperor's reign on the track over?"

But such questions also illustrate just how high a standard Haile is held to. Because although his two most recent track races— Edmonton, Hengelo—haven't gone so well, he certainly hasn't been inactive over the past year. In fact, he produced two outstanding road results on either side of his failed one hour world record attempt in Hengelo. Two months before Hengelo, on April 14, 2002, Haile ran the London marathon and set a world's best time of 2 hours, 6 minutes, 35 seconds for a debut performance. That result was deemed poor, though, because he was third. Even if it did take a world's best time of 2:05.38 from Khalid Khannouchi to complete the job.

"What happened in London was not what I wanted. It was my first big race after losing in Edmonton, and my plan was to do something very special like set a new marathon world record. I had excellent preparation for London, including winning the world half-marathon championships in Bristol a few months in advance. I actually started training for London the day after I lost my world 10,000-meter title in Edmonton. I began doing long runs on the roads around

Edmonton, building up my mileage and getting stronger. All the press were saying that I was finished after my bronze medal, and I wanted to change that story as fast as possible and create some good news about Haile Gebrselassie. Nothing makes me angrier than when people say I'm finished just because I lose one race. Such thinking is crazy. How can a whole career be wiped away with one defeat? It's ridiculous. The press, they never consider *why* I might have lost. They don't examine the cause, which in Edmonton was my high fever only two days before my race. Instead they say, 'Haile Gebrselassie has lost . . . Haile Gebrselassie's track career is finished.' For the London marathon my plan was to show everyone that I'm fine. But unfortunately I had some trouble with my fluid intake and my pacing, some simple planning mistakes about how to approach the marathon. Back in Ethiopia no one could understand how I lost. They weren't used to seeing me lose and were very upset. They said to me, 'Are you selfish? Why didn't you win?' The fact that London was my first real marathon, or that the marathon is a hard event and very different from what I had been doing before on the track running 10,000 meters, didn't matter to them. Ethiopian people are funny that way. They think it's better for me not to compete than to lose. Which was why they were so happy after Doha."

Doha, Qatar, December 13, 2002, and six months after his DNF in Hengelo, Haile set a world's best time for 10K on the road (his 16th world record)—27 minutes, 7 seconds. In the process, he claimed a million-dollar bonus that the event's organizer had put up for anyone who could run a new world record.

"I think the promoter in Doha thought his money was safe," Haile likes to joke now. "He knew I was coming off problems in London and Hengelo, and that I had this calf injury. Although my reason for running Doha wasn't about the million dollars, believe me. I wanted to test my shape before committing myself to track again. But my preparation went surprisingly well. Once my calf began to heal, I was running very good workouts. In fact, after one session I did on the road I knew that million dollars would be mine. I was running two times 5000 meters on a slightly hilly course and Doctor was there timing me. For the first one I ran 13:20. I remember exactly what Doctor said. 'How is that possible, Haile? This isn't the track.' I told him not to worry, and ran the next one even faster. 'I think that million dollars will soon be in my account, Doctor,' I said with a smile as I pulled on my sweats. 'According to this performance, Haile,' he said back to me, laughing, 'there's no question about it.'"

But road racing isn't track racing. Running well on the road is about pushing hard from the front, almost like a full-blast endurance time trial. The close quarters of the track are missing. There's no lap counter, no scoreboard clock. The course is open and expansive, not tight and intimate. Narrow lanes are replaced by wide shoulders. The exact distance each step forward takes you is less pronounced on the road. While a track's score of white lines mark every increment of your progress. As a result, the intensity's higher on the track, the pressure's stronger. And it's not Haile's fitness that anyone's questioning in advance of his race in Birmingham tonight—Doha certainly confirmed that he's in shape. It's whether he can handle the tactics of hard-fought track racing after such a long absence. Will his speed be as sharp as it once was? Can he reassert his dominance? Those are the real questions on everyone's mind, including, of course, Haile's.

When lunch ends Haile makes his way down to the lobby to check the start list. As he walks out of the elevator and into the crowded lobby, it's obvious that his presence affects others. Heads turn, conversations stop. Various white middle-aged men rush up to him from all angles, each with his own agenda: a journalist requesting an interview, a representative from Adidas making sure he has all the equipment he needs, a meet promoter hoping to entice him to his event, and a fan requesting an autograph. Hailu and Abiyote wait patiently while Haile deals with each inquiry. Finally moving on, Haile greets other friends and acquaintances who are gathered in the hotel's busy lobby. His handshake is bright, and every contact he makes involves some easy small talk.

When Haile eventually reaches the large easel in the corner of the lobby where the start lists are posted, he traces his finger down the list of entrants in the 2-mile like an expectant schoolboy at term's end checking to see if he has been promoted to the next grade. Once he finds his name and reminds himself of the start time, *8:24 P.M.*, he scans the list again to confirm whether there have been any last minute scratches or additions to the field. There haven't. Approaching Haile's side, Stephan Kreykamp puts his arm around Haile's shoulders and pulls him close. He whispers into Haile's ear. "Looks okay, don't you think, Haile?" Stephan also works for Jos, and he reminds Haile that his car to the stadium leaves at 6:45 P.M. It's now 2 P.M., and all that's left for Haile to do is collect some bottled water and fruit from the athletes' hospitality room before heading up to his room, where he'll relax by himself until it's time for him to get ready.

The lobby certainly doesn't quiet down following Haile's exit. This is still a public space, after all, with the normal goings on of any major metropolitan hotel: guests checking in and out, taxis arriving and departing, hotel staff carrying bags and opening doors. But when a hotel also serves as the headquarters for a major international track meet, it takes on an added hustle and bustle.

Jos, for example, works the lobby like a political fund-raiser. Here in one swoop he can touch base with any number of sponsors and promoters and discuss future deals for Haile, or any of the other 140 athletes from some 26 countries his company Global Sports Communications currently represents. This includes Olympic champions Gabriela Szabo (5000m), Million Wolde (5000m), Nils Schumann (800m), and Reuben Kosgei (Steeplechase). He meets journalists here, too, some from Belgium and Britain, others from Germany and France, and he answers all of their questions in their native languages. At the same time, he acts like a big-city editor and pushes story ideas on them—"Are you investigating . . . ? What about doing an interview with . . . ?"

At present, Jos employs 14 people to help him handle all the work generated by Global's expanding operation. He has even had to move his company into a new, larger office building that can also house as many as 30 visiting athletes. Still based in his hometown of Nijmegen, Jos symbolizes the local boy who made good. But expansion has come at a cost, too, as Jos now spends an increasing amount of time on the road and away from his wife and two young children.

But in many ways Jos is a victim of his own success. He seems to know how to select those athletes capable of becoming competitive at the highest international level. From city to city across Europe— Berlin, Stockholm, Rome, Zurich, Paris—one weekend to the next, the track circuit rolls into town ready to perform. This encompasses a six-week indoor season contested over the winter months, followed by almost five months of outdoor action beginning in May. And at practically every stop along the way, Jos is there with a dozen or more of his athletes ready to compete. The tour hardly frequents America, however. Track in the United States is a minority sport, relegated to virtual obscurity except in an Olympic year. But across Europe, where there are sold-out arenas and stadiums, prime-time television coverage, and six-figure cash prizes on offer, many track stars are household names. So it goes that for months at a time athletes, coaches, managers, promoters, and the press all regularly check into and out of different hotels, making the hotel lobby the unofficial epicenter of each point on tour. In the hotel lobby, for example, athletes can gaze at one and other and try to determine who looks ready: *Is he limping? Has she gained some weight?* There's a constant air of display in the lobby, like a catwalk. Just watch the elevator doors open and see how heads turn and judge, assess, and evaluate.

In the lobby it's all legs and arms and exposed abs. Not to mention big egos accompanied by loud, spirited talk. But so much of this self-posturing that the athletes put on is an act—most are better at convincing others that they're in shape than they are at convincing themselves. It's in this way that races can actually be won or lost in the hotel lobby. The lobby is where the psychological warfare begins. The great British middle-distance runner Sebastian Coe was one athlete who definitely staged his appearance in the lobby. "The moment I walked into the hotel lobby my whole demeanor would change. I would do my utmost to look confident and exude a strong presence, even if I didn't quite feel that way."

And why not put on such a show? Everyone's vulnerable in the hotel, and easily intimidated. No one's in uniform; everyone's out of his or her element. Distance runners in particular only appear impressive when they're running. Only in movement do they become smooth and strong. Standing around a hotel lobby in jeans and a T-shirt they're reduced to something absolutely ordinary: skinny, small, quiet. But at the track, before a crowd, where it's possible to run, stretch, and bend, they become sportsmen. Up until that point, however, a great deal of time needs to pass, and most of it is spent in and around the hotel. Books, magazines, television, music, video games . . . these become the distractions athletes rely on to pass the time. And to a certain extent, the athletes who can manage the boredom of waiting around the hotel the best tend to have the longest and most successful careers. This doesn't make them boring people, however. Rather, they have the mind-set to relax as time passes. They don't let the pressure get to them. They don't become anxious or impatient while they wait for their event. Jos actually believes this is one of Haile's greatest attributes: "When everyone else is getting jumpy and nervous, like at an Olympic Games, somehow Haile seems to remain totally unaffected."

"Maybe it's because I'm used to waiting for things," Haile says by way of explaining his prerace composure. "In Ethiopia we're not so familiar with having what we want when we want it. The roads are slow going; phone lines and computer connections fail regularly. Life for us is not so scheduled and organized. Not like it is in Europe. In Ethiopia you might wait for a bus for hours, or a store may not open when it says it will. This is something normal. Not that I like it very much, and the more I travel I see that this must change. But that will take time, too. So what I usually do in my hotel room before a race is simply lie down and wait. Maybe I'll sleep, or read, or listen to music. Or I'll watch television. Mainly, though, I just want to have some peace and quiet before I have to head to the track. That way I can think about my race and consider in detail what it is that I need to do."

For his race tonight, the plan circulating inside Haile's mind as he relaxes in his room is quite simple: hold a fast pace. Indeed, world record pace. He needs to run 2 consecutive miles at just above four-minute-mile pace. Quite impressive, really, when you consider how difficult it is to run one four-minute mile, let alone two back to back. Haile has memorized the exact lap times he needs to hit for each of his 16 trips around Birmingham's banked 200-meter oval. The meet promoter, Ian Stewart, has organized two rabbits to help Haile get there. The first rabbit will take Haile through the mile; the second will carry on for two more laps. It will then be up to Haile to manage the last six laps on his own. And it's exactly how he'll do this that he's rehearsing in his room as he waits for the shuttle to the track: *Lock in early to the rhythm and pace . . . track the rabbits' heels . . . keep things rolling once I'm on my own, and concentrate and relax. Concentrate and relax . . .*

❖

The most vocal section of the Birmingham crowd comes from the Ethiopian corner, where Haile's London-based fan club of over 2,000 expat Ethiopians sit. And when Haile is introduced over the PA as part of the opening ceremonies along with a number of other stars like Jonathan Edwards, Colin Jackson, and Kelly Holmes, the Ethiopian corner reaches a frenzy.

For the expat Ethiopian, Haile represents a powerful connection to home, an export to celebrate. These people love their country, and many of them live abroad out of economic necessity or for personal safety following the numerous political changes that have occurred in Ethiopia over the last few decades. All of them wear scarves or hats lined in green, yellow, and red, the three stripes on the Ethiopian flag. They wave banners, take photographs, and shout and sing songs in Amharic. Some are fully dressed in their traditional national costumes, and most come as an entire family, young and old alike, to see the man all Ethiopians revere.

This is a degree of sport celebrity vastly different from what you might associate with a pop star or a football player. These supporters' attachment runs far deeper than the superficial recesses of fanaticism or escapism. For Ethiopians everywhere Haile is a lifeline to progress and development. His presence on the tracks of Europe and America makes Ethiopia a topic of discussion, not another neglected African nation. And to begin to address some of Ethiopia's many problems, discussion is the necessary first step.

The support Haile receives when he is away from home competing even stirs his emotions: "To hear all the Ethiopian people cheer for me when I'm running in Europe makes me very happy. I see the three colors of the flag, and hear the songs, or look into the faces of all the Ethiopian people who have come to watch me and immediately I'm inspired. I want to run even harder because of that; I want to show my supporters my appreciation and give them my best performance possible. I remember in 1999 when I came to Birmingham and broke the indoor world record for 5000 meters and the noise from the crowd was incredible. I thought they must all be Ethiopians. I felt like I was running back at home."

After completing a lap of honor together with the evening's other celebrity athletes, Haile makes a quick exit from the track floor and returns to the warm-up area two floors below. It was here where he first settled when he arrived at the arena from the hotel half an hour earlier. Headphones cover his ears and emit an energetic reggae beat. He's dressed in a dark blue Adidas sweat suit, and seated on a metal folding chair. By his feet Haile keeps a knapsack, which he slowly unzips to remove a powder-blue racing top. Then, just like anyone else who has ever run a race, he pins his number onto the front of his singlet, taking great care to get it centered.

When it's time to start warming up—always one hour before his race—Haile summons Hailu and Abiyote and the three of them begin to jog clockwise around the windowless, rectangular warm-up area. Their heads are lowered as if in prayer, and their faces hold a placid expression. One circuit around the rubber floor—four adjacent tennis courts minus their nets—takes them approximately one minute. Haile's stride is light and smooth, as if he's making quick tick marks on the ground. When the balls of one of his feet touch down, the heel of the other instantly rises. Viewed from behind he gives the impression of levitating.

After 10 minutes, Haile about-faces, and the threesome resume their pace in the opposite direction. Haile isn't moving extraordinarily fast; he appears comfortable and well within himself. But isn't that always how an expert makes his work appear: simple, as if you could even do it yourself?

"During my prerace warm-up I try to take things easy," Haile explains. "I relax my whole body as completely as possible in order to feel smooth, light, and comfortable. I want to be calm and in total control. The most important thing is that I feel my muscles warming and lengthening as I jog. Like there's something inside my body that's expanding or growing. My chest, it should be opening up, and my legs, they should be strengthening."

It's a lively place, this warm-up area, more like the backstage of some grand theatrical production than sport's equivalent of the green room. Present are practitioners from every discipline—distance runners, sprinters, hurdlers, throwers, jumpers—all preparing in their unique way. Imagine a gathering of singers, dancers, and actors where each person is inside his or her own private pre-performance routine. What a scene that would be: a wide space resplendent in voice, sound, and movement. Such is the setting beneath the track floor in Birmingham tonight as all manner of bodies move through intricate and specific phases of mobility and flexibility: a shotputter executing a pert sideways shuffle, a hurdler spread eagle on the ground, and a pole vaulter walking on her hands.

For the other 2-milers warming up, Haile's presence is clearly a distraction. As they watch him progress through his routine they can't help but question the efficacy of their own. *Maybe I should change direction midway through my jog?* Haile, as you might expect, is oblivious to what anyone else around him is doing or thinking: "The other people in the warm-up area don't concern me. I have to be totally inside myself there. Otherwise I won't be able to bring out the performance I want."

When he finishes jogging, Haile initiates a hard stride through the center of the warm-up floor. Quickly, Hailu and Abiyote fall into step behind him. Three more strides follow, where roughly at 10 meter check marks Haile gradually accelerates, coming to a stop just short of reaching top gear.

Still occupying the middle of the warm-up area after their last stride, the three Ethiopians move into a series of drills. To begin they shuffle softly and rotate their arms in wide propeller-like circles while simultaneously spinning their trunks as if they were wearing hula hoops. It's a complicated choreography that they make look natural. Next, they bound down the floor with their legs far in front of them and their front knees rising alternately. All of these moves are synchronized, too, and as Haile, Hailu, and Abiyote carry on down the floor they begin to resemble a military brigade or a cheerleading squad. It's these drills that Haile uses to simulate and rehearse the foot placement, knee lift, posture, and arm swing of his running action. And as he completes one sequence after another his face is pure concentration.

For the next step in his routine, Haile spreads his feet wide apart and comes within inches of reaching a full split. He bends forward and rests the palms of his hands on the ground. He then executes a series of long stretches. This is not the customary stiff pose of the long distance runner who can barely touch his toes. Here is where one sees the origin of Haile's speed and explosiveness. His ankles, knees, and hips are supple and elastic as he holds each stretch for 10 seconds or more. He's spring-loaded and deft; even when he's stationary he appears to be moving like a beam of light shimmering in the night sky, or, to be more specific, like a star. Add to this his bottomless endurance reserve and you have a seemingly unbeatable combination of athletic skills.

Forty-five minutes after beginning his warm-up routine, Haile is still attending to every signal his body transmits: *power . . . speed . . . coordination . . .* He's completing a checklist in his mind, matching expectation with sensory feedback. Like a shop owner reviewing his inventory, Haile knows exactly how he should be feeling at each stage of his warm-up. And as he sees it, "It's my job during the warm-up to make sure that I arrive at the starting line in the final necessary state."

When the call comes for all 2-milers to check in and proceed up to the arena floor, suddenly everything begins to happen much faster. Haile and the 13 other 2-milers are pushed into an elevator. When they reach the track floor they're told, "Sweats off and spikes on, gentlemen." A line of marshals leads them onto the track. There's barely enough time for Haile to get a feel for the track's bounce and put in one last acceleration. When the Ethiopian supporters spot him sprinting hard into the first turn they start to chant over and over, "Haile, Haile, Haile." Haile acknowledges them with a quick thumbs-up and a big smile before finally taking his place behind the white starting line.

Introductions are made over the PA system . . . Haile shakes down his arms, smiles, and then exhales deeply. A second later the gun sounds and he's away, straight into third place behind the two assigned rabbits.

The initial laps proceed right on schedule, at close to four-minute mile pace. The pack has transformed into a long thin line. Haile's head is down, his chest is out. On the backstretch of each lap his eyes rise to check his position from the giant scoreboard screen.

The clock reaches three minutes; Haile takes two deep breaths and his chest expands a further 2 inches, flattening out all the creases on his singlet. His strides are sharp and high; he's steady and perfectly tuned as he propels himself off each bank and ricochets down the corresponding straightaway. This world record attempt is clearly on.

Haile's arms pump steadily as another lap is completed. The closed angles his elbows form slice evenly through the air.

Here comes the mile split: 4:03, and rabbit number one jumps into the infield as rabbit number two takes over.

Almost immediately Haile's chomping at his heels. He shouts, "Faster! Run faster!"

When finally the second rabbit veers into lane six, his job complete,

Haile assumes the spotlight.

He's alone at the front now, and whatever his lead might be over the second-place runner doesn't seem to concern anyone. The rest of the field is running in complete anonymity. Haile wants this world record. The crowd want it, too. The noise they're generating is absolutely sonic. And from the deep expression written across Haile's face it appears that more than wanting this record he actually needs it. It's as if he's trying to escape a future he's not ready to face. *I'm only twenty-nine years old . . . there have to be a few more good years in me.*

Haile's absolutely glowing now as the lap counter turns to three . . . then two. He's brimming with speed and power. But more importantly, he's beginning to answer the questions he carried with him into this race—*Can I get back on top after the losses and injuries? Can I be the dominant one again? . . . Yes, I can! Yes, I can!* And for this he seems a lighter man, relieved of the burden of proof. For this record will soon be his; his return to the top will be confirmed.

When it's official, a new indoor two mile world record of 8:04.69, a whopping five-second improvement, Haile delivers a flourish of waves and bows and smiles to the ecstatic crowd. He blows kisses in the direction of the highest section of seating above the first turn, where his Ethiopian supporters are absolutely delirious.

"Thank you, thank you, Birmingham," come his words over the PA when Jon Ridgeon, the on-field master of ceremonies finally catches up to Haile. "It's great to be running like this again and back on track," he adds. "I feel like my old self. I'm so happy . . . so very happy. I couldn't have asked for a better start to 2003."

10

Atlanta, July 29, 1996

To win an Olympic 10,000-meter title one must first reach the starting line unscathed. To feel fresh and injury-free following the months of hard preparation and final tune-up races is crucial; to progress easily through one's semifinal, with the pace not exacting too heavy a toll, is vital. An Olympic 10,000-meter final is too rare—only once every four years—and too spectacular to approach feeling anything less than perfect.

When Haile arrived in Atlanta, to run the 10,000 meters at the 1996 Olympic Games, he was unscathed; he was smooth all over like a polished chestnut; he was full of lightness and confidence. The preceding months had gone exactly as planned—hard workouts, a string of victories. He was the 10,000-meter world record holder and two-time world champion. To many observers his victory in Atlanta was a mere formality, a tick in a box, as simple as switching off the lights before going to bed.

On Wednesday afternoon, July 17, Haile checked into his room at the Olympic village. It was a spare but comfortable space: a single bed, one small window, four cinder-block walls painted white, a gray linoleum floor. To brighten it up he could have brought a few reminders of home with him. Maybe a framed photograph of his girlfriend, Alem, to place on his bedside table. Her wide smile and soft brown complexion would have raised the color of the room. A small wooden or stone carving, or any other type of memento, would have dampened the room's echo. As it was, Haile's sentimentality only went so far as to bring the engagement ring he was planning to give Alem upon his return to Ethiopia. That had been his proposal to her: "If I win the gold medal in Atlanta, Alem, will you marry me? We can have our engagement in the airport, exactly when I return, to announce to everyone our intention to marry. It will be a great day of celebrations and festivities." And so it was that part one of Haile's plan fell into place: Alem had said yes instantly. Whether he would win the gold medal remained to be seen.

After he unpacked his bags and stored his clothes in the closets and drawers, Haile needed to get outside. There were all those hours he'd just spent cooped up in an airplane to exercise away. He decided to visit the warm-up track next to the main Olympic stadium to test out his new spike shoes and to get a feel for the track's surface. Besides, his room was no place to spend any time. The Olympics were in town. There was an entire village to explore, new people to meet, events to watch, and all varieties of food to sample in the 24-hour cafeteria. There were also the finishing touches Haile needed to apply to his shape as the nine-day countdown to his 10,000-meter semifinal began.

The early tactics in an Olympic 10,000-meter final tend to be gentle and subtle. There's looking, mainly: assessing the bounce in a competitor's step—his reaction off the ground, his speed in bringing his legs around—or reading his expression—excited, hesitant, afraid? Listening is also important: tuning in to a rival's breathing—is it short and shallow or deep and full? Inside a tight pack of lean and brightly colored distance runners all moving forward from bend to straight, bend to straight, it's rare that anyone speaks. A few words relayed early on to a teammate perhaps. Nothing of any real consequence is ever shared.

Haile felt extremely secure in his tactics leading up to Atlanta. He knew that his rivals wouldn't be able to sustain a hard enough pace to tire him out, or sprint fast enough to outkick him. What could they do, then? Well, Josephat Machuka, in the 1992 10,000-meter final at the world junior championships had resorted to violence. Machuka had led the entire way, and when Haile passed him on the final straightaway the Kenyan slung his right arm forward and punched Haile in the back. It was a reaction brought on by frustration more than anything else, as if to shout, *What can I possibly do to beat this man?* Since then Haile's stinging finish has vanquished a long line of Kenyan stars. Try as they might to tire him out by setting a furious pace, or putting in a long, hard run for home, Haile just waits. He waits like Yifter used to. After all, why lead, why do the early work when you can simply sit and wait? Wait to make your move and win when you choose.

The tactical precision needed over the course of a 10,000-meter race makes long distance running something like a moving game of body poker. A runner's cards are his lungs and his muscles, and he can only play them for what they're worth. At any point someone could bluff with a surge, or feint confidence by jumping to the lead. By the last lap, of course, all is usually revealed.

The poker player analogy becomes even more relevant when a runner has something to hide. A good poker player knows how to conceal his hand, especially when he's holding a weak card. Little did Haile know as he ran around the warm-up track adjacent to the main Olympic stadium that Wednesday afternoon in Atlanta after just checking into his room at the Olympic village that over the next 12 days he would have to partake in the hardest game of concealment he'd ever played.

To heighten the advantage of their powerful corps of sprinters, including Michael Johnson—who was attempting a historic and rare double over 200 meters and 400 meters—the Atlanta organizing committee had laid down an extremely hard surface inside the Olympic Stadium and around the warm-up track. It's well known that hard running surfaces have a stiffer rebound effect. They don't absorb an athlete's energy, or cushion his feet. Instead, he gets sprung forward into his next step, his next stride. All the better for running fast times and setting new records. And the tracks used in Atlanta and manufactured by Mondo had a shock absorption rate of 35.6 percent, just inside the accepted minimum of 36 percent.

But 10,000-meter running is hardly sprinting. It's an event that takes close to half an hour minutes. And 30 minutes of racing, or for that matter even training, on what's basically a concrete surface wearing only a pair of thin spike shoes can spell danger for a distance runner's feet. Haile discovered just how true that was when he returned to his room following his test run around the warm-up track and removed his socks and shoes.

Initially the blister on his left big toe was small and harmless. Nothing to worry about. What distance runner hadn't had a blister before? Just pop it and let it drain. Which was exactly what Haile did before he went to sleep.

In Haile's phone calls every day to Alem from the Olympic village it was all good news and cheer. He reported all the excitement from his first Olympic Games. He told Alem about the athletes he was meeting from around the world, his impressions of America, and how different it was from home—"It's all so big here, Alem . . . the roads, the buildings, even the people; so many people are very fat." And Alem was full of positive wishes, saying exactly how she wanted Haile's race to go: "Don't leave it to the very end, Haile. Please, try to save us the worry." And always Haile told her that he'd do his best.

In his calls home Haile never mentioned to Alem his long, lonely

days, or his sleepless nights spent crying into his pillow, or that he had-
n't run a single step since the first day he had arrived in Atlanta. He
could have told her all of this. She loved him so much and wanted to
know what ever he was thinking or feeling. He could have told her
that he was seeing a doctor every day to try to find a solution to his
problem—anything to help him run, anything to manage the pain
and keep his Olympic dream alive. It might have taken some of the
pressure off him if he had. But Haile couldn't see why he should both-
er Alem, or cause her to worry about something she couldn't fix. "I
have to find a solution myself," he believed. So he continued to call
her, and among the other bits of news they discussed were their plans
for their engagement party: the dress Alem would wear, the priest to
get to bless the occasion, who to invite, and how much cake and
champagne to buy. And as Haile listened to Alem go on about one
detail or another, he held the engagement ring he was intending to
give her in the palm of his hand. The soft gold felt warm against his
skin. Like Alem's fingers tracing the texture of his face. Haile knew he
had to win these Olympics. He had to win for so many reasons.

"It was when I woke up after my first night's sleep in the Olympic
village that my tragedy really began . . ." That night, in Atlanta's swel-
tering heat and humidity, the tiny blister that Haile had popped and
drained before going to sleep had become infected. His entire left foot
was swollen; the skin across his toes was bubbling and wet with puss.
At first when he stepped out of bed he didn't know what to do or what
this might mean. For a moment he even thought he must be dreaming. *Yesterday I was fine? What is this? Where did this come from?* So he
rubbed his eyes and looked back down at the floor. But nothing had
changed: raw, pink skin. He walked across his room, confident that
this couldn't be such a serious problem. But it was. He couldn't put
his whole weight on his foot; a hot, burning sensation raced up his leg

as if someone was dipping his foot into flames. So he sat back down on his bed and tried to view the situation with an air of detachment. He grabbed his foot and brought it up to his face. And as if he was inspecting a piece of silverware for dents, Haile examined it from side to side and up and down. What he saw frightened him: masses of raw, pink skin. And at that point a tiny shiver traveled up his spine and he knew what was happening to him was real. But he didn't panic. He repeated over and over that there were still many days to go before his semifinal race—eight—and that it was just a few blisters for God's sake, and weren't some of the best doctors in the world here at the Olympics? It was then that he picked up the phone and called Jos.

The first course of treatment involved creams and ointments that were cool against Haile's foot. The doctor he saw spoke positively. Jos spoke positively. And Haile had no choice but to think positively.

"There's still time before your race, Haile," said the doctor. "Just don't do any running, meanwhile. Rest. Lie in bed with your foot up and give it plenty of air."

But as calm as Haile tried to remain, he couldn't help asking himself over and over why this was happening to him—*Have I disappointed God?* He couldn't help touching his blisters even though he knew he wasn't supposed to. And every hour he'd get out of bed and jog in place in the center of his room to test if there had been any improvement. He tried to pull his spike shoes on over the blisters—he couldn't. He wondered if bigger shoes he borrowed from friends would feel better—they didn't. He was worrying too much; he wasn't allowing his body to rest and respond on its own time.

Eventually Haile was reduced to wearing sandals only. He also couldn't put those finishing touches on his shape. When the rest of the Ethiopian team would head out to the practice track for some final hard-paced intervals, Haile would remain back at the village. It was an incredibly boring time, and lonely, and even scary: *Are my dreams of becoming an Olympic champion over?* And that was what brought on the tears, especially at night: the terror working away inside him that his gold medal was almost certainly lost.

Semifinals over 10,000 meters are an exacting process done to eliminate a couple of dozen competitors and pare the final field down to a manageable size. In Atlanta the men's 10,000-meter semifinals were scheduled for 9:15 P.M. and 9:55 P.M. on Friday, July 26. Haile was listed to run in heat two. And as far as everyone knew he'd be there. The press were easy to placate. "Yes, I'm excited about my first Olympics," Haile told reporters. "Yes, my preparation has gone well." Coaches and team managers from various countries who saw Haile every day in the Olympic village cafeteria thought he seemed content and happy enough. When a few Kenyans asked Haile how come they hadn't seen him at the practice track with the rest of Ethiopian team, Haile just mumbled something about running early in the morning on his own. What cause did they have to suspect he was lying? None, of course. But then *lying* probably isn't the right word. Haile was just keeping his cards close to his chest.

The two 10,000-meter semifinals were full: 21 runners in heat one representing 20 nations, and 21 runners representing 19 nations in heat two. The procedure to reach the final was straightforward: The first six finishers in each semifinal would advance automatically, with the remaining six finalists determined by time as the six "fastest losers."

Such a qualifying procedure for the 10,000 immediately creates a tactical conundrum, especially for the runners in the first semifinal. Run slowly, conserve energy, and allow the race to dawdle and your only likely chance of making the final is as an automatic qualifier. It's a good card to play if you're certain you can position yourself wisely over the last lap and avoid getting boxed in or outmaneuvered into a nonqualifying position. The other option, to run a fast race and push the pace, can extend your odds as far back as there are fastest-loser spots up for grabs. The cost, of course, is a more demanding effort and the risk of not fully recovering for the final just three days later. Whereas those runners in the second 10,000 semifinal, with the results of the first semifinal before them, can target the exact time they need to run to earn one of the fastest-loser positions. But of course if someone knows he can't run that fast, he'll have to hope for a slow pace and gamble that he can kick himself into a qualifying place. But usually semifinals in the 10,000 go to form—unlike heats in the 800 meters or the 1500 meters where a mistake is more pressing and difficult to mend because the speeds are too fast, and momentum rides harder and stronger. Over 10,000 meters the truth in talent, ability, and experience tends to come to the fore. That's not to say, however, that upsets still don't occur.

The doctor Haile had continued to see every day to treat his blisters finally advised him to scratch from his 10,000-meter semifinal. The creams and ointments just weren't working. Everyone could see that. Haile's foot was still a grotesque, painful mess. The doctor told him that even if he did manage to make it through his semifinal, the damage he would do to his foot in the process would make it impossible for him to run in the final. "Better to salvage the rest of your season than end it here in your semifinal," he said. But Haile had just one question. He asked the doctor if he risked doing any permanent damage to his foot by running. Apparently he wouldn't. "Then it's just a matter of the pain?" Haile clarified. "That's right," the doctor said. "The pain." "Then I have to try to run. I have to forget my pain. This is the Olympics; it might be my last chance to win a medal."

A large pack of distance runners circling a track can be an untamed, unruly horde. Nothing is constant or predictable. From a surge to a slowdown, the pack assumes a life of its own like an ocean swell or a mountain breeze. And in Haile's semifinal this was certainly the case. He was battling for some kind of advantage; he was trying to keep his pain and all his lost days training a secret.

Through the early laps Haile was buried among all the tall bouncing bodies fighting for a position in the final. The shadows cast off their shoulders bathed him in cover. He was looking in every direction with eyes rounder and brighter than a cue ball. He was pushing hard into the track each step of the way. It was a sharp twisting action. Each step down, forward, and then up . . . down, forward, and then up. The friction, the grinding, the heat . . . for him it was like walking barefoot over broken glass. In the later laps, Haile was making even greater contact with the ground as he tried to keep his Olympic dream alive: He needed to dig deep; he couldn't falter. And as trying as it must have been, he maintained perfect form and the perfect poker face throughout it all and managed to win his heat in 28:14.20.

But this was only a problem half solved. There was still the damage to assess, and a decision to be made. All along, though, Haile knew that he'd be back out on the track to take his position in the final. It didn't matter what the doctors or anyone else had to say. Three days were what he had to get ready.

They ended up being three very long days. Haile could do no running. He could only sit in his room and wait. And while he waited, he prayed. He prayed for courage and strength, and of course for good luck, too.

For this Olympic 10,000-meter final on July 29, 1996, everyone would be watching Haile. He was the odds-on favorite. The 17 other runners on the track would be watching him. A live audience of more than 70,000 people would be watching him. And a worldwide television audience in the billions would be watching him. Except for only a few people like Jos, who would be watching Haile on a television screen at the warm-up track, no one knew about his blisters and what he had had to overcome just to get this far.

Alem wouldn't know. She'd be watching Haile on television with dreams of marriage running through her mind.

Haile's father and his brothers, and sisters, and nieces, and nephews, and aunts, and uncles would be watching him on television back in Ethiopia none the wiser.

Even Miruts Yifter would no doubt be watching.

No one, though, would be watching Haile closer than Paul Tergat. Tergat had completed a perfect run-up to these games. He had reached the starting line unscathed following months of hard preparation and final tune-up races. He was feeling perfect.

Tergat's view, of course, would come from the inside. And after six laps he had a good fix on Haile. He was one position behind him in eighth place. Over the next few laps the pace slowed and then sped up. And it slowed and sped up again. The order changed; the configuration of the pack went from a bunch to a line, and from a line back to a bunch. Not a single one of the 18 runners fell behind. Everyone was still in contention approaching the final 2 kilometers. And this was what led Tergat to act.

If Tergat had known about the injury his Ethiopian rival was carrying, he might have acted sooner. Had he known about the blisters on Haile's foot, the skin peeling back from under his toes, the blood seeping through his socks, he might have applied more pressure and surged to the front with as many as eight laps to go instead of waiting as he did.

As it was Tergat's move with five laps to go was still a serious gesture, and Haile knew it. Everyone did. Everyone in the race, everyone in the stadium, everyone in Ethiopia. Jos's guts were rattling. Alem covered her eyes, silently cursing Tergat and berating Haile, *Why are you making this so hard on us? Pull away, pull away, just win now.* From his position in fourth, Haile moved out wide and chased after Tergat, the only runner in the pack to do so. In a matter of 10 strides he was there, only inches behind the tall Kenyan. The noise from the crowd was thunderous. Tergat kept steaming ahead with his eyes focused and determined. He didn't dare glance back for fear of what he might see: someone close to him. Worst of all, Haile. But with three laps to go Tergat's nerves got the better of him: a quick snap of his head to the right. Then his looks became more frequent and Haile began to realize that he must be frightened. With this realization a tiny shiver shot up Haile's spine . . . *I can win. My God, I can win this race.*

Entering the final lap with the bell sounding, and sounding to Haile and Jos and Alem and everyone else back in Ethiopia like the most concentrated and beautiful symphony ever performed, Haile dropped his chin with a quick pop as if to tap free a cork and allow the air to escape from a bottle. It was the trigger that he had been waiting to pull. And in a blink his lead was 10 meters . . . 20 meters. His stride was open, wide, and long. He was alone: his blue shoes, red shorts, and green shirt a solitary blur of beauty, a solo performance befitting only awe. Down the entire homestretch there was never a break or a falter. A dancer in perfect steadiness until the curtain dropped. How could this be? It even seemed impossible to Haile to have escaped this tragedy in the making. For he looked over his shoulder eight times in the final 50 meters: *Am I alone, yes, Am I alone, yes, Am I going to win, yes, My God, am I going to win, Yes, I'm going to win, Oh, I'm winning, I'm winning, I'm winning* . . . And with his arms stretched forward as if he was reaching out to embrace the globe, or take hold of Alem, Haile crossed the line and became Olympic champion. His run and jubilant pose continued well past the finish line. Maybe he was planning on running all the way home? But then Ethiopia came to him on a crooked stick that he began to wave during his lap of honor. And when Haile reached a section of Ethiopians sitting trackside, they all rushed forward to feel his sweat in their hands, some even bringing it to their mouths; the moist taste of victory. The sweet taste of success. Sweet like wedding cake washed down with champagne.

11

Haile at Home

With two quick toots of his horn the large green metal gate swings open. Accelerating quickly, Haile pulls inside, stopping within inches of the whitewashed cement wall. In one simultaneous action he cuts the engine, opens the door, and steps outside. Two other Mercedes are parked in the driveway; a swing set and slide rise from one half of the lawn, plastic garden furniture from the other. The green gate is shut by now; the boy responsible for that has also removed Haile's gym bag from the trunk and scurried out of sight. Now climbing the steps to the front door, a life far more intriguing than the demands of running and racing is set to unfold for this multiple Olympic and world champion.

"Eden, what are you doing home in the middle of the day?"

Haile's eldest daughter replies in English. "I'm playing. There is no school today, Daddy."

Eden is five years old, and her name means "heaven." She attends an English school and her teacher, Mrs. Jones, is British. Eden's favorite color is pink, and she likes the number eight best of all because it's so easy to make.

"Why is there no school today?" Haile says straight into his daughter's wide face.

"It's a holiday, Daddy, May 1."

"Okay, all right. Good girl. Then where are your sisters?"

Enter daughter number two, who comes rushing into Haile's legs, her head meeting his knees squarely. "Oh, my goodness, Melat," Haile shouts as both girls laugh wildly. "And what about Bete? Where is she?" This is Haile's youngest, named for the holy city, Bethlehem. "She is having a nap upstairs," Eden quickly explains.

Now slowly moving hand in hand through the hallway, Haile guides Eden and Melat to the living room, where he begins to quiz them in English.

"Sing the song you know, Eden."

"What song?"

"Little Star. That one."

The performance begins without pause, accented with twirls and sweet expressions. Three-year-old Melat, whose name in Amharic means "miracle" joins in when she remembers the words.

"Okay, very good, girls. Very good." Haile is smiling broadly and quick to offer praise. "What about some counting in English?"

The sofa where Haile and his daughters sit forms the focal point of a sunken living room decorated with comfortable, soft furnishings. A life-sized stuffed leopard fills one corner, a television another. Three small steps lead up to a dining area fitted with six cushioned chairs around an oval mahogany table. Built-in bookshelves, cabinets, and well-stocked glass trophy cases form the walls.

Eden and Melat soon become more playful and begin to record laps around the coffee table—one, two, three . . . Haile watches them, all the time sipping a bottle of Pepsi in his left hand. The girls' laps quickly turn more spirited, punctuated by headfirst crash dives into the corners of the sofa. Their white pleated dresses rise above their heads, giggles fill the room. Dad pays close attention heightening the girls' delight.

"Oh, very fast. Very fast girls."

Eden and Melat then decide to involve their father more directly in their fun and target their next dive straight into Haile's stomach.

Feigning shock and surprise, Haile crashes back against the sofa and offers his attackers exactly what they want: a loud shriek and a startled expression. "Oh, my goodness, I didn't see that coming. You two are very clever." This only reinforces a repeat performance . . . and another . . . and another. Soon Haile's defenseless, pinned against the couch, and that's when the tickling begins. He begs for mercy. "No, no, not there, Melat. That's my worst spot." Pillows ricochet off the wall, limbs and feet head in every direction, the girls pant heavily in between bursts of laughter, and their father is loving every moment. This, after all, is the true result of Haile's 10,000-meter victory in Atlanta. This is everyday family life around the Gebrselassie home.

When Haile returned to Addis Ababa from Atlanta, a rollicking sea of faces and smiles greeted him at the airport. He stepped off the plane to the home-grown sounds of drums, bells, whistles, and songs. Celebration filled the sky. Alem reached Haile with a deep, everlasting embrace. She was a vision of beauty in her ivory-white engagement dress, her hair pulled back, and Haile's entire family by her side. Tables and chairs had been set up inside the airport to accommodate 2000 guests; the priest was there; engagement rings were to be exchanged. Haile was prepared to receive a gift far more precious and wondrous than his Olympic gold medal. This would be his greatest prize, and what he had also gone to Atlanta to secure: the promise of marriage from his true love, Alem.

Now eight years on from their airport engagement, Haile and Alem have a strong, loving family. Alem is the perfect balance to Haile's willful, stubborn side. She works subtly to both support and influence his opinions, and together they have both prospered.

Haile and Alem were married in the winter of 1996, and two years later Alem gave birth to Eden. Haile would love to add a boy to the family fold, but he knows he can't go on trying until he succeeds— "That would be acting irresponsibly to the problems of overcrowding in Ethiopia," he feels. Moreover, according to African distance running lore, it would probably take him a number of tries. "In Africa we believe than an athlete who's in good shape will only have girls," Haile explains. "Some men even stop training for a year to try to have a son." But Haile's not about to stop running for anything. Particularly with the start of the 2003 outdoor season around the corner, and the opportunity to regain his 10,000-meter world title at the end of the summer in Paris. He's training harder than ever—endless 400-meter repetitions below 60 seconds, searing tempo runs through the forests of Entoto, and gym session after gym session. And following a brilliant indoor season that included not only a new 2-mile world record, but a world championship title over 3000 meters in Birmingham on March 16 (7:40.97), what reason could Haile possibly have for thinking that his dominance won't continue once his outdoor season opens in Hengelo over 10,000 meters on June 1?

Rivals can emerge from the most interesting places. Faraway, exotic places. When the American miler Jim Ryun was leading the world it was in distant Kenya that his chief competitor, Kip Keino, lived and trained. The New Zealand middle-distance champion John Walker had to keep his eyes on Tanzania, and Filbert Bayi, in order to maintain his supremacy. Ryun and Walker knew little about their rivals— the language they spoke, the landscape they ran over. For all intents and purposes they were from different worlds. But then that's what makes rivalries what they are . . . the differences.

Indeed, Haile's early rivals were different from him—Paul Tergat, Daniel Komen. Kenyans are not Ethiopians in so many matters pertaining to custom, language, food, religion, and culture. And what fuels a rivalry, raises the stakes, attracts interest, and forms sides but differences? Crosstown rivalries, by contrast, present all manner of problems—the Yankees and Mets, Manchester City and Manchester

United, Sebastian Coe and Steve Ovett. Who to support isn't necessarily intrinsically prescribed. Families may divide, friends might come to blows as choosing sides becomes based on something subjective or idiosyncratic and not, for example, clear-cut nationalism. And now for the first time Ethiopians understand how difficult it is to favor one son over another. That's because after Hengelo they were left with the two most dominant distance runners in the world and precious little to tell them apart.

Over the early laps in Hengelo, Haile appeared sure of victory. When the rabbits dropped out he automatically assumed the lead, unconcerned about who was in his wake. This was confident front running born from years of experience and insight. By the 6th kilometer he looked poised to notch up another win in front of his Hengelo home crowd. He was up tall and on his toes, his eyes were wide, his breathing was sound, and he was clear of the field bar a young and inexperienced teammate—a 21-year-old, just a boy really. What reason could Haile have had to doubt his success?

Abundance, splendor, riches . . . These aren't conditions that Ethiopians have enjoyed of late. So to have one man leading the world of distance running is fantastic in itself, a cause for streets to be renamed and holidays decreed. But to have two men at the top is to be blessed with incredible wealth. For a decade Haile has run unchallenged at home. His victories were always safe and predictable, like the sound of chimes at noon. But now in Kenenisa Bekele he must weather his first serious domestic threat. And as fellow countrymen, and practically fellow everything else, it's hard to say what exactly might fuel this rivalry.

Haile and Kenenisa both train under the watchful eyes of Doctor; they're both managed by Jos; they belong to the same tribe; and they grew up in neighboring villages. Amharic is their native tongue, and so they see the same headlines: *Kenenisa's Hengelo Kick a Wonder* . . .

Haile's Hands Full Now. They both live in Addis Ababa and hear the whispers that circulate town: *Haile is through . . . Kenenisa is the new Emperor.* They can't escape each other's influence. In such a distance-running-mad nation, it's impossible for them to inhabit separate planes. There is nowhere for them to hide: They are two rivals as similar as brothers or best friends.

. . . Finally with five laps to go in the Hengelo 10,000 Haile surged in an effort to drop Kenenisa. By that point he had no other choice. A lap earlier he had signaled to Kenenisa to pass him and help with the pacing as they had discussed the previous day. But Kenenisa refused. He remained exactly where he was, right on Haile's heels. And it was at this point that Haile realized he might have a race before him. He knew as well as anyone that if someone follows you, it is much easier for him to attack.

In a stride-by-stride comparison it's remarkable how similar Haile and Kenenisa are. Yes, Haile's nine years older—a fact made clear by his rougher, more weathered complexion. But the way they both rise off the ground and touch down again is almost identical: graceful, lithe, flowing. Their strides overlap in complete synchronicity, like an eclipse of the sun and the moon. Their proportions match and rhyme like a tight poetic couplet. Only Kenenisa is not so open and extroverted as Haile. His features can even seem frozen or firm, unyielding like a statue's. Midrace, or late in a race, he gives little away. He's like a moving sphinx whose steps are silent and breaths invisible.

By kilometer number 9 Haile was becoming seriously concerned: "With two laps to go I sensed I was in trouble." He was flicking his head from side to side, shaking out his arms, rolling his shoulders, and wavering inside his lane. Despite his repeated attempts to drop Kenenisa, nothing had worked. He was still there. And Haile had to accept the fact that all the front running he had done had been to Kenenisa's advantage. While he had been blind for most of the last 23 laps, Kenenisa had been able to tuck in and cover all of Haile's moves . . .

Frozen in space, Kenenisa's appearance is statuesque. His body is hard, defined, and erect. His elongated neck, sharp jawline, and straight nose appear like features carved from a wooden mask. Even in full flow he is steady and efficient. Like the ideal butler, he remains poised and balanced. It's possible to imagine him running with a pile of books stacked neatly on top of his head. His skin is also polished and clean, like gleaming black granite or freshly cut onyx. He has a porcelain doll's face attached to a solid base: those chunky thighs, such staunch calves.

And it was precisely his solid, powerful legs that worried Haile the most with one lap to go: "I knew Kenenisa's strength . . . how well he could sprint. For example, I have been watching him in training the last three years. I saw him on television at the world cross-country championships when he outkicked all the Kenyans. But Hengelo was his first 10,000 meters on the track; I wasn't quite sure what to expect from him. Although I did know that he would wait for me to make the first real move."

That first real move finally came with 300 meters to go, when at the top of the backstretch Haile burst into action. *That's surely it,* almost everyone in the crowd believed. *The master applying his final stroke, showing the young pretender what true genius is.* Shouts and screams could be heard around the stadium—"Go Haile! Go Haile!" Events were playing out exactly as everyone expected. But upon closer inspection, something appeared terribly wrong. Instead of the driving force forward he normally was when he dropped down a gear and made his move to sprint home, Haile's back was arched and his hips were thrust in front of him, turning his body into a backward letter C, when he should have been more like a forward slash leaning hard into his work. He appeared to be fighting a storm, like he was being blown backward by a firm breeze. He was working against himself, overstriding, and squatting down. He simply wasn't advancing with his normal, routine ease. And Kenenisa sensed it.

To the average spectator in Hengelo, of course, Haile's form appeared perfectly fine. But Kenenisa was far more than a spectator. He was an actor, a real player in the plot. As such, he had the ideal vantage point to notice any mishaps in the script. And while a runner's stride might look to the uninitiated like a single continuous act, to someone as practiced as Kenenisa it had become a sequence of intricately calibrated adjustments of foot to ankle, knee to hip, elbow to shoulder, and so on. Where a fan might just see fluidity, Kenenisa would see geometry; what would be nature to most people would be machinery to Kenenisa—parallel lines, extended planes, points of impact. And these minute and individualized calibrations make all the difference between a measured stride of ease and one of struggle. A runner in command finds a better way; Kenenisa knew that. A jogger's legs might say, *I lift, I'm sinking . . . , I lift, I'm sinking . . .* Whereas the professional's legs should say, *Lift, forward, drive . . . lift, forward, drive . . .*

With 100 meters to go Haile tried to drop down another gear. But like a hollow wall there was nothing inside, and the empty sound echoed throughout the track world. Kenenisa was shoulder to shoulder with Haile now and even beginning to pull slightly ahead. A battle seemed imminent, a struggle to the end: the tight to and fro, tug and pull of two determined men. But Haile's mind overwhelmed his chances: *I can't match his sprint. He is too strong for me.* And with 50 meters to go he knew he was going to lose. The crowd knew, too, and they were struck dumb. Instead of mad screams as Kenenisa poured it on and bounded across the line in 26:53.70, 0.9 of a second ahead of Haile, there was only silence. No one seemed to know how to respond to this revelation, this upset, this changing of the guard.

The hordes of Ethiopians present stood still with their flags at ease and their voices mute. *What does it mean to rejoice in Kenenisa over Haile? What does it mean not to?* The Dutch fans just applauded politely, and Jos stared into the sky from his position on the backstretch contemplating which of his athletes to approach first: *Do I console Haile or congratulate Kenenisa? How will the other react to whatever decision I make?* The only person who seemed clear about what had just happened was Kenenisa, as he told IAAF news editor Chris Turner.

"Before this race I thought I could run well. My training was good and I knew I was in shape. But I was afraid for much of the time . . . I didn't know what might happen to me after 7 and 8 kilometers. That was new territory for me, that was why I didn't take Haile's offer to come to the front. This was my first 10,000 meters . . . I didn't want to risk anything. *Hold on,* I told myself. *Wait until the last possible moment before making any kind of move.* Because believe me when I say, I was afraid of what Haile could do. He is such a tough guy after all. But I think my tactic of waiting put extra pressure on him. And now after beating Haile for the first time I have more confidence, especially for the world championships later in the summer. That's when I expect I will meet Haile again over 10,000 meters. I hope the result will be the same. I will try to beat him there, too."

Haile versus Kenenisa in Hengelo wasn't the first time they had met. That was at the inaugural Great Ethiopian Run on November 25, 2001, a 10K road race through the streets of Addis Ababa that Haile won comfortably in 30:30 with Kenenisa finishing in third. But Kenenisa has metamorphosized since then. Four months later on March 23 and 24, 2002, in Dublin, he won the short course (4K) and long course (12K) races at the world cross-country championships, respectively, and then repeated the feat the next year in Lausanne on March 29 and 30. Across the sports world his "double-double" was proclaimed "astounding" and "incredible," especially for a runner so young. Those victories also represented something that Haile had never achieved: true international success at cross-country. But Kenenisa's outdoor track season in 2002 failed to live up to the promise he showed over the country in Dublin. A heel injury reduced his fitness and curtailed his calendar, thus making 2003 his true international track debut. And after winning the 10,000 in Hengelo in a world's leading time, he's certainly off to an impressive start. But will he be able to sustain his form throughout the summer and prevent Haile from regaining his world 10,000-meter title? To do so would be tantamount to a *coup d'état*. But then Kenenisa has never been afraid to defy authority and follow his own path.

The second of six children from the small town of Bukoji in the fertile highlands of Arssi, just south of Addis Ababa (the same region where Haile comes from, and also Derartu Tulu and Fatuma Roba), Kenenisa knew at a young age that he didn't want to become a cattle farmer like his father. As he explained to the writer Sabrina Yohannes, "I wanted to excel in my studies and become a teacher, a doctor, or a civil servant . . . I wanted to work in something that required in-depth knowledge and provided opportunities for growth."

Kenenisa was equally ambitious when it came to sport. He imagined excelling against the best runners in Ethiopia, not just his schoolmates. Early on, however, when good results were slow to come, he wasn't sure if he had the makings of a champion. But as Yohannes reports, it was Kenenisa's physical education teacher, Sentayehu Eshetu, who explained to his young student that he had to be patient. "It'll come gradually," Eshetu said. "Don't expect to suddenly be able to challenge the others. You have a lot of work to do."

Finally at the 1999 world cross-country junior championships, Kenenisa had his breakthrough when he placed ninth. Two years later, at age 19, he won that junior championship, and in an astonishing rise to the top he was a senior world cross-country champion the following year. But Kenenisa knew he had to prove himself on the track to be considered a "real" champion: "Track is not cross-country, and my times for 5000 and 10,000 meters are not even the leading ones in Ethiopia, let alone the world. This is something I want change." And so following his double success at the 2003 world cross-country championships, Kenenisa's immediate goal became to represent Ethiopia over 10,000 meters at the world track championships.

To make the transition to track Kenenisa had to become more comfortable around the confines of a 400-meter oval. First he had to shake the dizzy spells he experienced when he ran around a track; he had to develop his pacing skills, and learn the internal rhythm of lap times. And time was pressing: Hengelo, which would be Kenenisa's only real opportunity to run the necessary qualifying time to make Ethiopia's world championship team at 10,000 meters, was scheduled for just 10 weeks after the cross-country season. But then this is a young man who knows how to target and achieve what he wants.

Kenenisa carries with him a strong independent streak. Unlike other Ethiopian runners, he won't be lured into following anyone else's pace. Not even in practice, and not even Haile's. Although he shares the same training track as Haile, he prefers to run in a different group. And when it comes to warming up for races, he refuses to get in formation and mimic Haile's routine. He'll head off by himself, jog at the pace he wants to, and perform his own set of drills and exercises. This is unusual among the Ethiopian squad, where an unwritten code places the individual's needs beneath those of the group's. None of this is to say that Kenenisa doesn't respect Haile or Ethiopia's tradition of great runners. Rather, he believes that he belongs to a different era. "The past was all Haile," he explained after his victory in Hengelo. "But now these are the years for me. This is the start of a new generation in Ethiopian distance running."

Haile's post-Hengelo comments reflected a similar sentiment. "I have always known that the future would catch up with me . . . that a takeover was imminent. For many years I always won in Hengelo. Now I have company . . . and Kenenisa is very young and talented and I respect him very much. I think I will struggle to beat him from now on. But I will not give up . . . I can't give up. It must just be that I need more speed . . . more speed has to be the answer. That is why I will go home now . . . to work on my speed. But I will be back. I will be back for more races very soon."

Kenenisa, however, didn't go home after Hengelo. Instead he carried on winning. He went to Oslo on June 27 to compete in the prestigious Bislett Games, where he faced a hungry squad of Kenyans. Sammy Kipketer, Eliud Kipchoge, Abraham Chebii, James Kwalia, and Albert Chepkurui were all keen to run the young Ethiopian into the ground. The distance would be 5000 meters, and when the pack reached the first kilometer in 2:34.11, Kenenisa was placed comfortably in fourth. Over the next five laps he began to surge in and out of the lead. At 3 kilometers (7:45.13) he was fixed up front with a string of seven tucked behind him. The next two laps proceeded in exactly the same fashion. But then suddenly the Kenyans decided to move. And as if on cue they all rolled over Kenenisa and into the lead. So surprised was Kenenisa by their challenge that he dropped backward through the pack in one great free fall.

With just 200 meters remaining Kenenisa looked well beaten in fifth place. The Kenyan vanguard appeared unstoppable. Then slowly they began to fade just as Kenenisa discovered a second life. He accelerated around the final turn, and when he hit the homestretch he passed an exhausted Chebii and a wrung-out Kipketer. With 30 meters to go he held an advantage of less than an inch. But it was enough, and Kenenisa now had his second victory in two starts. He had upstaged Kenya's best, and set a new meet record of 12:52.26 in the process. It was a massive 20-second improvement over his personal best.

Four days later on July 1 in Lausanne, Kenenisa was on the line for another 5000 meters. And again he won. Pundits across the track and field world were declaring him "devastating" and "unbeatable," "possibly the most versatile distance runner of all time." Doubts over his ability on the track disappeared. Jason Henderson, writing for *Athletics Weekly*, proclaimed, "Kenenisa can do it all . . . sustain a hard pace, insert killer surges, exact scintillating sprint finishes." More importantly, Kenenisa also seemed to possess the one intangible that separates the best from everyone else. Just like Haile, he knew how to get himself into the lead and stay there.

While Kenenisa was busy extending his winning streak across Europe, Haile was back home sharpening his speed and preparing for his next outing: 5000 meters at the Paris Golden League Meeting on July 4. He completed countless sets of sprint drills—butt kicks, high knees, bounds, and hops—along the backstretch of Ethiopia's national stadium. Written into his training program were short, intense repeats over 200 and 150 meters. Doctor was there encouraging him, monitoring his technique and execution: "Drive the arms, Haile . . . knees up . . . push, push, push." So by the time Haile boarded his plane for Paris, he had a renewed sense of confidence and determination. Paris, he believed, "will mark a new beginning to my season."

Through the early laps in Paris Haile seemed comfortable and well in charge. After four laps he drew alongside the pacemaker, Martin Keino, and shouted at him to speed up. The Parisians, who love such displays of élan, hooted and stamped the ground. By 3000 meters (7:44.62), Haile was in the lead. But not for long, as half a lap later the Kenyan Benjamin Limo took it back. By the final lap the front pack was bunched so close together that it was impossible to determine who was in command. But soon the true business would be at hand, and someone would certainly try to distinguish himself by breaking for home. Ultimately it turned out to be Haile who shot free from the pack with 300 meters remaining. It was a true power move, and within three strides he was well clear. But again, as at Hengelo, his sprint faltered. The acceleration he normally relied on just wasn't there. This enabled Abraham Chebii to get past Haile on the top of the homestretch. The crowd in the Stade de France was alight. Moments earlier the prospect of Haile losing had seemed absurd. But now with Chebii alone in lane two storming toward the finish line it would only be a matter of seconds before the unheralded Kenyan would secure the greatest victory of his career (12:53.73 to 12:54.36), beating, as he said to reporters, "the big man."

Not since July 15 and July 30, 1994, had Haile lost two races in a row. Immediately Jos became concerned. He sensed something was wrong, and that Haile's defeats weren't just a case of losing to better men. As he had in Hengelo, Jos also noticed in Paris that "Haile just didn't look like Haile when it came time to sprint. He's all bent backward and sitting down. His hips are too low, not up and out; he isn't driving with his arms or pushing off with his toes. That's not Haile. Something's not right."

Jos was anxious to test his hunch, and he confronted Haile with the facts. "I know something is wrong, Haile. Your style is completely off. And if we are going to make it better you need to tell me."

Haile's next race, another 5000 meters, was just seven days away in Rome. There he would face Chebii again, and also Kenenisa. To have any chance of evening the score with his two young rivals he had to find his missing sprint finish.

After a number of long conversations with Jos in the days leading up to Rome, Haile finally admitted that his groin had been bothering him the last few weeks, and that he couldn't seem to shake a persistent cough.

"Why didn't you say something earlier, Haile?" Jos wanted to know. And in his typical unassuming fashion, Haile replied, "Oh, you know, Jos, this was my problem. I thought I needed to solve it myself. I didn't want to worry anyone else."

But a series of medical tests that Jos quickly arranged for Haile revealed that he had bronchitis. And apparently it was all the coughing associated with the bronchitis that had irritated Haile's groin and as a result restricted his ability to sprint. Medication was prescribed to treat the cough, after which Haile's groin would hopefully heal, thus enabling him to resume normal speed training. But this chain of events would take time, and with the world championships only six weeks away, and Rome just a couple of days away, it didn't seem like there was time enough to reverse the course of events. Nevertheless, Haile presented a brave face to the media at the press conference in Rome. Journalists from America and across Europe all wanted to know the same thing: What did Haile think about Kenenisa and Chebii? "I expect Chebii and Kenenisa to be my strongest competitors tomorrow," Haile told them. "And if my time is good here I think it means that I will do well at the world championships."

But in all honesty, Haile had no chance against Kenenisa and Chebii in Rome. He was sick and injured and they were eager, confident, and fit. Everyone knew it. Jos considered scratching Haile from the race. Haile sensed his predicament, too. For as he wandered around the hotel lobby the day of his race he appeared distant and distracted, almost as if he wished he was in another place and another time. What else could explain why he was talking about running the world half-marathon championships in Portugal three months away in October instead of his race that was just six hours away? But to dream of Portugal was to escape Rome. Haile's season was spinning out of control, and a road race months away must have felt like a safer option than the track and these youngsters and their fast legs. At the press conference he had declared Kenenisa "the Prince." He even mentioned returning to the marathon, where he felt his lapse in speed wouldn't be so problematic. To many journalists those comments indicated that Haile knew his track career was over. And in their notepads they scratched out possible leads . . . "Gebrselassie's passing the torch . . ." "Rome to be Ethiopian's swansong . . ." "The Emperor dethroned . . ."

Kenenisa, by contrast, was without distraction in Rome. The day of the race he appeared focused and calm. In the morning he sipped his tea quietly in the hotel's restaurant. In the afternoon he chatted with teammates in the lobby. He was a man in demand, and for anyone who asked he gladly posed for a photograph, answered a question, or signed his name. At the press conference the day before he had predicted an exciting race: "It will be a good competition . . . and no matter what, the final result will be fast. How couldn't it be with such a world-class field of Ethiopians and Kenyans?" Over the course of the question-and-answer period he took a loose, relaxed pose while Haile was forced into acting as his translator. Here it was a full day before their race and Kenenisa already had Haile exactly where he wanted him: working for him up front while he sat back and watched.

As the echo from the starter's gun reverberated through Rome's Olympic stadium, signaling the commencement of the men's 5000 meters, the requisite positions on the track were filled posthaste: Behind the three rabbits Kenenisa settled into fourth, Haile went into fifth, and Chebii was farther back in the pack. The pacesetters led through the first (2:33.51) and second (5:08.01) kilometers right on cue. By the third kilometer (7:45.60), Kenenisa had moved into first, with Haile in second, and Chebii monitoring both of them in third.

A lap and a half later, however, the pace began to slow drastically. By 4 kilometers (10:29.38) the lead pack had swelled to seven. But all eyes in the stadium remained on only three men: Kenenisa, Chebii, and Haile.

A rough stretch of jockeying for position ensued over the next lap until suddenly Haile bolted to the lead. His change in speed was drastic, and so definitive that it left everyone trailing except Kenenisa and Chebii, who instantly attached themselves to Haile's rear. Questions rang out across the press box: "Six hundred meters, isn't that a long move from home?" "Is this a setup, some sacrificial ploy to help Kenenisa?" "Can he honestly expect to beat those guys like that?"

Haile powered past the finish line to the sound of the bell and the roar of the crowd: one lap to go. Of course it was impossible to know what was going through his mind. Was this a move he had made with confidence? Was it the only tactic he could come up with to kill his younger rivals' speed? Or was it something more desperate? A last throw of the dice to try to win back control of his empire?

The truth revealed itself with 150 meters to go when Haile veered hard into the second lane. "I was racing to help Kenenisa," he later commented. "I knew that I could do nothing else. And I wanted Kenenisa to win. He is from my country, and he is my friend, too."

With the opening Haile created, Kenenisa drove hard into the lead. For a second it looked like he was on his way to an easy victory, as Chebii appeared to be boxed in. But the young Kenyan's instincts were sharp, and before Haile could shut the gap he had opened for Kenenisa, Chebii darted past him and launched a ferocious kick of his own. His arms were gathering all the air he could hold, his stride was growing by the second. With 50 meters remaining he pulled even with Kenenisa. Behind both of them Haile was reduced to a spectator. And what he witnessed not only surprised him but everyone in the stadium.

In his last three starts Kenenisa had appeared untouchable. His combination of stamina, speed, and tactical sense had seen him dominate every one of his races irrespective of the situation. Now with Haile apparently working on his behalf, what could possibly prevent him from extending his winning streak? But Chebii wasn't willing to play the tragic loser. And when Kenenisa turned his head to the right and saw the Kenyan on his shoulder he was clearly startled. Believing he had a gap, he now realized that he had a battle on his hands. This was speed against speed and youth against youth, but also Kenya against Ethiopia.

For the Ethiopians in the crowd, taking sides was delightfully simple. "Come on, Kenenisa," they screamed. "Come on." Even Haile lent his voice in support, willing Kenenisa on from farther up the track: "Sprint, sprint, sprint." But it wasn't enough for Kenenisa. Chebii ran like a man possessed, for he, too, had the force of his nation behind him. And that added push was what possibly enabled him to squeak past Kenenisa in the final 10 meters, his arms raised in celebration over his 0.2-second victory, 12:57.14 to 12:57.34, with Haile coming home in third in 13:00.32.

In his comments to the press, Chebii was ecstatic: "I could see that Haile and Kenenisa were working together to try to beat me, but I prevailed in the end." Kenenisa, on the other hand, was quiet and eerily steadfast: "Yes, Haile and I had a plan. He had agreed to help me win by trying to take the kick out of Chebii and creating a gap for me. But it didn't go exactly as we hoped. It was not a good result. For my next race I will be better prepared. I will not make any kind of mistake."

Kenenisa's next race, of course, on August 25 in Paris, would be the 10,000-meter final at the track and field world championships. And to complete his preparations he decided to return to Ethiopia and build on the positives of his four-race European sojourn. For Haile, however, knowing exactly how to proceed from Rome wasn't so clear. His ongoing losing streak was making it difficult for him to remain positive and focused. Voices were running through his head: *Am I too old? Is there anything left in my legs?* Everywhere he turned he heard people declaring the end of his career. And as difficult as it was for him to admit, he knew there was some truth to that. When he spoke to the press in the mixed zone beneath the stadium in Rome, he offered an honest assessment of his situation.

"These youngsters are running like I was five years ago: They are very fast. But this is normal . . . you cannot control the whole world forever. Actually, I am so glad to have runners like Kenenisa at the moment. Ethiopia will hopefully not have too many problems at the world championships with talents like him. He is a very good athlete already, and still he is so young, only 21. Also, he is doing many great different things like winning at cross-country. I think we can expect him to improve a lot more in the next five or six years. In general, I see a bright future for Ethiopian distance running. The time when I was starting out there were only five or six of us, but today there are so many runners all trying to make the national team. In 1993, I remember, only two Ethiopian athletes qualified for the 10,000 meters at the world championships in Stuttgart. While today I would soon lose count of the numbers preparing for the 10,000 at this year's world championships. I am very confident about Ethiopia's running talent. I think it is only good news."

Despite Haile's conciliatory tone, this wasn't a concession speech. He knew deep inside that although he was losing races he wasn't actually running that poorly. When he finally had a private moment in Rome with Jos he told him that he was still happy and enjoying his life on the athletics circuit.

"Don't worry, Jos. I have plenty of motivation. When I analyze it, the times I'm running are better than other years. Besides 1998, when I got my 5000 and 10,000 world records, this has been my fastest start to any season. Believe me, Jos, I am in very good shape. It's just my speed that needs work. Over the last 400 to 200 meters I seem to lose my form. But I know it's still there inside me. I can feel it. Which is very good news because I was worried after Hengelo that I might have lost it forever. But now I know I didn't lose it. I just have to find a way to bring it out. With my cough diagnosed soon I will be able to resume normal speed training. And maybe there is enough time for me to be ready by Paris? Because honestly, Jos, my big problem this season has not been Kenenisa. It has been myself and the injuries. I just hope now there is time for everything to come right."

There was time. But not much. Looking at the calendar, there were 44 days until the 10,000-meter final in Paris when Haile boarded his flight from Rome to Ethiopia on July 12. That meant when he stepped off the plane back in Addis he couldn't afford to waste a single moment. He had to commit all of his energy to training, not to business, not to politics, and not to gallery openings and weddings. Otherwise, he had no hope of winning that fifth world championship.

As part of his final preparations for Paris, Haile decided to compete one last time over 5000 meters at the London Grand Prix on August 8. It would enable him to measure his progress, and chart how well his speed was coming on. He already knew that the medication the doctor in Holland had given him was working. His cough had cleared up; his groin was almost completely healed. He was getting back to full-bore speed training, but he wanted to assess how much farther he needed to go.

It was a hot night in London; the capital was in the throes of an unprecedented heat wave. The air was still and moist around the Crystal Palace Stadium. The men's 5000 was the last event on the program, leaving as much time as possible for the temperature to drop. As a result, Haile had a long wait in the warm-up area as event after event took place—the dashes, the field events, the Emsley Carr Mile. A small squad from Ethiopia had traveled to London, as the Ethiopian Athletics Federation wanted everyone on the team to Paris to complete their final preparations at home. But Haile had persuaded officials to allow him to travel to London, arguing that he needed one last confidence boost before the worlds.

When the 18 runners contesting the 5000 in London finally reached the track and toed the line, darkness had set in. The stadium lights glowed bright; the stands were full. No one in the capacity crowd had dared go home. There were nine runners spread across the inside four lanes, and another nine runners 10 meters up the track spread across lanes five to eight. They all waited for the gun. Everyone did, as a collective hush spread across the stands. There seemed to be a sense of concern for Haile throughout the crowd: *He has to win tonight. He can't lose four races in a row.* Even the meet director, Ian Stewart, didn't want to see that. So following advice from Jos he had put together a somewhat "soft" field. But this wasn't a case of the heavyweight champ facing a string of chumps to protect his title. Certainly not: The Kenyans Sammy Kipketer and Benjamin Limo were seriously world class, and more than prepared to take a good swipe at Haile. They knew he was vulnerable, after all, and that they might never get a better chance to collect such a prized scalp.

In the final seconds before the gun, Haile's ears turned toward the starter. He was tipping forward, a bundle of anticipation and energy. Then instantly the pack was released, breaking apart like a bag of marbles spilling across the floor. It was clear to see Haile's intentions: crossing the finish line with 12 more laps to go, he was in fourth place with his eyes wide and alert. He was out to show that although he might be down he was by no means out.

With five laps completed Haile moved into second. He knew that the rabbit had been employed for 3000 meters (seven and a half laps), and he was poised to take over precisely at that point. Indeed, two and a half laps later Haile was in the lead with Kipketer and another Kenyan, John Kibowen, right on his heels. Reluctant, however, to play pacemaker, Haile backed down. He began to look over his shoulder and assess the field. He stared directly at Kipketer as if to say, *You want a faster pace . . . then do it yourself.*

As a result, the 10th lap took 67 seconds to complete, and the lead pack tripled in size. Feet and elbows now began to collide, and more than one runner almost tripped. On the backstretch of the penultimate lap, Haile had had enough of the crowd and decided to make his move. It was exactly where he had surged to the front in Rome—with 600 meters to go. And as in Rome, the London crowd also gasped.

Haile was now exposed and vulnerable, an easy target for the others to track. But by the time he reached the top of the homestretch with 500 meters to go, he was alone. The others were struggling for the minor places while Haile's stride was long and tall, and he looked strong and confident. As the bell sounded signaling the last lap, he gave no signs of faltering. This was the true Haile Gebrselassie: in charge and in control. Jos, who had positioned himself along the backstretch, was pumping his right fist into the air and yelling when Haile sprinted past him with 200 meters remaining. "Faster, faster, faster. Keep kicking Haile. Thataway. Keep kicking . . ."

Haile's expression heading into the homestretch was pure joy. He was going to win and he knew it. On top of that he was sprinting effectively: His knees were high, he was pushing forward with each stride. He felt it himself, the old sensations returning: his hands rising, the wind rushing past his ears. *I'm on my way back*, he said to himself. And he repeated it. *I'm on my way back. I'm on my way back.*

Haile's winning time (12:57.23) was a British all-comers record, and within moments of crossing the line an Ethiopian flag found its way into his hands. He began his victory lap blowing kisses, bowing, and waving to the crowd. When he finally reached the backstretch and met Jos, the two of them jumped into each other's arms. Fixed in a tight, back-slapping embrace, Jos mouthed into Haile's ear, "You're ready for Paris now." And Haile agreed. He didn't say anything as such, but he didn't need to. His eyes spoke volumes. They literally sparkled: *I think I am, Jos. I think I am.*

There were now 16 days to go before the Paris 10,000-meter final and Haile's plan was simple: return to Ethiopia for one more bout of speed work. That didn't leave him a lot of time, and naturally it would still be tough going in Paris. The odds were clearly against him regaining his world title and defeating Kenenisa in the process. But if anyone could overcome the odds it was Haile. For example, what about Atlanta and all the problems he had had there? And then there was Sydney. Who could have predicted that? If Haile could win an Olympic gold medal under those circumstances, then certainly he was capable of doing anything.

12

Sydney, September 25, 2000

Ethiopians know too well that all reigns come to an end. It's their history to experience change, at times drastic change. Sitting governments expire, party leaders, warlords, tribal chiefs all revolve. Nature can vary across seasons and years. Rain may pour down, flooding plains and valleys, or drought can see swaths of green revert to a dry, static, close-cropped brown like the coat of a mangy dog.

Ruling emperors centuries back, Menelik I, Menelik II, certainly would have thought their power was well intact. Haile Selassie, Mussolini, Mengistu—all experienced a rise followed by a decline. Such is the course of Ethiopian history. Such is the course of sport . . . normally, that is.

In the buildup to the 2000 Sydney Olympics, Paul Tergat sensed that conditions surrounding the crowning of the next 10,000-meter Olympic champion were moving in his favor. Perhaps the reign of Haile Gebrselassie was finally coming to an end? After further losses to Haile following the 1996 Atlanta Olympics—in 1997, at the world championships in Athens, he watched defenseless as Haile kicked clear of him with one lap to go, cruising to an easy victory, and in 1999, at the world championships in Seville, it was the same again: Haile sprinting hard on the final lap following a slow early pace and Tergat repeating as runner-up—Tergat was determined to reverse his position.

For Sydney, Tergat was preparing like never before, tearing through his training like a runaway forest fire. News from the Gebrselassie camp raised his hopes. Rumors persisted late into the summer of 2000: injury, missed workouts, doubt, despair. Haile was apparently in trouble. Tergat understood that this was an opportunity he couldn't afford to squander. Perhaps luck was finally on his side.

Paul Tergat was born on June 15, 1969, in Baringo, Kenya, into the Tugen tribe. His was a polygamous family, and he was one of 17 children living under his father's roof in an arid region of the Great Rift Valley. He knew great hunger as a child, and his mother used to sing him to sleep to ease his stomach pain. He began running relatively late in life, after he had completed high school and joined the air force. Prior to that he had never thought too seriously about becoming a runner. As a boy he played volleyball, soccer, and basketball; he grew up next door to the school grounds, so transport was never a reason to begin running. Then in 1987 Tergat's father, Kipkuna Arap Tuetok, took him to the capital, Nairobi, to watch the final day of the All-African Games. It was a transformative experience for the curious 18-year-old: "That was the first time I had seen runners at close quarters. They appeared as normal human beings, not demigods as I had imagined. So I began running, too, but more because it was a good way to kill time and make friends in the air force." Tergat had no idea of the incredible talent that lay inside him until a coach spotted him running a routine race and persuaded him to take up the sport more seriously.

After only a few months of hard training, Tergat began to produce national-class times. His breakthrough was immediate and startling. He set ambitious goals and targets for himself. World championships and Olympic titles began to occupy his mind. And to organize and forecast what he imagined would be his future medal haul, he began to plan every detail of his training: "My upbringing gave me a strong will, a mental aggressiveness in what I wanted to achieve. Anything is possible in life so long as you approach it in a professional way."

Tergat was hungry to leave a mark on Kenyan track and field history. As he told Simon Hart of *The Daily Telegraph*, "When I first raced against my peers I was 20 minutes behind and I could taste the blood in my chest. But I studied them closely. I wanted to know their sleeping patterns, whether they ate different food. But the difference was purely in their training. I copied what they did and within one year I was level with them and even beating them."

Tergat went on to win five consecutive world championships in cross-country from 1995 to 1999. On the track, however, gold medals eluded him: so many occasions he was runner-up—Mr. Silver—in championship finals to his rival from neighboring Ethiopia. In Sydney, though, Tergat hoped to make amends.

Tergat's preparation for Sydney quickly became the stuff of legend: three killer sessions a day around the plains near his home in the town of Kabarnet, or in the nearby Ngong Hills. He ran possessed through the burning midday heat; he ran past packs of lions and giraffes. His wife, Monica Chemtai, always one of his strongest supporters, was even astonished by his resolve. "He is very strong and very determined." The three Tergat children, Ronnie, Harriet, and Lilly, hardly saw their father for all the running he was doing. Tergat can talk about those days now with a slight grin, the way a middle-aged family man might reflect on his wayward teenage years.

"I was a little bit crazy, then, yes," he says. "There were many times during my training for Sydney when I finished a workout semiconscious. I'd be so tired that I couldn't stand or eat. I could only sip some water and wait for my energy to return. And when I'd feel better after a few hours' rest, I'd go out and run just as hard again. But that was because I knew Haile would be training even harder. It's what I thought about when I considered stopping in the middle of a hard training session: Haile. I knew I had to punish myself to be able to outsprint him in Sydney."

Actually it's even a bit surprising that Tergat's career extended as far as 2000. In 1992, before his spate of international cross-country victories, he seriously considered quitting his newfound sport. That year Tergat had won Kenya's national cross-country championships, but he was forced to miss the world cross-country championships due to a last-minute injury. He was devastated as he sat in his hotel room in Boston watching the race on television.

Back in Kenya from Boston, Tergat undertook a course of rest for six months; he pondered whether he would ever regain his form. "My leg was not healing fast enough. And I thought, *Why continue? I have a good job with the air force . . . a pay slip to sustain my family?*"

But every athlete must learn to deal with defeat and cope with disappointment. It's an inescapable fact of sport, and so an important lesson to learn young. This period tested Tergat's commitment: "Now I believe to win or lose is part of sport. It's impossible to win all the time. I am a runner, after all, not a machine. Besides, I enjoy the excitement of competition. Nothing is more pleasurable. Running is in my blood, after all. It's not something I do just for medals and money. It's who I am. And I have always felt that as long as I can maintain my confidence my turn will come. In sport nothing is impossible."

But would Tergat's turn to claim victory over Haile come in Sydney? It appeared that it might following a final tune-up meet in Zurich a month before the game's opening ceremonies. Only Tergat didn't know as much. What he witnessed in Zurich was Haile doing his thing: running clear, easily beating him over 5000 meters. He had apparently forgotten Atlanta, and how clever Haile could be at disguising the truth. Anton Engels, however, Haile's physiotherapist, who was also in Zurich for that final pre-Olympic tune-up race, knew exactly what Haile was concealing.

When Haile began his build up late in 1999 to defend his Olympic 10,000-meter title in Sydney, Anton couldn't ignore what he was feeling every time he dug his fingers into Haile's right Achilles tendon. The scar tissue was thick: a crusty coating around the tendon and bone that shouldn't have been there. It wasn't going away, either. "Not without an operation," a host of leading sports medicine doctors across Europe had already determined. But this was an Olympic year, and surgery was out of the question. "I must run in Sydney," Haile told Anton countless times. "I have to win there." And so Anton's work became clear: to help a man who can only run on one leg win an Olympic gold medal.

It was Jos who brought Anton and Haile together following a desperate phone call in 1999. As a fellow Dutchman, Jos knew about Anton's work with a wide range of top international athletes. He quickly explained the situation over the phone . . . his leading athlete out with a serious Achilles tendon injury . . . it could possibly prevent him from defending his Olympic title . . . something had to be done to keep the pain in check. Anton agreed to meet Haile, and following a number of hands-on assessments and consultations he was prepared to present his diagnosis.

Jos and Haile sat in Anton's office waiting for the news. They had already been down a long road of X-rays and examinations with doctors and other specialists. While they waited to hear what Anton might add, they had to decide whether to trust his assessment. Something about the sandy-haired Dutchman agreed with Haile. He told Jos, "I think this guy is all right." Maybe it was Anton's modesty Haile liked, his admission that he might not always have the answer to every problem, but by asking enough people the right questions he would in the end. Or how he told Haile that an athlete must know how to heal himself: "I can perhaps show you the way, Haile, but the last thing I want is for you to be dependent on me. That's not healing someone, it's controlling them."

Since he was a boy, Anton had wanted to be a physical therapist. He was that amazed by the rehabilitation process he saw his father go through following back surgery: "How the body healed fascinated me. And unlike a doctor who sees a patient and then sends him home, I liked the idea of working more closely with people." A serious soccer player in his youth, as well as a keen all-around sportsman, it only made sense for Anton to specialize in sports physical therapy: "The entire time I was in university my goal was to open a sports clinic. I felt I understood athletes' needs and how important it was to be honest with them about an injury and what they could do to get better. The hardest part of my job, though, is telling an athlete his career is over. But life is about more than sport, and if it's time for an athlete to move on someone needs to tell him that."

Haile, of course, already had a rich and full life beyond sport—a beautiful and loving family, a thriving business, a tight-knit group of friends. But he wasn't ready to give up athletics just yet. That second Olympic gold medal weighed too heavily on his mind. And it showed as he waited with Jos for Anton's report.

"What's taking him so long?" he said more than once to Jos. "Do you think it's more bad news? I don't want more bad news." Haile's voice even began to quiver. "Jos, we need to be in Sydney."

Finally Anton's presence quieted Haile down. "Well, it's a very serious injury," he began. "To say that is not a question whatsoever. But can you continue running up until Sydney, that's what you want to know." Haile braced himself. He tightened his grip on the armrests of his chair and tried to slow down his breathing by thinking of his little girls' faces. Jos was tugging at his shirt collar and shifting back and forth in his seat. Anton, though, was just beginning to crack a smile. "Don't worry, you've found the right man now. I can help you get to Sydney."

Through an immediate series of intensive treatments beginning in late 1999, Anton got Haile back on his feet and training hard for Sydney. They spoke regularly on the phone. Anton traveled to Ethiopia, sleeping in Haile's house and working on his worn tendon day and night: massages in the morning before and after training, ongoing stretching and strengthening exercises, ice baths, hot towels, oils, ointments, creams, and additional massages following Haile's evening workouts. It was a rigorous protocol. But it was working. Haile competed indoors that winter and went undefeated. His outdoor season opened with wins in Hengelo, Nürnberg, and London. On every visit to Europe he met Anton for further work, more consultation, and increased reassurance that indeed he would make it to the starting line in Sydney. But then came the Weltklasse on August 11, the annual evening of athletics in Zurich considered by many to be the greatest single night of track and field in the world. Haile was scheduled to run his final tune-up race before the heats of the 10,000 meters began on Friday, September 22, in Stadium Australia, the venue for the 24th Olympic Games.

Injuries, so medical science claims, are clear physical episodes. It's the body's way of saying, Enough, and protecting itself. When a runner, for example, asks too much from his body and pushes too hard, his legs will answer back with pain. And the reply to pain can only come in one form: to limp. So it was that following Haile's victory in Zurich, after more than nine months of skirting the inevitable, he began limping.

"I don't know what happened in Zurich that was different from my other races. Of course there had been pain in every race and every day in training, too. I was never 100 percent, but I was managing. After Zurich, though, I couldn't walk. The pain was very bad. All I could do was sit down. Of course I didn't want anyone to see my pain, or worse catch me limping. I didn't want my rivals to know about my problem, especially Paul Tergat. So I just stayed seated in the stadium and waited until it was dark and everyone had left. Anton sat with me, too, just waiting. Then I limped back to the hotel and went immediately to my room, avoiding everyone, particularly the media. Anton and I even took a different route than normal to the hotel, just to make sure that no other athletes, like some Kenyans or Moroccans, saw me. I had to protect myself and my reputation. I wanted everyone to believe that Haile Gebrselassie was fine and ready to defend his title in Sydney. I couldn't let anyone see me limping so badly."

That night in Zurich Haile hardly slept at all. He was riddled with worry and fear: *Is my Olympic dream over? What can I do? Why is this happening to me, another Olympics and another problem?* He asked Anton and Jos to leave him alone in his room, to suspend their bedside vigil and the constant treatments of ice and massage. He said he would be okay: "Go back to your rooms and sleep. Let me take some rest and we'll see how I am in the morning." But Haile was only protecting them from the truth. He knew he was facing one of the toughest months of his athletic career.

Back home in Ethiopia, Haile was unable to train with the rest of the Ethiopian squad as they went through their final preparations for Sydney. They ran hard, exacting intervals on the track three times a week while Haile sat in the stands and watched, or just jogged or walked slowly around the infield grass. That was as much strain as his Achilles tendon could take. By now everyone inside the Ethiopian sporting community knew about Haile's situation. And they were all on edge. Somehow Haile managed to convince the Ethiopian press to keep his injury a secret from the rest of the world. As a result, on went a possessed Paul Tergat training like a madman, unaware that Haile was actually facing the possibility of not even going to Sydney.

"That was a horrible time in my life," Haile says now. "I didn't know what to do. Should I go to Sydney and hope for the best, or should I just pull out? But the Olympics are such an important event, it's not easy to know what is the best thing to do. My character also became very bad during this period. I couldn't sleep. I didn't want to see anyone. I was always angry, losing my temper and fighting with Alem for no reason, showing no patience or tolerance for anything. I was completely on edge. That was why I eventually decided, Enough: I had to make a serious test and decide whether to go to Sydney or not. And I remember that morning at the track very well. It was warm outside as usual, and the entire squad was there preparing for another tough session, one of the last. Doctor was on the infield grass watching me warm up, and I could see how hopeful he was. I could see hope in everyone's face. And I was praying that their good wishes would be enough for me. After some easy jogging on the grass I sat down on the high-jump apron to change my shoes and put on my spikes. I knew I must make my test in spikes, like real race conditions. My plan was to run a few 400s at race pace, and when I stood up I felt good. It was a nice sensation to be back in my spikes. I could notice my legs coming alive, and my mood improving: I was getting ready to run, getting ready to live again. But within the first 50 meters of my first warm-up stride down the backstretch I knew it was all over. I knew I was through. The pain was just too much. How was I going to run two hard 10,000-meter races within the space of four days when I couldn't even run a 50-meter stride? So that was it: I made my decision not to go to Sydney. I told Doctor . . . I told my teammates and wished them all good luck. I called Jos and Anton back in Holland. I told Alem when I got home. And I made an appointment to see the commissioner of sport that afternoon and give him my decision in person: I wasn't going to Sydney to defend my Olympic title."

The office of the commissioner of sport in Ethiopia is a wood-paneled rectangular room with two windows overlooking the busy avenue below and a soft brown leather sofa set against the opposite wall with a glass-top coffee table in front of it. The floor is a cool marble; the Ethiopian flag hangs inert from a chrome stand in the corner behind the door. Any two people seated on that sofa and chatting over a cup of tea would most certainly feel the dignity and influence of this space. What comes across are stately feelings of national pride, honor, and respect. And along with them a seductive sense of confidence and belonging. Other such places, heavy in their symbols, also transmit this emotional effect—courthouses, museums, churches. It's the idea of not being alone, that somehow there are powers beyond our understanding that influence our ideas, our conduct, and our decisions most of all. As Haile sat sipping his tea he must have come under such a spell.

"Thank you for meeting me, Commissioner."

"It's my pleasure, Haile. Always good to see you."

"I'm afraid, though, Commissioner, I have some bad news. I have decided not to go to Sydney. The problem with my Achilles tendon is too big after all, and will prevent me from doing my best."

"Haile, I'm very sad to hear that. Is there anything I can do?"

"I'm afraid not, Commissioner. There is nothing anyone can do."

"Will you at least consider coming to Sydney in a supporting role, Haile? You are a senior Ethiopian athlete; it would help the others immensely to have you there."

"I'm sorry, Commissioner, but I don't think that is something for me."

"Well then, Haile, your mind is made up."

"It is, Commissioner. And so now I must leave. Good luck in Sydney, sir."

"Thank you, Haile. Good-bye."

Now, it may take time for such spells to have their effect. These matters aren't so simple, like pulling a rabbit out of a hat, or sawing a woman in half. What we're talking about here isn't magic, but a type of transformation, or revelation. And despite Haile wishing the commissioner good luck, and the commissioner saying good-bye, and the two of them standing up from the couch and shaking hands, Haile wasn't out of the room just yet. He still had five steps to take to reach the office door, open it, and walk out. Five steps. And five steps taken slowly, as they would be in a somber office setting, can last as long as 10 seconds. Ten seconds. In 10 seconds a man can run 100 meters. That's the length of a track's homestretch. One-hundred meters. Over that much distance a miracle can occur.

"Just one last thing before you leave, Haile."

"Yes, Commissioner."

"Now I'm not trying to influence you. And of course the decision to run in Sydney is yours alone. But I just want you to know that I honestly believe that if you did come to Sydney, and you did decide to run, you would win the gold medal."

After reconsidering three serious points—first, how painful would it be; second, was there any risk of doing permanent damage; and third, what effect would a month's lost training have—and still being satisfied that pain is only pain, that surgery will ultimately correct any damage that might be done, and that winning is as much about self-belief as anything else—Haile walked out of his room in the Olympic village in Sydney on Friday, September 22, to take his position on the starting line for his 10,000-meter Olympic semifinal . . .

"I wore special shoes Adidas made for me . . . I did a lighter-than-usual warm-up. In the race, though, I didn't want to raise suspicions so I ran to win. I ran like normal instead of just trying to secure one of the last qualifying spots for the final. And, oh my goodness, there was lots of pain during that race, especially afterward, too. But I won [27:50.01]. I was in the final, and I had the weekend to get ready."

All day Saturday and Sunday Haile didn't leave his bed in the Olympic village. Teammates brought him food; Anton visited him and treated his foot. He only sat in bed with his foot elevated. That was his new job. And he did it well: "On Sunday morning I don't know how it was possible but I could feel something beginning to happen in my foot. Some kind of change was taking place. Like a tingling or a drying effect running through my blood. Or something electric or magical. My leg was healing, I knew it. I could feel it. And as boring as it was to spend two whole days lying in bed without anything to do, I actually wanted time to slow down even more. Suddenly every minute became significant to me. I thought a fraction more time here, or another second there might mean a little bit more improvement in my leg. And that was what I was asking for: more time, more improvement. It was only time, I knew, that stood in the way of a miracle."

Monday night, September 25, 2000, is often referred to in track and field circles as Magic Monday: the most spectacular single night in the history of track and field. Cathy Freeman completed her incredible run of pressure that night. Michael Johnson established himself as the greatest long sprinter of all time. There were 112,524 people in Stadium Australia to watch their races. It was a night truly meant for a magnificent happening. And yes, maybe even a miracle.

"That Monday night when I entered the warm-up area next to the stadium with Anton and Jos, Paul Tergat was sitting down on the ground relaxing. He looked up at me and said, 'Haile, how are you?' Just two words came to my mind. 'Very good,' I said. And it was at that exact moment when I believed I had a chance to win. So I began my warm-up feeling positive. Jos and Anton were watching everything carefully. I think they were more worried than me. Because you know it's sometimes harder to watch than to run. With each additional lap I took around the warm-up track, I felt my old rhythm returning. There was no limping . . . I was concentrating on making the pain disappear. I could see the other 10,000-meter runners, too, and not one of them scared me. Not even Tergat. And actually, I could sense that they were a little bit afraid of me. They still had no idea about my problem, I realized. Again I said to myself, *I have a good chance to win.*"

Perhaps it is harder to watch than to run. Watching affords no opportunity to exercise the tension and release the pressure. Where can it go as it builds and builds? There's not outlet, no escape. At least by running, the worry is shaken up and put into motion. But how could Jos and Anton just begin running around the warm-up track? They weren't dressed for it, first of all, and their roles demanded otherwise. They had to accept that. Anton would tape Haile's foot and help him with his stretching, while Jos had to consider what final advice to give Haile. This was important, the last words Haile would hear as he left the warm-up area and headed for the stadium. Those words would be with him up until the gun. For example, if an athlete's feeling overly tense, you might tell him a joke. Or perhaps he needs a final tactical instruction, or some positive affirmation such as, *You're the man!* Or, *It's all you out there tonight!* But the circumstances surrounding this night, and this race, and this athlete were so rare and unusual—a man vying for an Olympic gold medal running on one leg—that Jos was struck dumb. His years of experience guiding athletes into Olympic and world championship finals were reduced to nothing at this moment. He simply didn't know what to say. So when Haile approached him, holding his spikes in his hands and ready to follow the official into the tunnel leading out to the stadium's track, it was he who spoke, borrowing a phrase from Jos that he would use to psych up Haile before every one of his world record attempts: "Don't worry, Jos, I think it's world record weather tonight." And with that, Haile turned and walked into the tunnel, leaving Jos silently smiling and slightly shaking. They'd be apart for upward of 30 minutes.

And, oh, what a thirty minutes it was . . . "I knew I had to be up front right away to cover every move. The early pace was confusing with many surges and different tactics. But that didn't matter. I had to stay close to the lead; I couldn't give up the chance to win early on. I was feeling all right, though, not so bad. We passed the halfway mark in 13:45, a pack of about nine. I was really into the race at that point. At the 6000-meter mark I even briefly took the lead. I felt no pain in my Achilles whatsoever. I had simply forgotten about it. That was before the start of the 20th lap, when suddenly with 6 laps to go I felt very bad. Not from my injury, though. It was my breathing . . . it was very hard. And my legs they were tired and heavy. I began to think, *I can't make it. I've lost too many days of training. I'm not strong enough.* And for the first time in my career I considered dropping out of a race. I thought how nice it would feel to step to the side of the track and stop running, stop all the pain and confusion in my mind, just lie down and go to sleep. That was what I wanted to do, lie down in a heap and sleep. But thank God my mind changed. I realized that such thinking is crazy: *Oh, come on*, I told myself. *Only six more laps, you can run six more laps.* So I hung on. Somehow I hung on and kept running. I even found myself in the lead again, this time at the 9000-meter mark. And then with two laps to go I noticed something very, very interesting. I could see the pain on my competitors' faces . . . the three Kenyans: Tergat, Korir, Ivuti. And at the sound of the bell, with one lap remaining, I could hear them breathing hard. That was when I began to plot how I could win. I made the decision to attack with 100 meters remaining. And down the entire backstretch, as Tergat was surging to the front, I kept repeating to myself, *Wait. Wait. Wait.* And actually I thought I had no chance: Tergat was looking too strong and opening too big a lead. But I knew I couldn't chase after him sooner. I had to wait. My poor fitness wouldn't have carried my sprint any farther than 100 meters. Finally, on top of the homestretch with 100 meters remaining, I took to lane two, put my head down, and with all my power I began to sprint. And I can tell you that as I ran down the homestretch I was not in that stadium. The noise from the crowd was swirling around me like a fog. I was out of my body and unable to feel anything, not even my feet making contact with the ground. It was like no experience I had ever had before. Because I was pushing but relaxing, I was conscious but dreaming, I was running but float-ing . . . it was true make-believe, a real moment of magic. And that was the state I was in until I crossed the finish line. I even had to ask an official, 'Did I win?' And he told me I won. 'Yes, really, I won?' I said back to him. 'Are you sure? Are you sure?' I couldn't believe it. Just nine one-hundredths of a second. Oh, my goodness, so close. Oh, my goodness, I was so happy."

13

Coming Back

Celebrations following Haile's victory in Sydney were immediate. First, on his part, a long, drawn-out victory lap, slow like savoring the taste of a first kiss. The noise across the stadium built and built. It was something greater than fireworks, louder than a mechanical charge. This was beyond anything incendiary or electric. It was primal, voluminous, deafening.

Haile moved through it all waving and smiling; the drop in pace was pure relief: simple jogging in lane eight, sometimes just walking. The applause was too much for him to comprehend.

"Really, this is all for me? Wow! Incredible. So, so amazing."

Haile was transfixed by the 360-degree views—a capacity crowd on its feet cheering. He was soaking in the pleasure, relishing the satisfaction. He still couldn't believe his victory was true: "Oh, thank you to God for that." Or how it had been possible: "One month no training . . . all the time so much pain. This is a miracle for me."

Haile's teammate and bronze medalist, Assefa Mezgebu, joined Haile on his lap of honor. Draped across their shoulders was the Ethiopian flag; the stadium's lights high in the sky made night seem like day; time was lost following this fantastic, magical display; flashbulbs popped in every direction, illuminating Haile's and Assefa's glistening brown skin. At last the heavy work was done. Finally time to breathe.

Haile and Assefa reached a group of Ethiopian supporters on the backstretch who were literally falling over each other to touch their heroes. To thank them most of all. Arms came forward in all directions like a giant octopus rising from the sea.

Ethiopia's commissioner of sport engulfed Haile in one ferocious hug. Sweat marked his suit jacket. He was brimming with pride; Haile was laughing with delight.

"Good you came, eh, Haile?" he said.

"Yes, Commissioner. Very good. Very good indeed." More laughter followed. Laughter that was pure joy.

Back in Ethiopia, Haile's win had produced a wild torrent of hysteria and celebration: tears, shouts, leaps, horns, embraces. All of which would pale in comparison to the welcome Haile and his teammates would receive in a fortnight's time.

On his exit from the stadium Haile returned to the warm-up track where Jos and Anton were waiting for him. They never made it to the stadium. They had watched Haile on a small television that had been set up in the corner of the warm-up area.

Through every step of Haile's race Jos could hardly contain himself. He knew what Haile was up against—injury, lost fitness, a determined rival. At times Jos found it difficult to look and had to shield his eyes. The last 100 meters he was a wreck: *Will he . . . won't he . . . will he . . . won't he . . .* He was rocking in his seat, urging Haile past Tergat. He lost touch with the ground in those final 10 seconds. He stopped breathing; his ears closed, his features froze. But he wasn't numb. He had momentarily entered Haile's body: "Over the last 100 meters I was in touch with Haile's pain and his effort. It was excruciating . . . pushing forward, driving toward that line. I think I can say I definitely understood his struggle."

When at last Jos and Haile came together they held each other in a hug so strong that anyone who witnessed it would have said their souls must have touched. Jos was proud like a father. Haile was grateful like a son. Jos was repeating into Haile's ear, "That's enough, that's enough, Haile. You are the greatest runner ever. The greatest. You never need to run again. I will never ask you to run again." But Haile's thoughts were already moving forward, always forward. His response to Jos: "Time to fix my Achilles, Jos. I need to get healthy for next year."

Success on the track continued for Ethiopia in Sydney. On the back of Haile's and Assefa's medals came further wins: Derartu Tulu in the 10,000 meters, Million Wolde in the 5000 meters, and Gezahegne Abera in the marathon. Also in the women's 10,000 meters a silver medal went to Gete Wami, who also won a bronze in the 5000 meters, as did Tesfaye Tola in the marathon. In sum, eight medals for Ethiopia. It was more than any other African nation competing in Sydney.

Haile had been in the stadium every day to support his teammates and to shout and wave the Ethiopian flag. There was also an endless flow of invitations he had to manage, appearances he had to make, and receptions he had to attend. He never shook so many hands, smiled for longer, or signed his name that many times. The congratulations, the attention—would it ever end? Headlines poured forth from around the world. This was one story all the media could agree on: Haile Gebrselassie, The Greatest Distance Runner of All Time.

Nearing the end of the games Haile's schedule finally began to relent. One afternoon when there was no one from Ethiopia competing on the track, he decided to take in the sights of downtown Sydney with his friend Getaneh Tessema. It was a crisp, spring day. A gentle offshore breeze cooled the city. With his head back gazing up into the wide Australian sky, Haile imagined he could be in Addis Ababa. The clouds were as white, the air just as blue and endless. Lately he had been thinking a lot about home. It wouldn't be long now, only a few more days and he'd be back with Alem and the girls. He had accomplished what he came to Sydney to do. And a minute failed to pass when he didn't remember that last 100 meters—the struggle, the effort, inching past Tergat. *How did I do it?* Haile recognized that in his catalog of victories some wins were fleeting while others endured. Sydney 2000, he knew, was one race he'd never forget.

Haile and Getaneh continued their walk through Sydney's crowded streets. Haile picked up some trinkets for the girls: a stuffed koala bear, a boomerang. He bought a blue sweater for Alem. Buskers performed on every corner—jugglers, singers, magicians. Haile tossed a few coins into their hats. He was relishing this break from the stadium and the Olympic village. He knew that when he arrived home his responsibilities would return—parades, speeches, receptions. His diary would be full for months. But this day was his own, a rare chance for him to reflect on all that had taken place over the past week.

As their walk extended into the lunch hour, Haile and Getaneh looked for someplace to eat. "Let's get a bottle of red wine," Haile said entering an Italian restaurant. Getaneh was surprised, knowing what a teetotaller his friend was. "A whole bottle, Haile? Maybe just a glass." But Haile insisted. "Today I feel like having more than a glass." And so the wine flowed and time passed sweetly, peacefully. It was a perfect moment. And for that Haile was truly satisfied and inexpressibly happy.

October 6, 11 days after his gold medal performance, and Haile was on his way home. A reception was planned at the airport for the entire Ethiopian track team, followed by an official ceremony downtown. Haile had been through this before, following his gold medal in Atlanta four years earlier. He felt certain that he knew what to expect once the plane landed. But Atlanta had only produced three medals on the track for Ethiopia compared to eight from Sydney. And this welcome would need to reflect that difference.

To kick-start the whole affair a squadron of MiG jets had been dispatched by the Ethiopian government to escort Haile and his teammates home once they began their descent into Addis Ababa. It was a marvelous display that all the athletes loved.

On the ground millions of people had gathered at the airport to receive their heroes. Too many, in fact, for the police to contain. When the Ethiopian Airlines jet shut down its engines, the tarmac was overrun in a swell of delight. Gazing awestruck out the plane, Haile couldn't believe it: "People everywhere . . . This is not like after Atlanta. This looks like something much, much bigger."

And it was. The crowds continued out from the airport and onto the Bole Road. People crammed the median strip, hung from trees, and stood on roofs and bridges to have a view of their stars; they were 10 rows deep along the sidewalk. There was precious little space for Haile's chauffeured car to pass. Flags in everyone's hand cast the sky in green, yellow, and red. And in the air a helicopter hung suspended from a wire, the Ethiopian flag twinned with the Olympic flag.

Floats decorated with flowers, banners, and paintings of gold medals led the procession. Haile stood tall in an open-top car waving and bowing to both sides of the road and up into the trees, roofs, and bridges. He wore his Ethiopian team uniform with a necklace of flowers and his gold medal bouncing off his chest. He clasped a flag in each hand, and for miles and miles there were people, music, and song. In every direction there were people to acknowledge. As far as the eye could see there were people acknowledging Haile. The police on horseback and motorcycles had an easy job. There was no threat of panic or riot. This was pure love and celebration on display.

The motorcade's destination was Meskel Square, where another crowd in the millions had gathered. One by one each medalist was introduced to the mad throng. Last to be presented was Haile. The chorus began, "Haile, Haile, Haile . . . Haile, Haile, Haile." And it never waned all through his address.

For his next stop Haile arrived home, where Alem, the girls, the rest of his family, and a number of his closest friends were all waiting. A splendid banquet had been prepared; a band had been hired. Across the front entrance to the house a wide white banner said in English, WELCOME HOME HAILE.

It was beneath the banner where Haile found Alem. They kissed and everyone cheered. Haile's father greeted his son with pride; toasts, well wishes, and singing and dancing filled the next four hours. There was a cake decorated with the five interlocking Olympic rings, and the champagne was endless. A priest blessed the festivities, and a team of photographers preserved it all.

Haile and Alem cut the cake and served each other generous bites by hand just as they had done four years ago at the airport as part of their engagement ceremony. These celebratory quadrennial Olympic moments were fast becoming a tradition in the Gebrselassie home. The party continued long after Haile and Alem had snuck away to a downtown hotel room to spend the night alone and in peace. Then again, this occasion had never been for Haile and his teammates alone. It was a day for the nation. A moment when all Ethiopians could proclaim that their distance runners were the envy of the world.

As the euphoria of Sydney passed, Haile's thoughts turned to his next race, his next championship. To proceed he knew had to be do something about his Achilles tendon. In his mind surgery was the answer. But Jos, as always a presence in every decision affecting Haile's career, was hesitant. He wanted to exhaust every option and explore every possibility before Haile went under any surgeon's knife. He knew too well from his own experiences the difficulty of dealing appropriately with an injured Achilles tendon. He thought it best to proceed with caution and seek every opinion possible. Ironically, his thoroughness almost drove Haile to a premature retirement.

Things came to a head following a jam-packed one-day, three-nation tour of consultants that Jos had arranged for Haile. It was a mad itinerary, and by the end of it all Haile was fed up: "In just one day I visited doctors in Switzerland, Paris, and Helsinki. Anton was with me and every minute we were renting cars, jumping into taxis, or running to catch our next flight. I had to have different visas for each country and so I was all the time shuffling paperwork. And still we came away without an answer about having surgery. When Jos told me we needed more opinions, I became very angry. 'No, Jos. No more doctors. I've had it. I'm through. No more running.' Right away he tried to change my mind. 'Haile, it's like your races when you wait for the final homestretch to make your move,' he said to me. 'That's being patient. We need to be patient now, too, and make sure we find the right doctor.' But I didn't agree. I thought, *That's it. Maybe now is the time for me to retire.* But Jos insisted that I see one more doctor who was based in Bern, Switzerland. I agreed, but only on the condition that if we decided surgery was necessary I'd have it then and there. No more delays, no more debates. And I can say now that at the time I was only thinking that I had a 25 percent chance of ever running again. After seeing so many doctors already, I didn't think there was anything anyone could do to help me. But this doctor in Bern, Dr. Peter, he was very impressive. He made a good argument for having surgery, and I was quickly convinced. Anton was also with me and he agreed that what Dr. Peter was suggesting was the best approach we had heard. So the next day I was in the operating room having my leg cut open. Because I only had a local anesthetic I was talking to the nurse asking her what was happening and how it all was going. I could hear the saw cutting through my bone, but there was a screen at my waist so I couldn't see for myself how my leg looked. The nurse also kept telling me that I really didn't want to do that."

For 10 days following his operation Haile remained in Switzerland to attend physical therapy, slowly testing the mobility of his leg, learning exactly what exercises to do back in Ethiopia. To pass the time between his therapy sessions he sat in bed and drew pictures for Alem. He was remembering Asela and the countryside around his home: the birds, the color of the fields and the sky. He was feeling positive about the future, and drawing gave life to his ideas and impulses. He could sense his leg healing, and everyone around him was optimistic. "You'll be back on the track as good as ever," Dr. Peter said. "Thank you, Doctor," Haile said. "Thank you."

However, when Haile returned to Addis the reception he received was something completely different, and totally unexpected. "When I walked off the plane," he explains, "I was using my crutches and my foot was heavily bandaged. Everyone in my family was at the airport to meet me: Alem, my brothers, my sisters . . . And when they first saw me after I came through customs they began to scream. They were shouting and crying and falling to the ground. I didn't know what was wrong. I even began to look around the airport thinking that something terrible must be happening somewhere. But there was nothing, and I quickly realized it was because of me they were so upset. 'What did that doctor do to you,' Alem screamed. 'Look at you. Now you are handicapped.' My sisters especially were angry. 'Why have you done this? Risked so much just to carry on running. You should have stopped instead of doing this to yourself, becoming a cripple.' As fast as I could I explained that my crutches and bandages were not permanent. 'This is nothing,' I said, lifting my crutches in the air and pointing at my bandages. 'It's only what I must do to help my leg heal.'"

But Haile could see that his family didn't understand. Elective surgery for sport was something that didn't occur in Ethiopia. And so

Alem and Haile's sisters continued to cry, and his brothers and his uncles shook their heads. To remedy the situation Haile had to take a drastic step. Back at home he unwrapped the bandages on his foot. "Look," he shouted. "My foot is fine, it's still there." And what he did next would have shocked Dr. Peter. He laid down his crutches and began jogging around the living room floor. "See, I'm not handi-capped," he said. "I can still walk. I can still run. It's only time I need to be 100 percent again. The bandages and the crutches are just to help me."

And time it would certainly take, more time than Haile expected. What followed was a long process of coming back. He began his reha-bilitation by aqua jogging, lifting weights, and cycling. Dr. Peter had told him to follow this program for six weeks. "No running until then, Haile." But Haile quickly lost his patience; after three weeks he was running again. It was a stop-and-go process at first. He had to accus-tom his leg slowly to the hills and the long runs. It ended up taking months, not weeks, for Haile to regain his form. And along the way the losses mounted: Edmonton in August 2001, London in April 2002, and Hengelo in June 2002.

But Haile refused to lose hope. Instead he became more philo-sophical about running and his future. "I cannot let mistakes or prob-lems depress me. When I lose, for example, I need to spend a great deal of time thinking why did I lose. Was it a tactical mistake? Didn't I prepare well? Or in the case of Edmonton, London, and Hengelo, was I injured? Then I can only do my best to correct the problem next time. Setbacks in training or in competition are common, after all. They only strike you hard because you cannot predict them. But one cannot become desperate in the face of defeat. I have to maintain my composure; I have to be patient; I have to persist and aim for the next challenge. That's because my victories are not just for me, they are for all of Ethiopia. That is the responsibility I must live with."

At last in early 2003—three years from the date of his Achilles surgery—Haile began to feel his true form returning: His workouts were becoming easier; his legs had that spark again; he was recovering from his sessions without trouble. Furthermore, his spirits were buoyed by the summer's world championships and the Olympics the following year. In both cases there was the chance to make history. He could become a five-time world champion at 10,000 meters, and the first three-time Olympic champion at 10,000 meters. He could show the world that he was still a force. And he seemed to be well on target when in February he ran easily a new indoor world record for 2 miles followed four weeks later by an indoor world championship over 3000 meters. But then indoor track isn't outdoor track, and a few months in an athlete's career can make a world of difference—fortunes can reverse that quickly. So Hengelo in June proved to be a shock defeat for Haile, as did further losses in Paris and Rome in July. He was ill and injured; he was despondent and questioning his next move. While all the time young Kenenisa Bekele was gathering strength and building momentum.

But Haile wasn't begrudging of Kenenisa's success. That has never been his style. "Haile's not a person who worries," his friend and former pacemaker Worku Bikila explains. "He doesn't experience a lot of regret or jealousy. If someone else is accomplishing something, Haile is happy for him to accomplish it. If he doesn't succeed at something, well then, he didn't succeed. And if something doesn't work out, he just creates a way to improve the situation. Haile, you know, is always happy and always joking. I remember shortly after I had my first child Haile had his. He said to me then, 'Well, I was waiting for my pacemaker. When you began, then I realized I had better start, too.'"

Over his long career, Haile knows as well as anyone that life at the top of sport can be fickle: One man's up while another's down. And on August 8 he sensed a turn of fortune. His British all-comers record for 5000 meters at the Crystal Palace on a hot and humid London night that ended his three-race losing streak had come without trouble. Hope swelled again through Haile's veins; winning the world championships in Paris seemed possible. It would all be a matter, he felt, of how the race was run, and how well he could execute a favorable plan.

Ethiopia's tactics in Paris for the 10,000 meters were totally team oriented: Do whatever's necessary to sweep the medals. This was what Doctor had told Haile, Kenenisa, and the third member of Ethiopia's 10,000-meter squad, Sileshi Sihine. "Who gets which medals doesn't matter," Doctor repeated again and again in the days leading up to the final. "It only matters that we win all three." Haile understood Doctor's instructions. He assumed that his teammates did as well. "Don't worry, Doctor," Haile assured the old coach. "We will break the others early, especially the Kenyans. We can sort the medals out for ourselves after that."

The plan that had been hatched for the 10,000-meter final in the Stade de France, Sunday night, August 24, involved Haile, Kenenisa, and Sileshi taking turns leading until they had such a gap that they didn't have to worry about losing a medal. It was a strategy that everyone in the field expected the Ethiopians to follow. Meb Keflezighi, the American record holder for 10,000 meters, was confident in his pre-race forecast: "The Ethiopians will run away and create their own race for the medals. And Haile will lead that charge."

But Haile held back at the start, and it actually ended up being Keflezighi who took the early laps. He led through the 1st and 2nd kilometers (2:52.01 and 5:36.76, respectively) with the other 21 starters in a neat row behind him. By the 3rd kilometer (8:24.72) still no Ethiopians were at the front. It was Salim Kipsang from Kenya who was setting the pace. Haile was in 10th, and Kenenisa and Sileshi were only somewhat closer to the front.

Two laps later the picture remained unchanged. The pace was modest, too, consisting of laps in the region of 67 seconds. Wasn't anyone going to try to make an impression? Where were the Ethiopians? Then entering the homestretch to complete lap number 10 matters changed: Haile cut sideways from his position in the middle of the pack and into lane three, where he then shot into the lead. It was a serious move. One only had to look into Haile's eyes and observe his stride. The former was narrowing while the latter was widening.

Now on the backstretch of lap 11 it was Ethiopia one, two, three—Haile, Kenenisa, Sileshi—with the rest of field beginning to break apart.

Haile completed that circuit in 64 seconds, the fastest lap of the race thus far.

Lap 12 was another 64, and on the backstretch of lap 13 Kenenisa took over and led his teammates through the halfway point in 13:52.33.

Kenenisa held on to the lead for two more laps, running a 64 then a 61. He looked smooth and under control. But so did Haile, so did Sileshi. The others in the race, though, were beginning to suffer. That 61 had broken the lot except the defending champion from Kenya, Charles Kamathi.

John Cheruiyot, also from Kenya, and who would finish in fifth, later commented on the Ethiopians' midrace antics. "It was so tough. The pace was too fast. It seemed like they were going for a world record."

By lap 15 Haile was back in the lead, determined not to let the pace slacken. He ran a 62, pressing all the way. Kamathi was barely hanging on. It was a relentless, suicidal pace, and even Haile was anxious for some relief. On the backstretch of lap 16 he signaled to Kenenisa to take over. Kenenisa quickly obliged and led his three teammates and Kamathi through a 63 lap.

Still not satisfied that they were doing enough to break Kamathi, Haile took control once again and ran the 17th lap in 62. But Kamathi wouldn't fold, so Haile pushed on with another lap in 64. He wanted the Kenyan out of the race; he wanted revenge for the world championships in Edmonton two years earlier when Kamathi had grabbed the gold medal in the 10,000 meters; he wanted a sweep guaranteed for Ethiopia. But he shouldn't have had to do it on his own. Three times over the course of the 19th lap he looked over his shoulder and moved wide to create space for Kenenisa to come through, only to be rebuked.

It was at this point that Haile began to consider his options. *Do I slow down and force Kenenisa to take the pace? Why isn't he helping? This is what we agreed to do . . . to share the lead until everyone else in the race was gone. But if I start playing tactics and we lose a medal . . . ?*

Hence the crux of the problem: Haile didn't know how to fight his countryman. Kenenisa was a friend, not a rival. Moreover, Haile was team leader, the flag bearer for Ethiopian distance running. He was Kenenisa's mentor and role model. How then to turn against his prodigy?

As Haile continued to run at the front of the pack, he began to imagine what people would think back at home if he started working for himself: *So selfish and greedy to try his own tactics to win.* Kenenisa, of course, would be forgiven for running for his own cause. Such is the liberty of youth; such was the burden Haile carried as he found himself chained to the lead, obliged to serve everyone but himself.

Lap number 19 was back down to 61 seconds and for all intents and purposes the race was over. The Ethiopians' lead was now half a straightaway: Kamathi had quit and walked off the track, only to comment later, "They [the Ethiopians] were too strong." But Haile still wouldn't back down, and he turned in a 63 for lap 20. There were now just five laps to go.

On the homestretch of the 21st lap, Haile again moved out into lane two to encourage one of his teammates to help with the work. This was unprecedented front running from a man who had won both of his Olympic gold medals and all four of his world championship titles by playing coy and running from the back. But for this championship Haile seemed to have lost his will to run selfishly. And when his teammates again refused to assist him, he didn't slow down or move out into lane three and cut behind them to force them into the lead—tactics he would have certainly employed had there been two Kenyans or two Moroccans on his tail. Instead he kept things moving at the front all on his own.

Lap 22 took 63 seconds, lap 23 62 seconds. Haile had covered the last mile in a blazing 4:12, the last 2 miles in an incredible 8:22. With only two laps to go he seemed resigned to his position as pacesetter. He was now beginning to hug the rail and contemplate how to beat Kenenisa. *Perhaps another hard lap will break him?* So he ran a 61 for the penultimate lap. But it had little effect. Kenenisa was right behind him and just as balanced and steady as ever.

Haile answered the bell with Kenenisa in tow. Sileshi was 20 meters off the pace but absolutely secure in third. Ethiopia would have their sweep. This was now assured. Who would get gold and who would get silver, however, remained in the balance.

On the backstretch of the final lap it began to look like Kenenisa was the favorite. With 200 meters to go he pulled alongside Haile's right shoulder. They were even now: two men in the same position to win. This was the point where Haile needed to sprint; he needed a deep surge and a change of gears to hold off his challenger and transform what had so far been an epic endurance contest into a spirited half-lap dash. His knees should have begun to rise higher; his arms should have begun to pump faster, and his feet should have started to react quicker. But nothing happened. Nothing changed. He was stuck, unable to fire his kick.

Kenenisa sensed as much, and as young people are so apt to do he turned his back on his elder. By the middle of the final turn his lead was 10 meters. Halfway down the homestretch it was 20 meters.

Haile gamely pushed on, never slowing but never accelerating. Across the line Kenenisa (26:49.57) waited for Haile to finish (26:50.77), and immediately they embraced. Haile's smile was still wide in defeat, and he and Kenenisa stood arm in arm waiting for Sileshi to secure the bronze (27:01.44). Then the three medalists, who were 17 seconds clear of the fourth-place finisher, Ahmad Hassan from Qatar, began their victory lap with the Ethiopian flag held high above their heads. There was pure delight from the Ethiopian supporters in the crowd. In fact, there was pure delight from everyone in the crowd. What they had just witnessed was one of the most impressive displays of distance running ever put on. In sum, Kenenisa and Haile had both run their final 5000 meters under 13 minutes (12:57 and 12:58, respectively).

Through his victory Kenenisa clearly established himself as the leading distance runner in the world, and without question the man to beat heading into the Athens Olympics in a year's time. "I am Haile's successor," he told the world at the postrace press conference. Haile spoke more of the collective victory. "The most important thing tonight was to have three Ethiopians on the podium. We had team tactics and obviously they worked. Gold is no doubt better than silver, but I am as happy for Kenenisa as I am for myself."

Haile was also happy because he could see now that he still had a future on the track. "My time tonight was good," he said. "I still have some speed . . . I'm still very strong for the track." And in an effort to assert his reclaimed form even more deliberately, he decided not to return to Ethiopia with the rest of his teammates following the world championships but to go to Brussels instead to try to break his own 10,000-meter world record. This attempt, Wilfried Meert, the Ivo Van Damme Memorial meet director, took seriously. "When the greatest distance runner of all time specifically asks you to set up a world record race, it means that he truly believes he can do it. And the 10,000 in Brussels is a tradition we are very proud of, and now for this year's meeting it might be more special than usual."

When Haile entered the Roi Baudoin stadium in Brussels on September 5, the African drums that have come to typify this meeting were already in full swing. There was a sold-out crowd of 47,000 people, all of them anticipating a highly charged men's 10,000 meters.

The early pace was firm and steady and Haile was on the mark, sitting comfortably and running relaxed behind the initial pacesetters, Kenyans Martin Keino and Shadrack Korir. A third Kenyan rabbit, Leonard Mucheru, brought Haile through 5000 meters in 13:15.58. For a new record the pace would have to pick up. Haile needed to run 13:06 for his second 5000 meters. He began his quest gamely, pushing ahead with a fresh configuration of splits in his mind. But to his surprise he wasn't alone. An unheralded Kenyan, Nicholas Kemboi, whose best time for 10,000 meters was only 28:19.77, was hanging with him. Soon he and Haile began sharing the lead, and this race which had been billed as nothing more than a world record attempt was now a competition, too.

At the 8000-meter mark (21:17.01) Haile calculated that he needed to run just over 60 seconds for the remaining five laps to lower his record. He knew that was a tall order. It was the end of the season, after all. And what a long and trying season it had been: the three-race losing streak, the rise of Kenenisa, the injuries and illnesses, the world championships only one week before. Further, Haile felt his left calf tightening, something he knew would pose a problem if he was to push hard for the record. Also complicating matters was the pesky Kenyan running in his shadow. "I didn't know who this Kenyan guy was. His name, or anything about his ability. So my tactics needed to change. It was more important, I decided, to win than to set a record. I wanted to show everyone that I could still win a hard competition."

Immediately Haile drew on his experience and began to observe Kemboi's stride and to listen to his breathing. He was assessing his challenger's condition, and the feedback he was receiving fed his confidence.

Haile began to test Kemboi, moving the pace around with a series of surges and slowdowns. With one and a half laps remaining he made a push for home. But it wasn't enough. He could see from the scoreboard screen that Kemboi was still there. Instead of panicking, though, Haile braced himself for a second move. He waited and waited until he was down to just half a lap. Then with 200 meters remaining he sprinted hard. It was a splendid display: hands and knees high, torso tall, head still. A gap opened between him and Kemboi that quickly tripled like some exponential math formula gone mad. Haile would win unchallenged with a huge smile on his face. There was no question about it, he was back and as good as ever. He had closed with a 56.6 last lap; his final time (26:29.22) was the year's fastest, and the third-fastest all-time. "I can still do it," he pronounced afterward. "Everything feels perfect. This is my message to Kenenisa and every other 10,000 meter runner in the world: See you in Athens August 20, 2004."

14

The Road to Athens

Homer said there was "no greater glory" than victory by hands or feet. Pindar described winning in sport as "the grandest height to which mortals can aspire." Centuries later their words still ring true, and no doubt these ancient Greek writers would be delighted that our greatest contemporary celebration of sport, the Olympic Games, has returned to their home: Home to Greece where the Olympics began. And for Haile and Kenenisa the road to Athens, and their first track race of 2004, began on the same day, and over the same distance, but an ocean apart.

Haile was in Boston, Massachusetts, on January 31 to run 3000 meters at the Adidas Boston Indoor Games, and he was talking about regaining the indoor world record he had set for that distance on January 25, 1998 in Karlsruhe, Germany (7:26.15), a record that he had lost just a few days later (February 6) to Daniel Komen, who ran 7:24.90 in Budapest, Hungary. However, Haile's motivation to improve Komen's mark wasn't just that he wanted to see his world record tally of seventeen increase by one. It was also about speed and preparing for Athens.

"One thing is for sure," he said from Boston. "If I want to win a third Olympic gold medal at the 10,000 meters I will have to work hard on my speed. And a 3000 meter indoor race is the perfect tool to test it. I am confident that I will run a fast race here; my aim is to do something special."

Across the Atlantic Kenenisa was also preparing to do something special over 3000 meters. He was in Stuttgart, Germany for his first ever indoor track appearance. "It will be something new for me to race indoors," he said, "and I'm looking forward to the challenge. I have spoken to Haile and other Ethiopian athletes and they say I should have no problems coping. But can I break Komen's record? Of course it would be my dream, but it is a very difficult record to beat."

As Haile ate his breakfast at the meet headquarters' hotel in Boston, news from Stuttgart was on his mind. While he chewed his toast he turned the pages of the *Boston Globe,* hardly noticing a single headline. The six hour time difference between the United States and Germany gave him the advantage for once: Now he could sit back and wait for Kenenisa to act first. It was Jos who finally gave Haile the news from Stuttgart. A text message arrived on his mobile phone from his colleague, Ellen van Langen. "Kenenisa wins 7:30.77."

It was a good time—the current world leader, seventh-fastest in indoor track history. Certainly it was a positive indoor debut for the youngster. But it wasn't anything spectacular or other-worldly. So as Haile sat with Jos and finished his toast and slowly sipped his tea, he drew in his mind a very specific race plan. *Now I have a more definite target today . . . break 7:30.*

In a few hours Haile would know whether he could open his Olympic campaign one step ahead of Kenenisa.

The Reggie Lewis Arena in downtown Boston had been sold out for weeks. Of the four thousand spectators on hand at least a third were expat Ethiopians. The noise that circled the 200-meter banked oval once Haile was introduced was tremendous. And when the gun sounded the entire crowd was on their feet. Reaching the mile mark in a shade above four minutes, Haile knew he needed to pick up the pace if he was going best Kenenisa's mark from Stuttgart, let alone

Komen's world record. But left to do too much work on his own after the pace makers dropped out with five laps to go, Haile couldn't hit the splits he needed over the last kilometer, and with two laps remaining he backed down and focused on securing the win instead. And that he did easily.

Now it was Jos who sent a text message to Ellen. "Haile wins 7:35.24," he tapped into his mobile phone as Haile jogged a victory lap, blew kisses, and bowed and waved to the crowd. Ellen gave Kenenisa the news. Both men now knew where the other stood— their Olympic campaigns were officially underway.

The decision had been made at the end of 2003 that Haile and Kenenisa wouldn't face each other at all in their build-up to Athens. Their first head-to-head meeting of 2004, given that everything fell into place and they both reached Athens, would be the Olympic 10,000-meter final on August 20. This was what Jos, Haile, Kenenisa, and Doctor had all discussed and agreed upon. It would allow Haile and Kenenisa to prepare for Athens with one less distraction and pre-occupation. As a result, separate competition schedules were drawn up. For Kenenisa his next stop after Stuttgart would be Birmingham, England on February 20 to run 5000 meters. After that he would focus on defending his world short and long course cross-country titles in Brussels on March 20 and 21. Haile's next race after Boston would be another 3000 meters in Karlsruhe on February 15, followed by a 2-mile in Birmingham. Next he would turn his attention to retaining his world indoor 3000-meter title in Budapest on March 6 and 7. Then following a hard spell of spring training, both men would open their summer season in Hengelo on May 31, with Haile running 10,000 meters and Kenenisa 5000 meters. After Hengelo new discussions would ensue to determine how they each would carry forward for the remainder of the summer and into Athens.

In Karlsruhe Haile had one objective: to surpass Kenenisa's world-leading mark for 3000 meters that he had set in Stuttgart two weeks prior. Although Athens was on his mind, too: "I really need another 3000 meters to keep working on my speed. Last summer, the races I lost to Kenenisa and also to Chebii, were always on the last lap. For this year I knew I had to do something about that." And what Haile did in Karlsruhe indicated that his preparations were well on course.

"There's a big difference between 7:30 and 7:29," he told reporters following his 7:29.34 world leading performance. "No one seems to respect a time for 3000 meters starting with 7:30 quite like they do 7:29. So after today's result I must say that I am very happy. I'm also healthy, now that some small injury problems I was having to my left hip and groin are finally settled."

For Jos, whose interests in the Athens 10,000 meter final would obviously be divided between Haile and Kenenisa, Karlsruhe was an important move forward for Haile. "Haile has seen a chiropractor and a few other top physiotherapists to sort out some problems to his back," he explained. "He is now sprinting better and he is beginning to reap the benefits in terms of speed, as his endurance base has always been good. Karlsruhe was only a step on the way, he will get faster."

But fast enough to lower his own world record for 2 miles five days later in Birmingham? That was what Haile was suggesting. "I would like to do something special in Birmingham as this is likely to be my last indoor race ever in Britain," he told Tom Fordyce of the BBC. "Next year I will step up to the marathon and once you move to the marathon it is hard to combine that with running indoors. I have to accept that I can't be number one on the track for ever. That is normal—look at the history of athletics. Nurmi was eventually beaten, so was Zatopek, so was Viren. I'm only a human being but I'm still fighting. Nobody likes to be defeated, and I want to win. But if something happens like last summer at the world championships, what can I do? Rather than be beaten, it is better to move up to the marathon. I don't want to stop racing on the track, but I must face it: I'm losing my speed. I cannot be like five or six years ago, and if you are losing speed you have to move up to the longer distances, otherwise the youngsters can beat you easily. Take Kenenisa, for example. He is an outstanding athlete. We train together so he knows my weaknesses and tactics very well. It's very difficult to beat him. If you plot our form on a graph, his line is going up and mine is going down. That is why there is no question as to how important it would be if I could break my 2-mile world record in Birmingham. Then I would show the world that I am not an old man yet."

But Haile wasn't the only one in Birmingham with record setting ideas. Kenenisa was also imagining that possibility, although he was keeping those ideas mainly to himself. Only Chris Turner, reporting for the IAAF, managed to get the shy Ethiopian to reveal what he was thinking ahead of his indoor 5000 meters debut. "Yes, if I try hard enough," he told Turner, "I can break the 5000 meter record tonight." However, for Kenenisa to lower Haile's record of 12:50.38, which he set in Birmingham back in 1999, he would need to run a lifetime best by nearly two seconds, not an easy trick for someone so new to indoor running. It's no wonder, then, that he downplayed his chances to Turner.

"Indoor racing is very different from running outdoors. But, regardless, wherever I run I listen to my body first and that is how I plan my races. It all comes from inside. So at the moment it is hard to know what my body is saying about how well I will be able to break records indoors. I will just have to let my body speak the tactics to me tonight."

Jos, though, wasn't of the opinion that Kenenisa should be so casual about his record breaking tactics. "If he wants to be considered the next Haile Gebrselassie, which some people say he can be, then it's not enough to win titles and championships—something he has already proven that he can do. He must start to set records, too. And to begin to accumulate more than Haile, more than 17, it would be good if he could open his account tonight. And that won't be easy. Only Haile and Daniel Komen have ever run below 13 minutes for 5000 meters indoors. This will be a very hard record to beat."

Little did Kenenisa know, however, that he was about to get some unexpected help in his record chase, and from a most surprising source. After Haile finished his lunch in the meet hotel, and before going up to his room to relax and prepare for his own race, he took the elevator down to the lobby to find Jos.

"I have an idea," he said to his manager. "Why doesn't Martin Keino set the pace for Kenenisa tonight."

Jos was confused. "Haile, we've arranged for Martin to help you. You know he's the best rabbit on the circuit."

"Yes, I know, Jos. But let Kenenisa use him. He has a harder record to beat."

"But, Haile, that's your record. . . . Are you sure?"

"It's fine, Jos. Kenenisa needs more help than I do tonight. Martin's the best. Let him help Kenenisa."

So Jos picked up his mobile phone and called the meet director Ian Stewart and the switch was made. That done, Haile headed up to his room for a nap. There were four hours to pass before he had to leave for the track.

The global expansion of track and field today has seen running become a true money sport. In 2003 more than $26 million in prize money and bonuses was awarded in competitions around the world. Women's 800-meter world champion Maria Mutola of Mozambique, topped last year's rich list by earning over one million dollars. Haile reportedly earned $167,000, with Kenenisa right behind him on $164,000. These figures, however, don't include confidentially negotiated appearance fees and other performance bonuses and incentives athletes might have either with meet directors or their sponsors, what is in effect the "real" money earned by today's stars. For a world record at the Birmingham Indoor Grand Prix, for example, a healthy bonus of $30,000 was on offer—certainly a strong incentive for any aspiring record breaker.

As a result of such high stakes running has had to change. Athletes need to be "sold" as stars and personalities, as the action on the track isn't always enough to draw a crowd. There needs to be music, raffles, on-field interviews, jumbo screens, hospitality tents, and merchandise for sale. Fans need to be able to identify with the athletes and know who they are: Thus the proliferation of personal stories, and the excessive promotion of accessible athletes. For Haile this often means endless press conferences, product launches, appearances, and television and newspaper interviews. And this year, 2004, "Haile versus Kenenisa" is one story that everyone wants to know about: Who's going to win in Athens? Can the Emperor be dethroned by his protégé?

Many of Haile's Ethiopian teammates, however, along with a number of the leading Kenyan runners, haven't quite grasped the dynamics of promotion and publicity that's such an integral part of international track and field today. Either they're too shy, or their English is poor, or the very idea of running as a business is a strange concept to them. While these athletes certainly expect to be paid for racing, they may not necessarily understand where the money comes from, or that there's actually someone on the other end who's interested in making a return. It's simply enough for most of today's top African runners, according to John Manners, an expert on Kenyan running, to know how much they need to earn to support their families and buy some land back home. In which case, they seldom develop a larger vision for how to market themselves, or how to help the sport grow. Whereas a truly successful athlete today has to be part entrepreneur, an identity that Haile has certainly created.

Haile has always recognized the social and political benefits that the growth of track and field can hold for the next generation of Ethiopian runners: more opportunities for travel and education, more money coming into the country, the creation of new jobs through athletes investing their winnings, and a positive image of Ethiopia for the rest of the world to see. In fact, Haile has almost single-handedly paved the way for Ethiopia's next generation of runners by endearing himself with the public, and convincing meet promoters that they can trust Ethiopians to run a good race. To help Kenenisa earn an invitation to his first international competition, for example, the Great North Cross-Country Run in Gateshead, England back in January 2001, Haile personally called the meet director, Brendan Foster, to ask him to give this new young Ethiopian a chance. Kenenisa won in Gateshead that day, and as a result we have this exciting new young talent on the scene. All thanks to Haile, then, who's not afraid to support runners who might eventually go on to break his own world records, or eclipse his fame. It's in this way that Haile acts as much as a brand maker as he does an individual managing his own career.

Imagine the product is Ethiopian Runners. Because of Haile's fantastic winning record, captivating personality, and the positive core values his success represents—hard work, honesty, dedication—sports fans across the world all have an understanding of what is meant by Ethiopian Runners. To turn up at a track meet where there are Ethiopians competing means something very specific. You can be certain that they will be running one of the longer races, and there's a strong possibility that they will perform well, probably even win, if not set some type of new record. Because of their consistency, and because Ethiopian runners are continually striving to improve and strengthen their position as the world's greatest long distance running nation, an emotional bond forms between spectator and athlete, loyalty is fostered, and as a fan or track consumer you feel like you've entered into a relationship where a promise has been made on the part of the brand to stay true to its goal. Subsequently, you begin to develop a deep commitment to said product such that you are likely to identify yourself as an Ethiopian supporter and cheer for Ethiopian runners above everyone else, perhaps even runners from your own nation.

But as shrewd as Haile's marketing and promotional instincts may be today, he hasn't always understood the business side of sport. He says, for example, "Early in my career when I learned that some distance runners in America and Europe were on a better contract with Adidas than me I couldn't understand why. How was that possible? If I was the world record holder and Olympic champion shouldn't I have a better contract than runners I can regularly beat? But then it was explained to me that Adidas can sell more clothing and shoes in America and Europe than they can in Ethiopia, so they tell me that my return value may not be as high as lesser runners. That was a hard point for me to understand. But now because I am a businessman, and I have to be careful about where and how I spend my money I understand what Adidas is doing. I am under a lot of pressure to make the right decisions and keep my businesses going just like the directors of Adidas. I have more people than my wife and children to look after. There is my father, my brothers, my sisters, my aunts, my uncles, my cousins . . . and their children, too. The list it just goes on."

However, in professing his willingness to accept the business model and how it operates in sport today, Haile will never allow market forces to completely control what he does on the track: "If one of my sponsors pushed me to win a race or set a record because they told me it would be good for their product I would be very mad. But thankfully that has never happened. Adidas, for example, has been very good to me and so supportive throughout my whole career, both during the ups and the downs. And that's important because I need to be comfortable with my sponsors. Once a large European brewery wanted to sponsor me but I told Jos no. 'Jos,' I said, 'I'm sure the money is good and it's a fair deal, but I would not be comfortable having a beer company's name on my shirt and so close to my heart.' And Jos honored my decision. He always does. He might pester me with more information about something that he thinks is a good idea, but he always allows me to have the final decision. And I think that's one reason why he is the best manager in athletics, and why we have had such a strong relationship that has lasted so many years. Really, we are like best friends."

Let alone market forces controlling him, Haile also won't allow national forces to influence too heavily the decisions he makes about his running. He is a man who runs for himself first, which is why he's carrying on to Athens—to try and make history and become the first athlete to win three 10,000 meter gold medals: his Olympic hat-trick—not because his country expects him to compete there.

"Success has to come from yourself," he believes. "My motivation is all inside, and it's still there after all these years. Otherwise I wouldn't be running any more. There are some people in Ethiopia who think that running for one's country must be the most important thing. These are some of the old men left over from our past communist days. They especially believe this when the Olympics and world championships are taking place. While I understand it's important that I represent Ethiopia well when I race, it cannot be my sole reason for running. I am not a soldier. If someone tells me it's my duty to do something for Ethiopia I feel very bad. I'm offended, actually. So I tell people, 'Please don't push me to do something for my country or something else. I run for myself and my country. And all my power I will put into winning for Ethiopia.' The feeling for wanting to do sport has to come from inside. No one can give it to you. I don't even care if the president or prime minister tells me to run for Ethiopia. I simply don't understand such an approach to sport."

But that's not to say Haile is immune to national pressure. His tactics in Paris last summer at the world championships where he led for most of the race were largely dictated by his fear of Ethiopia losing a medal. "Yes, I wanted us [Kenenisa and Sileshi] to break free from the Kenyans to secure success for Ethiopia," he says. "No, I couldn't give up the lead once we were clear from them and run more for myself. What if a Kenyan got back in the race and took one of our medals because I was slowing the race down and playing with tactics as a way of upsetting Kenenisa after he refused to help with the pacing? Okay, sure, that's what I should have done if I was only running for myself. But things aren't as simple as that. If we lost a medal I would have been the one to get in trouble. Everyone back home would have said, 'You should have known better. . . . As the older one, why did you let this happen?'"

Clearly, then, Haile faces a dilemma: the tension between serving himself and serving the state. Can he run to satisfy his own interests? In Athens he hopes to try. Although the pressure on him to spearhead a sweep of the medals by setting a pace that no one besides his two teammates can tolerate will be enormous. But then Athens is still half a year away, and a lot can happen in the meantime. More to the fore of Haile's mind is supporting Kenenisa as he prepares to run his first indoor 5000 meters. As such, he leaves the warm-up area below the track in Birmingham where he arrived from the hotel an hour earlier and pushes through a set of heavy double-doors where he steps out into a large concrete foyer and sits down to watch Kenenisa's race on television.

Joining Haile in front of the television are his teammates, Abiyote Abate and Kutre Dulecha. As Haile waits for Kenenisa's race to start, he exhibits some clear signs of nervousness: His feet are tapping, and he's speaking incredibly fast to Abiyote and Kutre. The anxious movements he's making in his metallic seat create a harsh scraping sound against the concrete floor causing a number of people nearby to wince. Finally, in an effort to try and calm down, Haile crosses his legs and leans back in his chair, but only a second later he's leaning forward again staring up at the television attached to the wall and tugging on his fingers as if to separate them from his hands.

Over the early laps Kenenisa is invisible behind the three pacesetters. And at various points his race is minimized into the upper right-hand corner of the screen when a British interest appears in a field event. Obviously Haile would have a better vantage point trackside, but with his own race scheduled to begin in just over an hour, he doesn't have time to negotiate the different levels of Birmingham's National Indoor Arena. Better to stay down in the bowels, he's decided, close to the warm-up area.

After 3000 meters (7:47.27), Martin Keino drops out and steps onto the infield having completed the perfect rabbiting job. The compact, muscled figure of Kenenisa fills the screen. Seeing the relaxed expression on his friend's face, Haile shouts, "He can do it." Although the BBC's commentators, Brendan Foster and Steve Cram, are quick to point out that Kenenisa is eight tenths of second behind Haile's record setting pace from 1999. But then almost on cue, and seemingly in response to Foster's and Cram's calculations, Kenenisa runs a 29.96 second lap to get back on record pace. He then runs a slightly faster lap, 29.92, and then 30.45, and suddenly with seven laps to go he is 1.7 seconds ahead of Haile's pace.

As subsequent laps pass—30.53, 30.85, 30.57—Haile reads each split out loud when it appears in the upper left hand corner of the screen, repeating as he does, "He can do it. . . . He can do it."

Also visible on the television screen as Kenenisa completes each lap is Jos. He is urging him on, waving his arms and leaning out onto the track to scream, "Lift . . . rhythm, pick it up . . . faster."

By the time Kenenisa has just four laps to go, a crowd of athletes, officials, and coaches have gathered around the television Haile is watching. As Kenenisa powers on, now ahead of Haile's record schedule by a comfortable 2.8 seconds, they glance over at Haile to try and gauge his reaction. Is he jealous? Resentful? But Haile's ongoing chant indicates otherwise: "He can do it. He can do it."

Kenenisa completes his twenty-second lap in 30.74, and the lap after that in 31.16. Now with two laps to go the strain starts to mark his face. In fact, he's losing much of the advantage he had previously built up. Jos was obviously right when he said, "This will be a very hard record to beat."

For his penultimate lap Kenenisa runs 31.10 and loses more time: he's six hundredths down on Haile's schedule and there's just one lap to go. Foster comments over the TV, "Bekele is tiring . . . he's struggling . . . his legs are heavy." But Haile remains steadfast. He's rocking back and forth in his seat. "Come on Kenenisa," he's pleading. "Come on."

When Haile set this record five years ago he ran his last lap in 28.6, but Kenenisa's going to need something even faster. It's obvious from the tortured expression on his face that he's trying his hardest. His eyes are wide open and pure white like a car's headlights at midnight; the bones on his face mark his skin with deep ridges. He's reaching well below the surface, trying to make his mark, trying to approach the line in the sand that Haile's drawn and cross it. This is new territory for Kenenisa. He's never set a world record before, and it's going to be close.

For a few agonizing seconds the outcome hangs in the balance and Haile is speechless as he watches the screen, watches perhaps as his own piece of history gets wiped away. It's a liminal moment for him. He's between spaces—a world where he remains the record holder, another where he doesn't. He appears poised, though, to accept the outcome either way.

But reality quickly asserts itself and what's about to occur becomes evident. With 100 meters to go Haile is out of his chair and on his feet. He can see from Kenenisa's high knee lift and strong arm action that he hasn't given up.

"Yes, Kenenisa," he shouts. "Yes. Yes." And when the clock stops at 12:49.60, a new world record by 0.78 of a second, Haile bursts into a torrent of claps and high fives with everyone around him. Then a second later he's off. "Time to go warm up," he shouts to no one in particular, and he's through the double doors and back inside the warm-up area. There is exactly one hour before the start of his own race and his attempt to match Kenenisa by setting a new world record for 2 miles.

Unfortunately, Haile couldn't match Kenenisa on this night. The early pacing he received was erratic and unbalanced. He could never establish the even rhythm that's so crucial when it comes to breaking long-distance running world records. With a lap to go Haile shook off Jos's enthusiasm and encouragement. He was in the lead and just wanted to finish. But on the backstretch of the final lap his legs began to slow. He looked weighted down; he was straining to swallow enough air, and the lines in his brow grew more and more pronounced. *Am I going to make it?* he was wondering. Also noticing that Haile was in trouble was Markos Geneti, a 19-year-old Ethiopian, who was in second place and closing fast. Around the last turn with 50 meters to go Geneti was poised to pull even with Haile. But Haile was oblivious: the volume of noise surrounding him made it impossible for him to hear his countryman approaching. In fact, when Geneti pulled alongside Haile, Haile stumbled slightly from the shock. And in the fraction of a second that it took him to regain his composure and mount a response, Geneti had opened a small lead and there simply wasn't enough ground left for Haile to claim it back. In a flash they were both across the finish line, Geneti first in 8:08.39, Haile next in 8:08.65.

For the many expert track and field commentators on hand in Birmingham that night a real sign of change was evident: Kenenisa claiming his first world record, and Haile losing to an unheralded teammate. No disparaging comments were passed, simply honest assessments: "The future is in question for Gebrselassie," wrote *Athletics Weekly*. The news that came later in the week, that Haile had decided to forgo the indoor world championships to rest a few niggling injuries, followed a few weeks later by Kenenisa's defense of his short and long course world cross-country titles—his "triple-double"—only seemed to confirm what many people were already thinking: The track career of the greatest long distance runner of all time was at its end and his successor had arrived. And what happened in Hengelo on May 31 when the 2004 outdoor season opened certainly didn't help to reverse anyone's opinion.

Among those in Hengelo to keep an eye on developments and assess Haile's and Kenenisa's Olympic progress was Doctor. Even he was hesitant to predict Haile's future. "Athens will be very difficult for Haile. We shall see. These youngsters today are strong, very much like Haile was 12 years ago when he first began running well internationally. I remember even earlier than that, back in 1987, when I first saw Haile run. Immediately I knew he would be a champion. It was all because of his ambition. He wanted to succeed so badly; he wanted to change his life, and match the achievements of Miruts Yifter. And his progression was very fast. Although initially he was hesitant to pass our senior runners like Fita Bayesa and others. He had too much respect for them; he didn't believe it was right for him to overtake them. I made him train on his own for a few weeks and then I showed him the times of the others to get him to see that he was running faster. When he realized he should be ahead of them I let him back into the group. I had to do something similar with Kenenisa last year.

It was very hard for him to imagine passing Haile in training: no one passes, Haile, you see. That's what all the young boys grew up thinking. When Kenenisa saw that his times in training were better than Haile's, he began to develop enough confidence to run ahead of Haile. Now they train together often, and the workouts they complete are amazing. Before coming to Hengelo, for example, they did a 20-lap controlled time trial, passing 5000 meters in 13:15. And remember, this is at altitude. Because of what I see in training every day, and because I'm constantly measuring various parameters, new world records and the amazing things these boys do never surprise me. I predicted every one of Haile's records. Likewise I wouldn't be surprised if Kenenisa did something special here tonight. He is in excellent condition, and Haile's world record of 12:39.36 could be under threat."

Clearly Haile and Doctor have developed a special relationship over the years. And Haile gives tremendous credit to Doctor. "Doctor is an excellent coach. He understands running very well. He was quite a good runner himself, actually. In 1964 he was selected to run in the 800 meters and 1500 meters at the Olympics in Rome. But instead he chose to go to Hungary and study coaching. I'm glad that's the decision he made. His system for training us is very effective. There are no secrets behind his methods. To begin with he has great raw material, so many young boys and girls with very strong ambition. Next are his schedules combined with our hard work. The result is bound to be success. Doctor is also like a teacher for us. Sometimes he knows he must be firm, other times gentle. He is tough but fair. He is like our father for all of Ethiopia's runners."

And like a true father, Doctor couldn't have been prouder as he watched his two greatest athletes run in Hengelo. Both races were thrilling, both races gave a clear insight into the future. First to approach the line was Kenenisa in the 5000 meters, followed 45 minutes later by Haile in the 10,000 meters. And this is something of what Doctor would have seen . . .

Slightly cool and cloudy conditions are the measure of the day as the athletes in the men's 5000 meters walk onto the track from the holding area beneath the south stands of the Fanny Blankers-Koen Stadium. They're quickly slotted into their lane positions; the only competitor introduced to the crowd is Kenenisa and polite applause follows. Seconds later the race is off.

The first 400 meters passes in 58.50 seconds, the next in 63.24, the third in 62.78. Kenenisa is tucked behind the two rabbits as a long line of runners, all running smoothly, are in tow.

Leading is David Kiplak from Kenya, followed by Luke Kipkosgei, also from Kenya. No wind is upsetting the field; the flags that line the stadium's upper rim are limp. Nothing extraordinary is taking place just yet.

On the backstretch Jos reads out splits and as usual instructs Kenenisa to run faster. Dressed in a gray suit with a mauve shirt and a red tie, he busily configures times in order to give Kenenisa an accurate account of his progress.

With eight laps to go Kenenisa is still in third. Then on the backstretch of the fifth lap he moves past Kipkosgei and into second. Kiplak is struggling to maintain the pace Kenenisa wants. He can feel the eager Ethiopian pressing against his heels. When he realizes that he's only getting in the way, he steps off the track at the same moment that the infield clock freezes to mark the 2000 meter split—5:05.47.

Kenenisa is now in the lead. With him, however, is his teammate, Mulegeta Wondimu, whose best 5000 meters is only 13:26.01. Clearly he won't be close to Kenenisa for long, but he is using this opportunity to try to lower his personal best.

Pressing hard from the front now, Kenenisa's ambition begins to show: his expression is intense, his stride is sharp followed by a smooth, clean lift off. He and Wondimu are 70 meters clear of the field. But then Kenenisa begins to separate himself from his country-man. He is in complete flow: arms rhythmic, head steady. His all-gray Nike uniform hugs his light, taut form. With every step his lead widens and when he reaches 3000 meters (7:37.34) it's obvious that this race is over: it's just a matter of time now. But what will the time be? A new world record perhaps?

On top of the homestretch, across from the 100-meter starting line, a mass of Ethiopian supporters wave Ethiopian flags, clap, twirl, jump, and scream. Kenenisa storms down the backstretch of lap number 7 in response to their urging.

The pace continues. Kenenisa's knees punch on; with each stride he ingests another giant gulp of the track. He shows no signs of slowing, and everyone in the stadium is standing now. The announcer screams his support: "It's Kenenisa Bekele, ladies and gentleman . . . this is world-record pace."

By 4000 meters (10:07.93) a slight breeze has risen but Kenenisa isn't bothered. He storms around the second turn, his eyes intent, eager to pass the finish line and begin his penultimate lap.

Suddenly, though, the crowd becomes distracted by a new Dutch record in the men's pole vault. A busy buzz of national pride swirls above Kenenisa as his efforts are momentarily lost in the mayhem. But by the time he answers the bell the crowd's attention has returned. Photographers, too, are poised; a mob of them has gathered by the finish line.

The crowd continues to scream; the stadium announcer provides updates, interpreting Kenenisa's pace and explaining exactly what it might mean . . . "He's still on record pace, ladies and gentlemen."

With 350 meters remaining Kenenisa is leaning forward working for traction, pushing for pace. With 200 meters to go he passes a lapped runner. All eyes in the stadium are on just this one man. The noise builds even more as Kenenisa lifts himself into his final sprint.

And when he crosses the finish line "Simply the Best" blasts over the PA and he is mobbed by the press. He smiles easily for the photographers, recovering his breath instantly. He is holding up a bouquet of flowers in his right hand and a water bottle in his left. The infield clock behind him spells out the news: "5000m WR 12:37.35!" Haile's six-year-old record has been reduced by over two seconds.

As the remaining runners in the field cross the line no one takes much notice. Kenenisa is half-way down the backstretch on his lap of honor. He's waving the Ethiopian flag and anyone who can reaches out from the stands to touch him: everyone wants to find out if he is real, they want to feel a piece of distance running's future.

After an uneventful men's and women's 800 meters, the field for the men's 10,000 meters reaches the track. While Haile waits for the starter's orders a wall of photographers stand before him. What's he thinking as they snap away? Certainly he'd like to equal Kenenisa and set a world record of his own tonight. But is he ready? He knows now what kind of shape Kenenisa is in, and in less than half an hour he'll know where he stands. So will Doctor, so will Jos, so will the whole world—the Olympic 10,000 meter final is just 11 weeks away.

With the start imminent, Haile performs a few quick hops and the stadium approaches the hushed silence usually only reserved for the start of a 100 meter race. A moment later the 17 runners spill from the line.

By 400 meters (61.89) a single line has formed; Haile is in fourth. In front of him are the designated pacesetters: Francis Bowen and Martin Keino of Kenya, and Zersenay Tadesse from Eritrea.

At 1000 meters (2:38.75) Haile still holds fourth. The 10,000 is the last event on the track, and as the action in the pole vault and the shot put reaches a climax the crowds' attention momentarily shifts from the track to the field. But that's okay, as over these early laps both the runners and the audience need time to settle in.

When the lead pack reaches 1600 meters (4:15.20) Bowen drops out and Keino takes over the pacing duties as Haile moves up one position into third. In Haile's wake is his teammate, the 10,000 meter bronze medalist from last summer's world championships, Sileshi Sihine.

Haile is running directly on the rail not wasting an extra inch of distance. Dressed in a matching blue singlet and shorts his stride is light and direct against the red tartan track.

At 2000 meters (5:18.50) the order remains the same. These four—Keino, Tadesse, Haile, Sileshi—are packed tightly.

Haile's brother Tekeye, who lives in nearby Utrecht, is watching the race carefully from the side of the track. Jos is also watching carefully. And so is Doctor. And all the while the clock keeps running: the tempo builds and builds, the rhythm rises.

At 3000 meters (8:00.03) Keino drops out leaving Tadesse to manage the pace. Haile is in second, Sileshi is in third. The rest of the field is spread out and fragmented with almost everyone running alone.

Entering the homestretch to complete 4000 meters (10:39.03), and with 15 laps still to go, Tadesse unexpectedly drops out. This is the first glitch in the race's plan as he was supposed to carry on for a further two laps at least. Haile is thrust into the lead and Jos is furious. He is having strong words with Tadesse from his position in the infield. But Tadesse only waves his arms about and walks away.

The question now is whether Haile will have to bear the burden of leading the remainder of the race—another 6000 meters—or will Sileshi share in the work? Jos is adamant for Sileshi to do his fair share and he makes his feelings heard when he and Haile pass him on the next lap. Finally on the backstretch of lap twelve, Sileshi overtakes Haile and assumes the lead. He comes through 5000 meters (13:19.00) with Haile directly behind him. It seems now that a world record is out of the question.

At 6000 meters (16:03.28) Haile is back in the lead. The advantage he shares with Sileshi over the rest of the field is almost a full straight-away. At the start of the next lap (number 16) Sileshi again moves into the lead. Haile knows that Sileshi can't be taken lightly. He has been training with him and he is aware that he has a real race on his hands. Any idea of a new record has long passed from Haile's mind: he needs to concentrate instead on making the right moves to win. But as last year indicated, Haile seems to have trouble employing hard tactics against his younger teammates.

With six laps to go Sileshi is back at the front. At 8000 meters (21:25.02) he still leads—there are just five laps to go. It's obvious that neither runner will break the other. Their endurance just runs too deep; this will come down to a sprint finish. And perhaps doubting the potency of his sprint, Haile surges past Sileshi as they complete the next lap, leaving four more to go.

Haile leads through 9000 meters (24:07.31), and his stride remains crisp and light. With two laps to go he appeals to Sileshi to share the pace, but no help is coming. And Haile does nothing to force his teammate into the lead, or to turn the tactics to his advantage. Something he would certainly do if it was a Kenyan tracking him so closely this late in a race.

At the start of the final lap the question arises, Who will strike first? Around turn number one, nothing. On top of the backstretch, noth-ing. With 200 meters remaining and Haile still in the lead and Sileshi inches off his shoulder, again nothing.

Entering turn two for the final time Sileshi begins to apply some pressure. But Haile responds by gradually accelerating. And then in almost an identical replay to the 10,000-meter race run here last year, when Kenenisa struck from 150 meters out to beat Haile for the first time, Sileshi makes his move from exactly the same spot, and it's as definitive a strike as Kenenisa's was and he sprints away easily for his first victory over Haile, 26:39.69 to 26:41.58.

Jos immediately congratulates both runners as they head off arm-in-arm on a shared victory lap. Despite losing, Haile retains his "Mr. Hengelo" title as it's he the crowd hoist on top of their shoulders and parade down the homestretch. The photographers surround Haile, too, and all the autograph hounds. It has been a great evening for Ethiopian distance running: Haile remains loved by his fans, and the tradition of world record breakers lives on.

With barely a week for the world to digest Kenenisa's new global mark for 5000 meters, he was in Ostrava in the Czech Republic on June 8 to try and break Haile's 10,000-meter world record from 1998 (26:22.75). And again he got what he came for, putting on a remarkable display of front running to record a time of 26:20.31.

Afterwards Kenenisa spoke to Donald McRae of *The Guardian*. "The first 5000 meters was not good [13:14.42] . . . My pacemakers did not have such a good performance. I had to run on my own the last 12 laps and make up the time. It was only on the last lap that I felt I had the record. I had to run about 58 seconds and it was tough because I was very tired over the final two kilometers. If the pace is good for the whole 10,000 meters, then maybe I can take off another two seconds."

The writing certainly seemed to be on the wall now: it would be hard stopping Kenenisa in Athens. There was even talk of him attempting a 5000m/10,000m double. But when asked by McRae what he thought about his chances at the Olympics the youngster offered a surprisingly coy response. Was he concerned there might be someone out there who could spoil his plans?

"Yes, I want to be Olympic champion," he said. "But my year would not be a disappointment to me if I did not win in Athens. I am already world 10,000-meter champion, but the Olympics are a new game. Athens will be my first time and I do not know how I will feel. The Olympics are so big, bigger than everything. Maybe I will make some little mistakes in my running which would not matter normally, but at the Olympics everybody wants gold so much that you never know what could happen."

Was Kenenisa contemplating Sydney 2000 and how Haile had seemingly come back from the dead to claim the 10,000 meter gold medal? Perhaps he was being wise not to count Haile out too soon despite defeating him in their last three meetings. It just goes to show how infective a living legend's reputation can be. After all, it was Haile's first Olympic performance that inspired Kenenisa to become a runner. As he explains, "For the Atlanta Olympics in 1996 I was 14 and I watched Haile on television. On top of the television I also had a radio. I didn't want to miss anything. And now we will be running in the Olympics together. For me it is a big dream."

Noises concerning Kenenisa's Olympic chances were also coming from outside Ethiopia. Kenya's national coach, Mike Kosgei, who spoke to Omulo Okoth from the *East African Standard* said, "The Ethiopian explosion is a flash in the pan. Wait and see what team we select for the Olympics and you can forget about Kenenisa Bekele and the other Ethiopians. If you think they are sitting pretty ahead of the Games, you are terribly mistaken."

Curiously, one man not saying much about any Kenyan's or Ethiopian's chances in Athens, including his own, was Haile. "It's going to be very difficult," was all he would say. "I will try to do my best, prepare as well as I can, and we will see." Kenenisa wasn't sure, either, how his mentor was feeling about his prospects in Athens especially after having lost his two most prized world records in the space of just nine days. "I don't know how Haile is really feeling," he said. "He will always look happy because we are friends. But we are also competitors, so I don't know what he thinks inside." No one did, actually. After Hengelo all Haile would say to Jos was, "Don't worry, Jos. Don't worry. You worry far too much when I lose. It's just one race. I will be fine. . . . I will be fine. I will just go home now and train harder."

Kenenisa, though, continued to race. From Ostrava he traveled to Gateshead, England (June 27) to run 3000 meters. Conditions were windy and cold and he posted an uninspiring victory in 7:41.31. For his next start he was scheduled to run 5000 meters in Lausanne, Switzerland on July 6. However, in taking every possible precaution to arrive in Athens unscathed, he decided not to run after feeling a slight twinge in his right Achilles tendon. This proved a wise move and within a few days he was back in Ethiopia and training in full.

Similarly, Haile kept churning out one hard session after another. Through the trails around Entoto he was pushing himself like never before; on the track he was grinding out long, intense repeats. He was maintaining his strict gym routine, and doing all he could to hone his sprint finish. In short, he wasn't going to arrive in Athens unprepared. The opportunity to win a third gold medal at 10,000 meters was too important to him. "There is no question it would be my greatest achievement," he said. "It would be wonderful, something very special." In fact, so serious was Haile about preparing for Athens that he moved out of his house and entered a strict training camp set up by Doctor.

In early June Haile took up residence at the Ararat Hotel on the outskirts of Addis Ababa, handy both to the forests for long runs and the national stadium for speed work. All of those in contention for a spot on Ethiopia's Olympic team were brought together by Doctor to eat, sleep, and train as one. Only on Sundays did Haile go home to see his family and get his laundry done. In speaking about the value of such a camp he said, "Discipline is the key to running well. I may not like living away from my family for so long, but it is something that I accept I must do in order to run my best. It's all part of the many sacrifices that are required to be a champion."

However, hard training alone doesn't bring one championships. It's also important to become race fit, which was why Haile broke from camp to compete over 5000 meters at the London Grand Prix (July 30). "It's vital that I test myself before Athens," he said, "especially since I haven't had a race in two months. If I can run a good time in London, something around 13 minutes, and finish with good speed, it will mean that my Olympic preparations are going well."

And indeed, Haile, got the performance he was after. Running in a controlled, well-paced manner, he moved into the lead with two and a half laps to go. But when Craig Mottram from Australia made a push for the front with 450 meters remaining, Haile gladly fell back into second. And there he sat until the final 70 meters when he stepped clear of the tall Australian to win in a British All-Comers record of 12:55.51. It was exactly the confidence boost he needed. As such, there wasn't much more for him to do in the remaining three weeks before his next race: He would return to the training camp in Ethiopia before departing for Athens on August 16 with the rest of his Olympic teammates. That would then leave him with three days to put the finishing touches on his shape before the evening of August 20 and the start of the men's Olympic 10,000-meter final.

Athens, 2004. Kenenisa, Sileshi, and Haile lead the 10,000m final.
Photo by Mark Shearman

15

Athens, August 20, 2004

On Tuesday August 17 Haile checked into his room at the Olympic village in Athens. In three days he would be on the track to defend his Olympic 10,000 meter title. Or would he? News was beginning to surface that all was not well. Richard Lewis of the *London Times* had broken the story two days earlier. "Haile in race to beat injury," his headline read. Haile's left Achilles tendon was giving him trouble. All the speed work he had been doing over the last two months on the rock hard track in Ethiopia's dilapidated national stadium was beginning to take its toll. There was severe inflammation around his tendon and the bursa. He even flew to Munich to see the renowned sports doctor Hans Muller-Wolfhart after he had returned home from the London Grand Prix. And when Dr. Muller-Wolfhart completed his examination he prescribed immediate radiation treatment. But to be effective radiation treatment must be accompanied by complete rest—an option Haile was reluctant to consider.

"I love the Olympics," he said. "They are so special. I am praying everyday that I will be okay. If this was any other race I would pull out. But the Ethiopian people expect me to run. . . . I have to think about that, too. Athens is not only for myself. Besides, I have had injury problems before at the Olympics—blisters in Atlanta, my right Achilles in Sydney. It seems to be my curse. But on both occasions I managed all right. I won gold. I hope it's the same for me now."

But Jos was less optimistic about Haile's chances. "Even when he walks he is in pain," he said. "Since his race in London three weeks ago his Achilles has really gotten bad. It was there before, but it was under control. My advice would be that he doesn't run. But the pressure Haile is under from the Ethiopian Olympic Committee is just tremendous: They think he has to run for the Kenyans to be unsettled. . . . They want him in the race to support Kenenisa and Sileshi. Even the president of Ethiopia called Haile last week to urge him to run. But all of these people are only thinking short term: they want as many medals as possible so that Ethiopia looks strong, especially compared to Kenya. I'm concerned with Haile's future and his health. If he runs through this injury he could seriously hurt himself. But there is really nothing left for me to do. Haile said so himself. 'Jos, you need to understand the pressure I am under,' he told me. 'I have to run.' So I am sure that's what will happen."

Indeed, on August 18, the deadline for teams to announce their entrants in the men's 10,000 meters, Ethiopia's Olympic Committee submitted three names: Kenenisa Bekele, Sileshi Sihine, and Haile Gebrselassie. Haile's bid for a third consecutive 10,000 meters gold medal was on.

Friday night August 20, an hour before Haile was due to start warming up for his third Olympic 10,000 meter final, he sat quietly by himself rubbing his injured Achilles tendon. "It's so stiff," he kept repeating. In the last three days he had only been able to do a little light jogging. In fact, in the last three weeks his training had been severely curtailed by the pain running through his left leg. But he had been assured by doctors working in the Olympic village that he ran no risk of permanently damaging his Achilles tendon if he competed tonight. So here he was, on the warm-up track adjacent to the main Olympic stadium, beginning to prepare himself to step up to the starting line in just over two hours.

Concerning his chances he said, "If I win a medal it will be fantastic. If not, that's all right as long as an Ethiopian still wins the race. Ideally I hope the same thing can happen here as happened in Paris."

Haile was of course referring to the sweep of the medals in the men's 10,000 meters that he and his teammates achieved at last summer's world championships. In that race their tactics had been straightforward and incredibly effective: push the pace after 5000 meters and break the race wide open. Everyone in Athens expected the three Ethiopians to follow a similar strategy tonight. So when the first seven laps passed at a relatively comfortable pace, as slow as 70 seconds per lap, no one was very surprised.

It wasn't until lap eight that events began to turn. Haile moved to the front of the pack from his position near the back and led the field through the fastest lap of the race thus far (64.02). Three laps later, after split times of 64.31, 65.01, and 61.30 the three Ethiopians were where they wanted to be. They had inserted themselves into first, second, and third. The sweep was on. Haile, Kenenisa, and Sileshi were in position to control the race the rest of the way. And the order didn't change for the next seven laps: Ethiopia one, two, three. But Haile and his teammates had company. Hanging on gamely was Boniface Kiprop from Uganda and Zersenay Tadesse from Eritrea. But where were the Kenyans? Incredibly, they were largely absent from the proceedings. Only Charles Kamathi, the 2001 10,000 meter world champion, seemed to be making an attempt to remain in contact with the lead pack.

There were now seven laps to go in this Olympic final and the crowd was finally beginning to show some interest. No Greek athlete was entered, but one runner in the field was receiving a reception from the crowd as if he was a native—although, when compared to the other runners in the lead group, that athlete appeared to be struggling:

Haile's right arm had begun to flail about uncontrollably, his stride looked long and heavy not short and crisp, and he was open-mouthed and grimacing broadly. He was clearly in trouble.

Entering the first turn of lap nineteen Kiprop passed Haile without any resistance, thus pushing the defending champion into fourth place and breaking up the Ethiopian stranglehold on the first three positions. Down the backstretch Kenenisa gazed up at the scoreboard screen. He could see that Haile was in distress. Immediately he turned and looked at Sileshi as if to say, *What should we do?* They appeared lost without their leader. The Greek crowd was also stunned at this turn of events and a succession of gasps began to pass through the stands. Meanwhile, Kiprop continued his charge forward overtaking Sileshi next and then Kenenisa. It was now Uganda first, Ethiopia second and third, and Eritrea fourth as even Tadesse had managed to pass Haile, relegating the great man to fifth place. It had to be said that an Ethiopian sweep was now in serious jeopardy.

With Kiprop up front the nineteenth lap passed in a slow 66.02 seconds. But Kenenisa and Sileshi weren't about to do anything to up the tempo. They could see that Haile was slowly clawing his way back to the front after latching onto Tadesse's shoulder. Three times they looked behind them to check on their teammate's progress: Haile was definitely getting back into medal contention. *Come on Haile*, their actions proclaimed. *Come on, we're waiting for you.*

Kiprop covered the twentieth lap in 67.46 as the pace dropped further. There were just five laps remaining and it was beginning to look as if the medals would be decided by a mad sprint down the final homestretch. But that was a scenario the Ethiopians wanted to avoid. For anything can happen in a kick finish. However, Kenenisa and Sileshi continued to wait for Haile. They were deliberately laying off the pace to buy their friend more time. He was only a few yards behind them. This was an incredibly risky move, though. No doubt

Kenenisa and Sileshi would've preferred to be up front running hard and doing everything they could to open a clear advantage in order to secure their hold on the first two medals. Yet here they were allowing the pace to dawdle in an attempt to give Haile a second chance. So much for selfishness at the Olympic Games. This was their mentor and teacher who was in trouble, the man who had inspired both of them to take up running in the first place. No way were they about to set him adrift.

It didn't take long for Kiprop and Tadesse to realize what Kenenisa and Sileshi were trying to do. Certainly they didn't want Haile back in the mix. So nearing the end of the twenty-first lap they began to increase the tempo themselves in an attempt to drop Haile for good. And immediately Haile fell off the pace. He simply couldn't keep up. Kenenisa and Sileshi tucked in behind Kiprop and Tadesse to cover their move. It was at that point that Kenenisa took one last look over his shoulder. He could see that Haile was finished: his head was down, he was gasping for air, his stride was slowing. It was all over: Any chance of a sweep was gone. And so down the backstretch Kenenisa did the only thing left for him to do: he stepped out into lane two and surged past Tadesse and Kiprop. And with Sileshi right behind him they opened up an immediate advantage.

With three laps to go the battle for gold was now between Kenenisa and Sileshi; the battle for bronze was between Tadesse and Kiprop. For the first time in 12 years of championship 10,000 meter races (six world championships beginning in 1993 and three Olympic games beginning in 1996) Haile wasn't in the final fight for the medals. He was in fifth place, and that was where he would remain as Kenenisa went on to run an extraordinary last lap in 53.02 to claim his first Olympic gold medal. Behind him came Sileshi in second, Tadesse in third, and Kiprop in fourth. Kenenisa's winning time of 27:05.10 was a new Olympic record eclipsing Haile's mark of 27:07.34 that he set in Atlanta in 1996. The world now had a new 10,000 meter Olympic champion—a new name to be hailed as the leading distance runner in the world: Kenenisa Bekele.

For Haile his fifth place finish in 27:27.70 was by no means a disgrace. He had come into these games injured and short on training. He was there to witness the passing of the torch in distance running supremacy, and he couldn't have been prouder of how the future looked. As he commented afterwards, "I tried to win a medal tonight but it didn't work. Over the last four to five laps the pain became too much, and my fitness just wasn't there. Today it didn't happen for me. But it did happen for Ethiopia. Gold and silver is fantastic and I couldn't be happier if I had won myself."

Epilogue

How to address the future, speculate, and comment on what comes next for Haile Gebrselassie? The Athens Olympics may have marked the end of Haile's decade-long reign of 10,000 meters invincibility, but his "track record" will long remain secure.

The world won't soon forget the light, free stride of Haile Gebrselassie. He ran an incredible number of beautiful track world records, spectacular beyond belief, and he won every major championship available to him. He brought crowds to their feet; his body pulsed and surged, and his open smile could only have been heaven-sent. He ran with a full heart and performed like a star.

Haile's future is bound to involve more world records and championship titles—the half-marathon, the marathon. But it's been the track that has suited him best. In a stadium he can be close to the people; bright lights, music, and sumptuous victory laps fill the air. In the round, on a track, Haile shone brightest: His exquisite touch, his effortless rhythm transfixed audiences' imaginations.

Away from the track Haile's influence has been equally profound. And no doubt that will continue to be the case. He and Jos will seek bigger and better challenges. Haile's three girls and Alem will forever remain his pride and joy. And he will carry on using his fame to advance a number of social and humanitarian causes within Ethiopia. There are his recent ventures to promote Ethiopian coffee worldwide, and to market and sell *tef,* the staple of every Ethiopian runner's diet, to the West. And, of course, there are the schools he continues to build throughout the countryside. "Education is the most important factor to change people's lives for the better," he says.

Haile has brought a similar life-affirming message to all Ethiopians. On a high-rise building in central Addis Ababa his mural gazes across the city, where written underneath it in Amharic are the words: *You can*. Gareth Davis from *The Daily Telegraph* commented following a recent visit to Addis, "Haile is a man with a social conscience. . . . He is arguably one of the greatest athletes of all time and, like Muhammad Ali, his impact on society and individuals transcends sport."

So it is then that Haile will remain the people's champion even long after he retires from sport. "I am already preparing for the day when I can't run at the top," he says. "Maybe I'll do more business, or just become a jogger. I expect it to come, though—but perhaps not until 2012, that would be my fifth Olympics! But you know, it's only something normal for a sportsman to retire. You cannot control the whole world forever. People soon forget you because another champion comes along. But I will still have a long life to lead, and I want it to be a happy and healthy time. So with my family and my friends I have to plan for my life after sport. Believe me, I have already accepted the fact that one day not so far away the world will forget about Haile Gebrselassie."

That, it must be said, seems highly unlikely.

Acknowledgements

This book wouldn't have been possible without the support of a great number of people. Most importantly, I would like to thank Haile Gebrselassie for his extreme generosity, and for allowing me such open access into his life on and off the track. He was always willing to sit through yet another interview session and answer my scores of questions, and for that he has my heartfelt appreciation and respect.

A special debt of gratitude must also be extended to Jos Hermens whose confidence in me to tell this story was always a constant source of inspiration. Thanks also to the entire team at Global Sports Communications, particularly Ellen van Langen and Stephan Kreykamp.

To the dozens of people I met in Ethiopia who provided me with so many invaluable insights into Haile's life and Ethiopia's culture and running history, especially Richard Nerurkar, Alem Gebrselassie, Assefa Gebrselassie, Yasin Side, Getaneh Tessema, Getaneh Reta, and Girma Neda, thank you for your patience and good will.

Thanks also to Anton Engles for such considered answers to my many questions, and to Vicky Brennan for her insightful comments.

To my fellow track and field writers who directly supported this project, I would like to say thank you: Amby Burfoot, Jason Henderson, Steve Landells, Paul Larkins, Elshadai Negash, Marty Post, Chris Turner, and Sabrina Yohannes. Also thanks to Mark Shearman for providing such unforgettable photographs for the book.

Much of the initial research I did for this book was made easier because of the work done by a number of sports writers, academics, and journalists who I would also like to thank: John Bale, Kaleyesus Bekele, Bob Chappell, Tom Fordyce, Bob Frank, Mamo Gebrehiwot, Doug Gillon, Ed Gordon, Simon Hart, Jamie Jackson, Tom Knight, Elaine Larkins, Richard Lewis, Rod Liddle, Seppo Luhtala, Donald McRae, Duncan Mackay, John Manners, Dave Martin, Kenny Moore, Sue Mott, Peter Njenga, Justin Palmer, Richard Pankhurst, Bob Ramsak, Ejeta Seifu, Matthew Syed, Brian Viner, Zeleke Wa, and Jim White.

At Fast Track I'd like to acknowledge Steve Chisholm and Lindsay Impett, and at UK Athletics, Emily Lewis. Thanks for organizing such great track meets in the UK.

Throughout the writing of this book De Montfort University and the University of Bath were vital sources of support and for that I am very grateful.

My friends and family were of course always supportive and helpful, no one more so than Pirkko Markula, who was always my first point of reference for every decision I made about how to write this book.

Finally, without the backing and encouragement of my publisher, Garth Battista, this story of one of sport's greatest personalities would have never been told.

Jim Denison
Exeter, England 2004

Appendix A
Summary of Haile Gebrselassie's Races
(Compiled by Marty Post)

Date	Place	Time	Cat	Distance	Location	Race
20 Aug 04	5	27:27.70	t	10,000m	Athens	Olympic Games, final
30 July 04	1	12:55.51	t	5,000m	London	London Grand Prix
31 May 04	2	26:41.58	t	10,000m	Hengelo	Thales FBK-Games
20-Feb-04	2	8:08.65	t	2 miles	Birmingham	Norwich Union GP indoor
15-Feb-04	1	7:29.34	t	3000m	Karlsruhe	LBBW Meeting indoor
31-Jan-04	1	7:35.24	t	3000m	Boston	Adidas Boston Games indoor
05-Sep-03	1	26:29.22	t	10,000m	Brussels	Van Damme Memorial
24-Aug-03	2	26:50.77	t	10,000m	Paris	IAAF World Championships
08-Aug-03	1	12:57.23	t	5000m	London	London Grand Prix
11-Jul-03	3	13:00.32	t	5000m	Rome	Golden Gala
04-Jul-03	2	12:54.36	t	5000m	Paris	Gaz De France
01-Jun-03	2	26:54.58	t	10,000m	Hengelo	Thales FBK Games
16-Mar-03	1	7:40.97	t	3000m	Birmingham	IAAF World Indoor Champs
14-Mar-03	1	7:51.43	t	3000m	Birmingham	IAAF World Indoor Champs, heat
28-Feb-03	1	7:28.29	t	3000m	Karlsruhe	LBBW Meeting indoor
21-Feb-03	1	8:04.69	t	2 miles	Birmingham	Norwich Union GP indoor
11-Dec-02	1	27:02	r	10 km	Doha	QSI 10-K
02-Jun-02	dnf		t	1 hour	Hengelo	Fanny Blankers Koen Games
14-Apr-02	3	2:06:35	r	marathon	London	London Marathon
24-Mar-02	1	59:40	r	half-mar.	Lisbon	Lisbon Half-Marathon
24-Feb-02	1	35:42	c	12,000 m	Addis Ababa	Janmeda Cross-Country
02-Dec-01	1	41:07	c	<14,000 m	Dunkerque	Cross de l'Acier
25-Nov-01	1	30:30	r	10 km	Addis Ababa	Great Ethiopian Run
11-Nov-01	2	41:38	r	15 km	Nijmegen	Zevenheuvelenloop
07-Oct-01	1	1:00:03	r	half-mar.	Bristol	IAAF World half-marathon champs
23-Sep-01	1	28:07	r	10 km	Prague	Mattoni Grand Prix
26-Aug-01	1	1:04:34	r	half-mar.	Addis Ababa	Ethiopian Half-Marathon champs
08-Aug-01	3	27:54.41	t	10,000m	Edmonton	IAAF World Championships
25-Sep-00	1	27:18.20	t	10,000m	Sydney	Olympic Games, final
22-Sep-00	1	27:50.01	t	10,000m	Sydney	Olympic Games, heat
11-Aug-00	1	12:57.95	t	5000m	Zurich	Weltklasse GP
05-Aug-00	1	13:06.23	t	5000m	London	Norwich Union British Grand Prix
25-Jun-00	1	13:01.07	t	5000m	Nuremberg	Live 2000
07-Jun-00	1	13:01.6	t	5000m	Milan	Notturna Di Milano
24-Aug-99	1	27:57.27	t	10,000m	Seville	IAAF World Championships
11-Aug-99	1	12:49.64	t	5000m	Zurich	Weltklasse GP
07-Aug-99	1	8:01.72	t	2 miles	London	British GP
17-Jul-99	1	7:30.58	t	3000m	Nice	Nikaia '99 GP
30-Jun-99	1	12:53.92	t	5000m	Oslo	Bislett Games
27-Jun-99	1	3:52.39	t	1 mile	Gateshead	British Grand Prix II
10-Jun-99	1	7:26.03	t	3000m	Helsinki	Ericsson/GP II
06-Jun-99	1	3:33.73	t	1500m	Stuttgart	GER outdoor track
30-May-99	1	8:01.86	t	2 miles	Hengelo	Adriaan Paulen Memorial
07-Mar-99	1	3:33.77	t	1500m	Maebashi	IAAF World indoor champs, final

06-Mar-99	1	3:41.22	t	1500m	Maebashi	IAAF World indoor champs, heat
05-Mar-99	1	7:53.57	t	3000m	Maebashi	IAAF World indoor champs
21-Feb-99	1	7:31.25	t	3000m	Lieven	Gaz de Paris indoor
14-Feb-99	1	12:50.38	t	5000m	Birmingham	BUPA indoor GP
07-Feb-99	1	3:34.28	t	1500m	Stuttgart	Sparkassen indoor
24-Jan-99	1	7:26.80	t	3000m	Karlsruhe	Karlsruhe indoor
04-Oct-98	1	28:59	r	10 km	Scicli	Memorial Pepe Greco
05-Sep-98	1	7:50.00	t	3000m	Moscow	IAAF Grand Prix Final
01-Sep-98	1	12:56.52	t	5000m	Berlin	ISTAF GP
28-Aug-98	1	7:25.09	t	3000m	Brussels	Van Damme Memorial
12-Aug-98	1	12:54.08	t	5000m	Zurich	Weltklasse GP
08-Aug-98	1	7:25.54	t	3000m	Monte Carlo	Herculis GP
14-Jul-98	1	13:02.63	t	5000m	Rome	Golden Gala
09-Jul-98	1	7:27.42	t	3000m	Oslo	Bislett Games
13-Jun-98	1	12:39.36	t	5000m	Helsinki	Helsinki GP II
01-Jun-98	1	26:22.75	t	10,000m	Hengelo	Adriaan Paulen Memorial
03-Apr-98	1	3:37.9	t	1500m	Addis Ababa	National Championships
11-Mar-98	1	17:20	c	6000m?	Paris	FRA cross-country
19-Feb-98	1	7:31.70	t	3000m	Stockholm	DNG indoor
15-Feb-98	1	4:52.86	t	2000m	Birmingham	BUPA indoor
08-Feb-98	1	3:33.27	t	1500m	Ghent	Flanders indoor
01-Feb-98	1	3:31.76	t	1500m	Stuttgart	Sparkassen indoor
30-Jan-98	6	1:50.39	t	800m	Dortmund	Sparkassen indoor
25-Jan-98	1	7:26.15	t	3000m	Karlsruhe	Karlsruhe indoor
28-Sep-97	1	28:22	r	10 km	Scicli	Memorial Pepe Greco
26-Aug-97	1	12:55.14	t	5000m	Berlin	ISTAF GP
22-Aug-97	1	7:26.02	t	3000m	Brussels	Van Damme Memorial
13-Aug-97	1	12:41.86	t	5000m	Zurich	Weltklasse GP
06-Aug-97	1	27:24.58	t	10,000m	Athens	World Championships, final
03-Aug-97	1	27:55.36	t	10,000m	Athens	World Championships, heat
04-Jul-97	1	26:31.32	t	10,000m	Oslo	Bislett Games
25-Jun-97	1	13:01.51	t	5000m	Paris	Gaz de Paris
13-Jun-97	1	12:54.60	t	5000m	Nurnberg	Live '97
31-May-97	1	8:01.08	t	2 miles	Hengelo	Adriaan Paulen Memorial
09-Mar-97	1	7:34.71	t	3000m	Paris	World indoor champs, final
07-Mar-97	1	7:50.14	t	3000m	Paris	World indoor champs, heat
20-Feb-97	1	12:59.04	t	5000m	Stockholm	DNG indoor
14-Feb-97	1	7:31.27	t	3000m	Karlsruhe	International indoor meeting
02-Feb-97	2	3:32.39	t	1500m	Stuttgart	Sparkassen indoor
05-Oct-96	1	28:42	r	10 km	Scicli	Memorial Pepe Greco
14-Aug-96	2	12:52.70	t	5000m	Zurich	Weltklasse GP
29-Jul-96	1	27:07.34	t	10,000m	Atlanta	Olympic Games, final
26-Jul-96	1	28:14.20	t	10,000m	Atlanta	Olympic Games, heat
27-May-96	1	7:34.66	t	3000m	Hengelo	Adriaan Paulen Memorial
19-May-96	1	3:34.64	t	1500m	Chemnitz	GER outdoor
23-Mar-96	5	34:28	c	12,000 m	Stellenbosch	IAAF World Cross-Country Champs
04-Feb-96	1	7:30.72	t	3000m	Stuttgart	Sparkassen indoor
27-Jan-96	1	13:10.98	t	5000m	Sindelfingen	IHS Meeting
21-Jan-96	1	28:59	c	10,000 m	Seville	Cross Internacional de Italica
07-Oct-95	1	28:39	r	10 km	Scicli	Memorial Pepe Greco
15-Sep-95	1	13:13.99	t	5000m	Tokyo	Super Toto

09-Sep-95	1	7:35.90	t	3000m	Monte Carlo	Grand Prix Final
01-Sep-95	1	12:53.19	t	5000m	Berlin	ISTAF GP
16-Aug-95	1	12:44.39	t	5000m	Zurich	Weltklasse GP
08-Aug-95	1	27:12.95	t	10,000m	Goteborg	IAAF World Championships, final
05-Aug-95	1	28:10.66	t	10,000m	Goteborg	IAAF World Championships, heat
03-Jul-95	1	13:07.81	t	5000m	Paris	Gaz de Paris
17-Jun-95	1	13:04.20	t	5000m	Villeneuve d'Ascq	FRA outdoor
05-Jun-95	1	26:43.53	t	10,000m	Hengelo	Adriaan Paulen Memorial
27-May-95	1	8:07.46	t	2 miles	Kerkrade	Kerkrade Classic
25-Mar-95	4	34:26	c	12,020 m	Durham	IAAF World Cross-Country Champs
20-Nov-94	1	43:00	r	15 km	Nijmegen	Zevenheuvelenloop
19-Aug-94	1	27:20.39	t	10,000m	Brussels	Van Damme Memorial
02-Aug-94	2	7:37.49	t	3000m	Monte Carlo	Herculis GP
30-Jul-94	2	3:37.04	t	1500m	Hechtel	BEL outdoor
15-Jul-94	4	13:11.87	t	5000m	London	TSB
06-Jul-94	1	27:15.00	t	10,000m	Lausanne	Athletissma
10-Jun-94	2	13:10.79	t	5000m	St. Denis	St. Denis l'Humanite
04-Jun-94	1	12:56.96	t	5000m	Hengelo	Adriaan Paulen Memorial
17-Apr-94	1	19:27	r	7.2 k leg	Litochoro	World Road Relay Champs
04-Apr-94	2	27:34	r	10 km ?	Media Blenio	Media Blenio road race
26-Mar-94	3	34:32	c	12,060 m	Budapest	IAAF World Cross-Country Champs
30-Jan-94	1	30:23	c	10,000 m	San Sebastian	Cross International San Sebastian
23-Jan-94	3	28:10	c	10,000 m	Seville	Cross International de Italica
06-Jan-94	1	37:39	c	12,000 m	San Giorgio su Leg.	Campaccio Cross-Country
01-Jan-94	1	26:27	c	9,000 m	Durham	County Durham Cross-Country
26-Dec-93	1	25:14	r	9 km	D'Issy les Molineaux	Corrida D'Issy Les Moulineaux
17-Oct-93	1	36:08	r	13 km	Pettinengo	Pettinengo Road Race
03-Oct-93	1	17:53	r	4 miles	Groningen	Groningen Road Race
18-Sep-93	1	13:30.91	t	5000m	Fukuoka	Fukuoka GP
22-Aug-93	1	27:46.02	t	10,000m	Stuttgart	IAAF World Championships, final
20-Aug-93	2	28:17.95	t	10,000m	Stuttgart	IAAF World Championships, heat
16-Aug-93	2	13:03.17	t	5000m	Stuttgart	IAAF World Championships, final
14-Aug-93	1	13:25.27	t	5000m	Stuttgart	IAAF World Championships, heat
04-Aug-93	4	13:05.39	t	5000m	Zurich	Weltklasse GP
23-Jul-93	3	13:15.10	t	5000m	London	TSB Grand Prix
27-Jun-93	2	13:10.41	t	5000m	Durban	African Championships
24-Jun-93	3	27:30.17	t	10,000m	Durban	African Championships
28-Mar-93	7	33:23	c	11,750 m	Amorebieta	IAAF World Cross-Country Champs
13-Mar-93	3	30:28	c	11,000 m	Sardinia	Ala dei Sardi Cross-Country
06-Mar-93	3	32:36	c	10,000 m	San Vittore Olona	Cinque Mulini Cross-Country
31-Jan-93	2	29:16	c	10,000 m	San Sebastian	Cross Intl. De San Sebastian
24-Jan-93	2	29:39	c	10,300 m	Elgoibar	Cross Muguerza
17-Jan-93	2	27:54	c	10,000 m	Seville	Cross Internacional de Italica
08-Nov-92	1	13:24	y	5 km	Berlin	Berlin Ekiden Relay
19-Sep-92	1	13:36.06	t	5000m	Seoul	IAAF World Junior Championships
18-Sep-92	1	28:03.99	t	10,000m	Seoul	IAAF World Junior Championships
21-Mar-92	2	23:35	c	8000 m	Boston	IAAF World Cross-Country Champs/Jr.
15-Dec-91	2	13:35	y	5 km	Chiba	Chiba International Ekiden Relay
24-Mar-91	8	24:23	c	8,420 m	Antwerp	IAAF World Cross-Country Champs/Jr.
19-Jun-88	99	2:48	r	marathon	Addis Ababa	Addis Ababa Marathon

Appendix B

World Record Progression Men's 5000 meters

12:37.35	Kenenisa Bekele	(ETH)	31 May 04	Hengelo
12.39.36	Haile Gebrselassie	(ETH)	13 Jun 98	Helsinki
12.39.74	Daniel Komen	(KEN)	22 Aug 97	Brussels
12.41.86	Haile Gebrselassie	(ETH)	13 Aug 97	Zurich
12.44.39	Haile Gebrselassie	(ETH)	16 Aug 95	Zurich
12.55.30	Moses Kiptanui	(KEN)	06 Jun 95	Rome
12.56.96	Haile Gebrselassie	(ETH)	04 Jun 94	Hengelo
12.58.39	Said Aouita	(MOR)	22 Jul 87	Rome
13.00.40	Said Aouita	(MOR)	27 Jul 85	Oslo
13.00.41	David Moorcroft	(GBR)	07 Jul 82	Oslo
13.06.20	Henry Rono	(KEN)	13 Sep 81	Knarvik
13.08.4+	Henry Rono	(KEN)	08 Apr 78	Berkeley
13.12.86	Dick Quax	(NZL)	05 Jul 77	Stockholm
13.13.0+	Emil Puttemans	(BEL)	20 Sep 72	Brussels
13.16.4+	Lasse Viren	(FIN)	14 Sep 72	Helsinki
13.16.6+	Ron Clarke	(AUS)	05 Jul 66	Stockholm
13.24.2+	Kipchoge Keino	(KEN)	30 Nov 65	Auckland
13.25.8+	Ron Clarke	(AUS)	04 Jun 65	Compton
13.33.6+	Ron Clarke	(AUS)	01 Feb 65	Auckland
13.34.8+	Ron Clarke	(AUS)	16 Jan 65	Hobart
13.35.0+	Vladimir Kuts	(URS)	13 Oct 57	Rome
13.40.6+	Sandor Iharos	(HUN)	23 Oct 55	Budapest
13.36.8+	Gordon Pirie	(GBR)	19 Jun 56	Bergen
13.46.8+	Vladimir Kuts	(URS)	18 Sep 55	Belgrade
13.50.8+	Sandor Iharos	(HUN)	10 Sep 55	Budapest
13.51.2+	Vladimir Kuts	(URS)	23 Oct 54	Prague
13.51.6+	Chris Chataway	(GBR)	13 Oct 54	London
13.56.6+	Vladimir Kuts	(URS)	29 Aug 54	Berne
13.57.2+	Emil Zatopek	(SWE)	20 Sep 42	Gothenburg
14.08.8+	Taisto Maki	(FIN)	16 Jun 39	Helsinki
14.17.0+	Lauri Lehtinen	(FIN)	19 Jun 32	Helsinki
14.28.2+	Paavo Nurmi	(FIN)	19 Jun 24	Helsinki
14.35.4+	Paavo Nurmi	(FIN)	12 Sep 22	Stockholm
14.36.6+	Hannes Kolehmainen	(FIN)	10 Jun 12	Stockholm
15.01.2+	Arthur Robinson	(GBR)	13 Sep 08	Stockholm

Appendix C

World Record Progression Men's 10,000 meters

26:20.32	Kenenisa Bekele	(ETH)	08 June 2004	Ostrava
26.22.75	Haile Gebrselassie	(ETH)	01 Jun 1998	Hengelo
26.27.85	Paul Tergat	(KEN)	22 Aug 1997	Brussels
26.31.32	Haile Gebrselassie	(ETH)	04 Aug 1997	Oslo
26.38.08	Salah Hissou	(MOR)	23 Aug 1996	Brussels
26.43.53	Haile Gebrselassie	(ETH)	05 Jun 1995	Hengelo
26.52.23	William Sigei	(KEN)	22 Jul 1994	Oslo
26.58.38	Yobes Ondieki	(KEN)	10 Jul 1993	Oslo
27.07.91	Richard Chelimo	(KEN)	05 Jul 1993	Stockholm
27.08.23	Arturo Barrios	(MEX)	18 Aug 1989	Berlin
27.13.81	Fernando Mamede	(POR)	02 Jul 1984	Stockholm
27.22.47	Henry Rono	(KEN)	11 Jun 1978	Vienna
27.30.47	Samson Kimobwa	(KEN)	30 Jun 1977	Helsinki
27.30.80	Dave Bedford	(GBR)	13 Jul 1973	London
27.38.35	Lasse Viren	(FIN)	03 Sep 1972	Munich
27.39.4+	Ron Clarke	(AUS)	14 Jul 1965	Oslo
28.14.0+	Ron Clarke	(AUS)	16 May 1965	Turku
28.15.6+	Ron Clarke	(AUS)	18 Dec 1963	Melbourne
28.18.2+	Pjotr Bolotnikov	(URS)	11 Aug 1962	Moscow
28.18.8+	Pjotr Bolotnikov	(URS)	15 Oct 1960	Kiev
28.30.4+	Vladimir Kuts	(URS)	11 Sep 1956	Moscow
28.42.8+	Sandor Iharos	(HUN)	15 Jul 1956	Budapest
28.54.2+	Emil Zatopek	(TCH)	01 Jun 1954	Brussels
29.01.6+	Emil Zatopek	(TCH)	01 Nov 1953	Stara Boleslav
29.02.6+	Emil Zatopek	(TCH)	04 Aug 1950	Turku
29.21.2+	Emil Zatopek	(TCH)	22 Oct 1949	Ostrava
29.27.2+	Viljo Heino	(FIN)	01 Sep 1949	Kouvola
29.28.2+	Emil Zatopek	(TCH)	11 Jun 1949	Ostrava
29.35.4+	Viljo Heino	(FIN)	25 Aug 1944	Helsinki
29.52.6+	Taisto Maki	(FIN)	17 Sep 1939	Helsinki
30.02.0+	Taisto Maki	(FIN)	29 Sep 1938	Tampere
30.05.6+	Ilmari Salminen	(FIN)	18 Jul 1937	Kouvola
30.06.2+	Paavo Nurmi	(FIN)	31 Aug 1924	Kuopio
30.23.2+	Ville Ritola	(FIN)	06 Jul 1924	Paris
30.35.4+	Ville Ritola	(FIN)	25 May 1924	Helsinki
30.40.2+	Paavo Nurmi	(FIN)	22 Jun 1921	Stockholm
30.58.8+	Jean Bouin	(FRA)	16 Nov 1919	Paris
31.20.8+	Hanes Kolehmainen	(FIN)	Jun 1912	Stockholm
31.02.4+	Alfred Shrubb	(GBR)	05 Nov 1904	Glasgow

Appendix D

Olympic Champions Men's 10,000 Meters

2004	Athens	Kenenisa Beleke	(ETH)	27:05.10
2000	Sydney	Haile Gebrselassie	(ETH)	27:18.20
1996	Atlanta	Haile Gebrselaisse	(ETH)	27:07.34
1992	Barcelona	Khalid Skah	(MOR)	27:46.70
1988	Seoul	Brahim Boutayeb	(MOR)	27:21.46
1984	Los Angeles	Alberto Cova	(ITA)	27:47:54
1980	Moscow	Miruts Yifter	(ETH)	27:42.69
1976	Montreal	Lasse Viren	(FIN)	27:40:38
1972	Munich	Lasse Viren	(FIN)	27:38.4
1968	Mexico City	Naftali Temu	(KEN)	29:27.4
1964	Tokyo	William Mills	(USA)	28:24.4
1960	Rome	Pyotr Bolotnikov	(RUS)	28:32.2
1956	Melbourne	Vladimir Kuts	(UKR)	28:45.6
1952	Helsinki	Emil Zatopek	(CZE)	29:17.0
1948	London	Emil Zatopek	(CZE)	29:59.6
1936	Berlin	Ilmari Salminen	(FIN)	30:15.4
1932	Los Angeles	Janusz Kusocinski	(POL)	30:11.4
1928	Amsterdam	Paavo Nurmi	(FIN)	30:18.8
1924	Paris	Ville Ritola	(FIN)	30:23.2
1920	Antwerp	Paavo Nurmi	(FIN)	31:45.8
1912	Stockholm	Hannes Kolehmainen	(FIN)	31:20.8

Appendix E

World Champions Men's 10,000 meters

2003	Paris	Kenenisa Bekele	(ETH)	26:49.57
2001	Edmonton	Charles Kamathi	(KEN)	27:53.25
1999	Seville	Haile Gebrselassie	(ETH)	27:57.27
1997	Athens	Haile Gebrselassie	(ETH)	27:24.58
1995	Gothenborg	Haile Gebrselassie	(ETH)	27:12.95
1993	Stuttgart	Haile Gebrselassie	(ETH)	27:46.02
1991	Tokyo	Moses Tanui	(KEN)	27:38.74
1987	Rome	Paul Kipkoech	(KEN)	27:38.63
1983	Helsinki	Alberto Cova	(ITA)	28:01.04

About the author

Originally from New York, Jim Denison currently lives and works in England. He is the editor of *The Coach*, a bi-monthly magazine for track and field coaches, and his features on running appear regularly in *Athletics Weekly*. He is the author of *Bannister and Beyond: The Mystique of the Four-Minute Mile*. Denison is also a lecturer in sports sociology at the University of Bath.

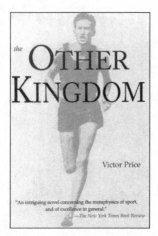

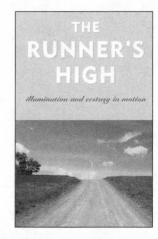

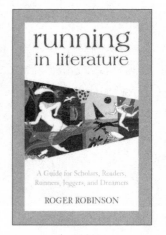

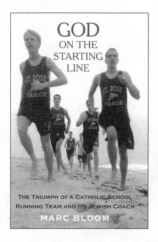